D0233012

DIGITAL CASH

DIGITAL CASH

THE UNKNOWN HISTORY OF THE ANARCHISTS, UTOPIANS, AND TECHNOLOGISTS WHO BUILT CRYPTOCURRENCY

FINN BRUNTON

PRINCETON UNIVERSITY PRESS

PRINCETON AND OXFORD

LCCN 2018964843
ISBN 978-0-691-17949-0

British Library Cataloging-in-Publication Data is available

Editorial: Al Bertrand and Kristin Zodrow
Production Editorial: Kathleen Cioffi
Text and Jacket Design: Leslie Flis
Jacket Art: Joey Colombo
Production: Erin Suydam
Publicity: James Schneider
Copyeditor: Jennifer McClain

This book has been composed in Arno

Printed on acid-free paper. ∞

Printed in the United States of America

10 9 8 7 6 5 4 3 2 1

"Pardon me, ma'am," she said. "But does she tell the truth?"

"Of course not," said Lil. "She tells the future. It's not the same thing, you know."

—BORIS VIAN, *RED GRASS*, TRANS. PAUL KNOBLOCH

I'm trying to get root access to the future. I want to raid its system of thought.

—JUDE MILHON

CONTENTS

DIGITAL CASH

THE PASSING CURRENT

This book tells the largely untold story of digital cash and the people who sought to build it—some to bring down states and nations and create a utopia of ciphers, some to be rewarded by the collapse of global order, and some to spur the genesis of a machine by which they could live forever. It explains how cryptocurrencies came to be: the preconditions, the technologies and subcultures, and the ideas, fantasies, fictions, and models of the future behind Bitcoin's first announcement.

The main argument of this book starts with the fact that it tells the story of *digital cash* in particular, rather than electronic money more generally. The work of making cash digital means creating an object that is trivial to transact over networked computers and easy to verify—to prove that it is what it appears to be—but impossible to forge or duplicate, and that can carry the information about what it is and what it is worth, without generating any information about how it is used or by whom.

This is a set of seemingly paradoxical and impossible demands: it must be available but scarce, unique and anonymous but identifiable and reliable, and easy to transmit but impossible to copy. It must have all these attributes in the context of technologies that were designed and built to make copies in their very functioning—costlessly, immediately, and perfectly.

The case I make to you is that the story of digital cash is best understood as a problem of knowledge in the larger history of currency itself. How do you know that a given currency token is valuable—that it can pass, that someone else will take it from you, that it can be settled and redeemed? The value of money in general—this intricate cultural microtechnology, this social medium—comes from powerful and often abstract beliefs about the way things are and the way they will be, as the first chapter of this book discusses in detail: the predictions, bets, and hopes that one kind of money will be accepted for payment of taxes, another will not be devalued by the market flooding with some rare metal or material, and that a social network of gifts, obligations, and reciprocities will hold for a third.

Zoom in from that lofty place to *practice*, to currency, cash, and coin. How do you know the value of this particular token of money? How are you sure of its identity, and how does it authenticate itself to you? We may know this through ductility, thermal conductivity, and sound: biting a coin, seeing how fast ice melts on it, the "ping test" of its chime when struck. We may know it from the smell and weight of a brick of compressed tea, the branding and bands on a cigarette, or through serial numbers, signatures, paper stock and fabric's "hand," and the security threads and watermarks on banknotes, letters of credit, or traveler's checks. We know all these things in the context of training, habit, and prior experience. With this in mind, how would you create a digital currency?

I want to convince you that we should understand digital cash as part of the challenge of *making digital data valuable*, and that many of the more puzzling aspects of digital cash resolve themselves when they're understood in terms of authentication, ownership, certainty, and proof for digital objects. The twin projects of digital ownership and digital cash always turn up together as the history told in this book unfolds, from building information marketplaces, to verifying anonymous statements, validating work and time, and battling counterfeiting and copying. In other words, this book is a history of how data was literally and metaphorically *monetized.*

The secondary argument I make is that the history of digital cash can also show us a particularly vivid example of the use of money and technologies to tell stories about the future. These stories are a way of making assertions, getting buy-in, placing bets, marshaling allies, and taking power in the present. Over the course of this book I describe several utopian and speculative monetary projects, major and minor. Each comes with its model of time, its stories and fantasies of history and the future, and its associated technologies—cryonics, varieties of cryptography, ocean-going cities—on which it draws for prospective value. All also face a translation challenge. They must explain and convince outside the small, homogeneous groups where they were created: those of almost entirely white American men from youth to early middle age, with backgrounds in engineering or software development—most of whom lived on the coast of California, shared political theories and beliefs, and knew one another through mailing lists and events.

All the speculative moneyers and mintmasters of this book work within their own particular historical condition: the Technocrats, diagramming prosperity with mechanical pencils on graph paper; the cypherpunks, undermining an anticipated totalitarian ultrastate; the Extropians, their frozen bodies launched like Pharaonic vessels into eternity, seeking disruptive chaos as fuel for a stellar motor; the libertarians and agorists and anarcho-capitalists and micronationalists and Objectivists and sovereign individuals, eagerly bracing for an oncoming collapse to validate their decisions, beliefs, and investments. Their work was in the prospective tense but required action in the present, from recruiting prototype communities to designing idea coupons to stockpiling weapons in anticipation of ruin—and all entailed either the production or the adoption of speculative currencies and digital cash. They shared this time frame with the seventeenth-century proponents of credit and fixed metallic money, who "aimed to explain and induce, persuade and gain momentum; if they succeeded in convincing an audience that could act, they could capture the future."[1]

The project of this book can be summed up in a single phrase. *Passing current* is a term in the world of currency for money that is generally accepted for exchange, passing from person to person. The idea of the cash in your wallet being "current money," though, holds true only because it is anticipatory money: the next person offered will take it, and it can ultimately be accepted in taxes or otherwise redeemed. Its present-time "currency," the fact that it passes, is a product of its futurity. "Passing current" also appears in physics and electrical engineering, including the development of the transistors and computational hardware used in creating digital cash: this book is partially a story about the work of moving electrons down wires. Finally, and metaphorically, the "passing current" evokes the elapsing of present time—the passing of this current moment between the documented and narrated past and the predicted, desired, and feared future. The story of digital cash lies at the intersection of those three passing currents: the social puzzles of money, the technological history of computing, and our sense of our historical and future condition.

This book therefore has two goals. When you finish it, you will have a portrait of the components, concepts, and ideas of digital cash from experiments in the 1980s to the creation of Bitcoin. In this, you will see how data was cashed in, so to speak, and the trade-offs and struggles that process involved (particularly the surveillance of payments and transactions). You will also have a history of several near futures told through experimental money, and the different ways prospective and anticipated events were applied in the present. This goes beyond the history of utopian currencies to the prototypes, images, narratives, functional systems, and speculative designs that worked as *techniques of futurity*. I hope to enrich what you know about currency (digital and otherwise) and computation, and to show you how powerful fantasies of the future were—and are—told using money, machines, and stories together.

With all that in mind: I hope with this book to give you an *experience*, a whirlwind tour of many different systems of utopian desire, future fantasy, and experimental life, including brief sketches of many of the personalities and practices involved— some of whom may seem wrongheaded, dangerous, even willfully perverse. The itinerary includes prototype countries and mathematical challenges, a financial system to bring its creator back from the dead, nonconductive liquids, Xanadu hypertext, leaf money, objective values, currency panics, private spaceships, public randomness, American Technocrats in capes, cryptographers in chadors, high-seas autonomous zones, Grace Hopper playing basketball, libertarian silver, geodesic schemes, broken time machines, idea coupons, forged signatures, a wall of lava lamps, and a tank of frozen human heads.

CHAPTER 1

SPECULATING WITH MONEY

We start with a utopian project in the United States at the heart of the Great Depression, a bizarre scheme to govern the whole North American continent as an industrial concern. Through the rise and fall of Technocracy Inc., we learn that money is a technology for managing time—futures, faith, and forecast—and it contains a model of society. Among other temporal modes embedded in money, "speculative currencies" deserve special attention. They act as systems for utopian practice—as cosmograms, a concept explained here that the rest of the book draws on.

TECHNATE

Howard Scott wore two costumes.[1] In the 1920s, he was the Engineer. In New York City's Greenwich Village he wore heavy boots, riding breeches, a leather jacket, a red bandana, and a broad-brimmed hat, and carried a slide rule and sometimes blueprints. It was clothing appropriate for keeping the sun out of your eyes on the construction site of a skyscraper, or laying an airstrip, or visiting a dam. Ayn Rand was still a teenager living in Russia, and *The Fountainhead* wouldn't come out until 1943, but Scott was already dressing like her architect hero, Howard Roark, ready to take off his jacket and start jack-hammering in the granite quarry. He had nothing in common with Roark, though, in ideology or in practice—aside from being a fantasy.

Howard Scott was a real person, but he was playing a character: he wasn't an engineer or an architect. He had nothing in particular to calculate with his slide rule. He was an eccentric, a neighborhood character, a command-economy orator delivering speeches in Village cafés about the importance of rationalizing life and increasing industrial efficiency.

In the 1930s, as the Depression rolled across the country shuttering factories, emptying fields and towns, and flooding roads and rails with refugees, Scott's costume changed: he turned up in a tailored gray flannel suit and a blue necktie. No longer the roughneck engineer, pretending to have just driven in from the oil rig, he was now every inch the rational organization man, the face of the firm. This was the uniform of the new technoculture, the vivid industrial fantasy he was about to tap with his political movement: Technocracy Inc.[2]

The United States at that moment was a cash-poor country. Strings of bank failures and runs encouraged hoarding cash and coin in socks, safes, strongboxes, "holes in the ground, privies, linings of coats, horse collars, coal piles, hollow trees."[3] We can hear a contemporary echo in the opening line of Nigel Dodd's 2014 *The Social Life of Money*. "They have been freezing money in Greece," he wrote, as the 2007–2008 financial crisis spiraled out of control and bundles of euros were stashed in "iceboxes, vacuum cleaners, bags of flour, pet food containers, mattresses, and under floors." In 1933, when Roosevelt declared an emergency banking holiday on taking office—buying time to pass a form of federal deposit insurance—the circulation of cash froze up still more.

Hundreds of cities and towns issued their own scrip, and Dow Chemical minted coins from magnesium. Stores in Detroit bartered crates of eggs and pounds of honey; shopkeepers, doctors, and pharmacists extended credit to customers and clients. The student newspaper *Daily Princetonian* issued $500 of their own currency in twenty-five-cent denominations in partnership with Princeton's merchants. The taxi dancers in New York's Roseland Ballroom—"ten cents a dance," in the words of the famous Rodgers and Hart song—took IOUs instead of dimes if you could show your bankbook to prove your funds, and amateur boxing tourneys accepted cigars, combs, and sacks of potatoes. Public transit ran on nickels, so Manhattan's Automats were besieged by commuters and good-timers in fancy dress trying to bum loose change.[4]

Technocracy's timing could not have been better: Scott and his acolytes stepped into a situation of deep monetary uncertainty with a utopia of scientific economics, promising to cure the Depression if brought into power. They enjoyed a rush of media attention in the United States for a few years, some serious, some mocking, but all publicity. At their peak, their vanguard were the closest the United States ever had to the hardcore Taylorizers and Constructivist machine-fetishists of the 1920s Soviet Union. They were an American version of the Bolshevik scientific management theorist Alexei Gastev and his Time League, who sought to use biophysics and chronophotography to entirely redesign society and everyone in it along factory lines: a sci-fi civilization of massified minimalism, with humans as perfected components in one continuous rhythmic engine.[5] Unlike the Bolsheviks, though, Technocracy presented itself as "beyond politics," coming instead from a framework of pragmatic engineering and—above all—"science." Their slogan was "Governance by science—social control through the power of technique."

To save American democracy from the Depression, it would be necessary to destroy it with a program of "Total Conscription!" of "the Men, Machines, Materiel and Money of the nation."[6] It was a program that would put Bolshevik "war communism" to shame, delivered with an upbeat American can-do attitude and a performance we could dub *engineering theater*. Dedicated Technocrats wore armbands and lapel pins with the "monad"—a symbol of oneness, for the unity of consumption and production—and gave quasi-military salutes. They got around by their own car and motorcycle corps, and cultivated a youth group called the Farads, a street team of avid recruits named after a measurement unit for electrical capacitors.

Their vision was a postscarcity command economy called the Technate that would include the United States, Canada, and (in some drafts) Mexico, run by autocratic master engineers. All activities they considered nonessential—political, artistic, ethical, social, intellectual, fun—would be curtailed, or eliminated altogether. This transformation would be underwritten by a new currency directly tied to energy, denominated in ergs and distributed as certificates. "A dollar may be worth—in buying power—so much today and more or less tomorrow, but a unit of work or heat is the same in 1900, 1929, 1933 or the year 2000," wrote Scott, in a 1933 article for *Harper's*, "Technology Smashes the Price System": money with an "objective value," that classic oxymoron, conflating an empirical quantity with a socially maintained principle.

Observe the sleight-of-hand trick of the "energy certificates"— more blatantly executed here than it will be later on. The certificates were *realer* than dollars, partaking of their ontological connection to "work or heat," rooted in the universe. They were realer in every way except that they didn't exist. But they *would*, the designs promised. The certificates were drafted in drawings and described in considerable detail: "made of water-marked paper and . . . issued in strips folded into rectangular booklets small enough to be carried conveniently in the pocket."[7] The energy certificates were realer than dollars—a more reliable store of value and unit of account, superior and unchanging—because they existed only in the future, when all of society would be rearranged appropriately for them. Not exactly proposals nor precisely prototypes, the Technocratic energy certificates—along with all the other speculative currency projects in this book— were what the historian of science John Tresch calls a *cosmogram.* A cosmogram is "at once scientific, artistic, technological, and political"; it is an object that contains a model of the universe and a plan for how to organize life and society accordingly.[8]

HOW TO DO THINGS IN THE UNIVERSE

Tresch's book *The Romantic Machine: Utopian Science and Technology after Napoleon* documents and revives a period in France between the fall of Napoleon in 1814 and the triumph of Napoleon III in 1852 when machines, positivist scientific work, quantification, and industry became vehicles for a capital-R Romantic way of living and thinking. He describes a moment when scientific and technological concepts and objects were starting points not just for empirical knowledge about the universe but for ethics, social transformation, aesthetics, the evaluation of our place in history, and the sheer rapture of experience.

Making this argument put Tresch in the delicate position of talking about things that did several sorts of work simultaneously: new buildings, calendars and organizational schemes, scientific apparatus, and public spectacles like panoramas and phantasmagoria. They all described a particular order of the universe, a set of arrangements and relationships, an orientation to the past and future, and how we should behave and act individually and as societies. They were simultaneously documents and objects: buildings you could stand inside, techno-operatic spectacles you could enjoy, maps and instruments you could use. "What's important," he writes of these diverse forms, "and why this is different than a cosmology, is that we're talking about a text that results in a concrete practice and set of objects, which weave together a complete inventory or map of the world."[9] These documents and objects work as a cultural technology.

Cosmograms are things, stuff, which order the cosmos and our place in it, embedding a system of relationships, roles, and actions within their operation. Examples range from the Biblical Tabernacle, Dogon rites, and Tibetan Buddhist mandalas, to encyclopedias, certain kinds of scientific projects, and library floor plans. What defines a cosmogram is not world-historical significance but the particular set of functions that it provides. From a user's perspective, it situates us in time and space (where and when are we?), establishes ontological levels (what is important?), and provides practices and models (what should we do and how should we understand?). In fixing reference points for members of a group, it establishes relationships and interconnections between different categories (significance and insignificance, superiority and inferiority, cleanliness and uncleanliness). In addition, it offers an image of the world as it could be, and it makes that image concrete with a set of practices and rituals to guide participation in the world—actions you can actually take. It is a model of the world with an agenda, an implicit utopian project expressed through an arrangement of objects and symbols.

Finally: Along with space, the cosmogram produces and organizes time and history for its users, particularly future history. It provides practices for maintaining that history and producing that future. It tells you what has been (which parts of history really matter) and what will be, whether by plugging into a religious cosmology, or the nineteenth-century gear train of Marxist dialectics, or the twentieth-century extrapolation of graphs. It tells you when *now* is, relative to what has been and what will be or could be, and how to behave with reference to when you are. It is a project of making the future into an object of knowledge.

SPECULATING WITH MONEY

Technocracy Inc.'s energy certificates were perfect cosmograms. They contained an entire—deeply bizarre—society and cosmos in miniature. They put values and prices on a world in which all of nature and all prior human activity were secondary, mere grist, for the goal of total industrial efficiency. The notes contained a convoluted accounting scheme ("a modified Dewey Decimal System"), which situated the bearer and all their possible purchases within an ontology of every role, service, and product available in the Technate. They encouraged and forbade behaviors in the Technocratic society. They also acted as a calendar of sorts: all energy certificates were to be expended within "a full balanced load period" of two years.

This two-year cycle installed one particular kind of time into the Technocracy notes: they would lose value and expire on a fixed schedule to spur investment and exchange rather than hoarding and speculation. This deliberate schedule was shared with other experimental currencies circulating during the Great Depression. There was a brief flourishing of stamp scrip and social credit projects in Austria, Canada, and the United States, money that rapidly and deliberately declined in value ("goes out of date like a newspaper, rots like potatoes, rusts like iron") unless it was put to use.[10] But Technocratic money carried a second temporal model aboard, one characteristic of money more generally: money tokens are artifacts of future time, when they will be next exchanged.

Many scholars of money have promulgated or debunked the classic origin stories of money, set in windswept dioramas of Ancient Times: money began as commodities and barter, or tax and tribute; as language, as gift, as quantification, as waste. Dodd's *The Social Life of Money* begins with six different purported starting points and alludes to many more. In theory and practice, our tales of money's origin shape the role it plays in our lives—but so do our stories of the future. The money we receive is *current* money, which we accept on the understanding that another (merchant, tax collector, bank) will accept it in turn, next, in the time to come.[11] We hold cash like the "strange white flowers" in the pocket of H. G. Wells's returning time traveler, relics of the future.

This fact seems a trivial point in the context of money and finance. Of *course* people hold assets and debts with an eye to stabilities and instabilities in "pasts remembered, futures anticipated, and time measured."[12] Money has always functioned within particular arrangements of time and history, as far back as we would like to go: we can talk about discounting receipts for grain storage in Egypt (*ostraka*), or the very complex *máš* debt and interest systems of Mesopotamia, woven into dynastic shifts and inherited hierarchies of power.[13] Investors arbitrage in the short term, with a mix of models, algorithms, and instincts: financial monetary temporality extends from sub-microsecond fluctuations to regular settlements of debt, from four-week Treasury bills to the 367-year-old Dutch water bond held by Yale University (still paying interest). It is premised on the unknown future, with systems of hedging unpredictable changes, including the perverse promise that other promises *won't* be honored and things will fall through.[14] Individuals and families, meanwhile, make complex bets about children, health, mortgages, education, retirement, from the next paycheck to the duration of a marriage. Part of this betting is the guesswork about what others will make of the future—and having to anticipate and account for the possibility that other people's bad guesses may warp your own.[15]

Financial professionals work with debt in terms of the rate of inflation of the currency in which it is denominated—how the value of the money making it up will change over the future life span of the debt. We may hold cash, gold, cartons of cigarettes, or bottles of detergent if we do not trust the near term of the banks: a mix of "reserve technologies," kept around in case other systems fail, as a house with electric lights will have candles in a drawer.[16] Investors make long-term studies to determine net present value for an investment in terms of the "time value of money," the discounting that reflects money later versus money now—and discounting models may have reshaped our sense of economic futurity in their own image.[17]

The commonplace blend of money between credit, coin, and certificates functions not just as a set of utilities but as an expression of *ordinary times*—and ordinary futures: "what people . . . *expected* the future to be like,"[18] wrote the cultural historian Rebecca Spang in her study of money in France through the time of the Revolution. "Based in repeated actions and regular expectations, these hardly conscious forms of trust sediment into an understanding of how the world—and, crucially, the other people in it—naturally work. In this way money is also an institution, or microtechnology, for the production and reproduction of shared norms and social cohesion."[19]

As money moves through our everyday relationships, roles, and reciprocations, it expresses still another kind of future temporality: the one we share with intimates, our kin, communities, and friends. (The awkward word *temporality* here describes not time itself but relationships to and ideas about time.) This is the future time in which money "casts shadows of both past and future on current interactions; both the relationship's accumulated meanings and the parties' stakes in its future affect what happens today," in the words of the monetary sociologist Viviana Zelizer.[20] Think of personal loans, sharing finances and accounts (or deciding not to), promising an inheritance or to love for richer or poorer, receiving an allowance, or keeping a stash of walk-away cash.[21] We earmark and discount money in relation to the anticipations, hopes, and fears we feel in our relationships and personal circumstances. Money is held and bestowed in the hope of future redemption, in both senses of the word: whether of the soul of the deceased through a religious donation or some shares of preferred stock set aside in trust for an infant.

One step beyond these intimacies lies the network of larger communities, affinities, and alliances. Christine Desan's *Making Money* uses a detailed analysis of coinage and the development of capitalism in early modern England to argue that money, whatever else it might be, is always also a group institution, an "activity designed to organize a material world" within particular communities.[22] It works to "measure, collect, and redistribute resources" for specific groups—often as expressions of existing frameworks of territorial power. The alchemy of making money reaches well beyond the state, Desan writes: "The community may be a state, but it can also be a collective organized along lines of loyalty, religion, or affinity to which people make recurring contributions of labor or goods," embedded within various frameworks of time, history, and the anticipated future.[23]

Finally, there is the last kind of monetary temporality: crisis and catastrophe. When money fails, "all close relationships are lit up by an almost intolerable, piercing clarity in which they are scarcely able to survive. . . . Money stands ruinously at the center of every vital interest."[24] So wrote the philosopher-critic Walter Benjamin in his notes on living through the post–First World War German inflation: all that delicate, human business of balancing promises, fears, and realities with friends and intimates was exposed at once when the future of savings, pensions, trusts, and set-asides collapsed into a present of immediate survival. This, too, is part of the experience of money: it's the sound of rats in the walls of the calm estate of "actual money"— which, in the splendid phrase of John Maynard Keynes, "lulls our disquietude," calming our "distrust concerning the future."[25] (Much of the last quarter of this book is set in that kind of time as it is imagined and anticipated.)

With this landscape of money and its futures in mind, what makes the temporality of a Technocrat's energy certificates different? They were a *speculative currency* not just in the sense of "financial speculation"—ways to make possible futures pay—but "speculative fiction," the imagining and narrating of futures. The certificates functioned neither as an investment vehicle nor a transaction tool, neither a safe-deposit box of Krugerrands nor a promise from a relative. Instead, they were cosmograms, a way of arranging the universe and generating what Tresch called "an image of the world as it could be"—and with it the practices, rituals, and communities that would enact that world in the present—in the form and with the particular cultural power of money.[26] Offering a path from now to then, they worked as platforms for utopian prospect and utopian practice. Now, rather than placing bets on the olive harvest, like Thales of Miletus, or on the financial probity of the Spanish monarchy, like the great Dutch bankers, money could be used to speculate as a cultural project that acts not only as a stake in the future but as an artifact from it.

THE REVOLT OF THE SCIENTISTS

Speculative currencies are not artifacts of *the* future, though: they express a specific and particular future, one that belongs to its time. Despite Technocracy Inc.'s constant performance of futurity, their organization was in every respect an expression of the science-fictional sensibility of the Great Depression period in the United States. Their prospective future, from which the energy certificates were addressed to us, was as much a product of that moment as the Empire State Building or Norman Bel Geddes's tome of "not far-distant future" design, *Horizons*. In 1932, W. A. Dwiggins, a calligrapher and designer of typefaces and books, proposed a redesign of the US currency "done," he wrote, "in the mood of the first half of the Twentieth Century.... It would tell of speed, and of enormous electrical potentials, of the air as a new highway, of a universe suddenly swollen to appalling size."[27] That was precisely the mood within which Technocracy and their money situated itself: "Our 1932 American currency," Dwiggins argued, should express "an enormous accretion of mechanicalized energy struggling to preserve a democratic form."[28]

The Technocratic future that Howard Scott propounded was one of streamlined Deco styling, flying-wing aircraft, and neat columns of totted-up figures. It applied the aesthetic of a corporate prospectus to every aspect of life, in a framework of unified, militant, totalitarian control by scientists, technicians, and engineers. The cafeterias of utopia would be catered by the visionary chemists of the New Nutrition movement of the interwar United States, who sought to make nature into "a chain of factories, an assembly line": edible fats and oils were waiting to be synthesized from "the oil shales with which our country is so abundantly supplied."[29] The whole continent would be fashioned in the image of a vertically integrated technology firm, the ultimate monopoly.

This was understood as the inevitable outcome in that particular corner of the age. Scott was a disciple of Thorstein Veblen—the economist and sociologist who wrote *The Theory of the Leisure Class* and coined the term "conspicuous consumption"—and Veblen's 1921 *The Engineers and the Price System* was something of a dry run for Technocracy. It came complete with a vision of a "Soviet of technicians" and a model of social change built on a down-tools strike by technical professionals, a socialist mirror-world version of Ayn Rand's strike of the "creative minds" in *Atlas Shrugged*. By 1933, H. G. Wells's *Shape of Things to Come* posited an inevitable World State dominated by technicians, scientists, and pilots, who set about abolishing religion, enforcing "Basic English," and instituting "completely abstract money, a money as abstract and free from association with any material substance as weight or measure."[30] That "completely abstract" money was to be the "air-dollar": a uniform unit of cargo in transit, with paper notes representing weight, volume, speed, and distance aboard an aircraft. For Wells, as for all our utopian minters of speculative currency, "there could be no Theory of Money that was not in fact a complete theory of social organization"—a cosmogram. The reordering of the world and human affairs around a new technological regime was symbolized and performed by the issue of new notes: the air-dollar, he wrote, "marked very definitely that the old static conceptions of human life with limited resources were giving place to kinetic ideas of a continually expanding life."[31]

That same year, Hugo Gernsback's incubator of modern science fiction, *Wonder Stories*, featured the story cycle "The Revolt of the Scientists." The series described a Technocratic financial coup. With chemical technology and "rays" that could transmute gold reserves to tin and erase the ink on all paper notes, the renegade technocrats wiped out debt and crashed the economy completely prior to their takeover.[32] This was not a unique premise. Stories about either the synthesis or chemical debasement of gold and silver, with consequent monetary chaos, had captured the public's imagination since the turn of the century— particularly in the pages of the science fiction pulps. As early as 1900, there was Garrett Serviss's thriller *The Moon Metal*, in which a gold megastrike at the South Pole upends the economy until the mysterious "Dr. Syx" presents a new metal, "artemisium," as the artificially scarce backing of value; in 1922, the protagonist of Reinhold Eichacker's *Der Kampf ums Gold* creates gold chemically to pay off Germany's war reparations and ruin the allied economies at a single stroke. (Eichacker's Germany, forewarned, rebased its currency from gold to platinum.) There is one difference with the Technocratic narratives, though: this disruption and coup was never a monetary disaster for them but a deliverance, forcing the world's hand and creating the future as it was supposed to be through a crisis in the technology of money.

The people this book studies organize themselves and their speculative monies in terms of powerful fantasies of the future. These are not the reasonable bets on future productivity or future taxation that Desan put in contrast to silver bullion, but technological and science-fictional imaginaries by which society might be irretrievably and utterly disrupted, with money as the mechanism of transformation and the escape route out of the present into the future. Their money is not just utopian but *uchronian* money, to take a word from the historian Reinhart Koselleck: a superior society realized not somewhere on Earth but somewhen, in a historical time to come, represented now through the currency that will pass.

After the fleets of gray cars with monad symbols, after the apocalyptic predictions and the obsession with conspiracies (particularly, for some reason, the doings of the Vatican) and the call for scientific vigilantes, the Technocrats lasted long enough to find themselves alone—stalled in what Koselleck calls a "former future." They were marooned in time, but in their moment the Technocrats demonstrated the role of speculative, utopian, and uchronian currencies: tokens for summoning their future to appear.

CHAPTER 2

SECURE PAPER

In this chapter, we study how cash and currency work in practice: the deeper history of producing, securing, and authenticating paper money—that strange class of printed documents we have all learned how to read. We follow counterfeiters and their foes, consider the problem of trusting documents, read an accidental treatise on sovereignty in an ordinary transaction, and learn about a secret constellation that all of us have seen and almost none can recognize.

OBJECTS MADE IN NEW WAYS

You likely carry many signatures on your person as you read this. In the United States, they are probably Timothy Geithner, Anna Cabral, Jacob Lew; in Brazil, Henrique Meirelles; in Malaysia, Datuk Muhammad bin Ibrahim; in Poland, Adam Glapiński; across Europe, Mario Draghi or Jean Claude Trichet. These signatures are the most widely reproduced samples of handwriting in existence, their little paraph swashes of personhood riding in discreet corners of the world's banknotes, along with national monuments, blandly introspective portraits of notables, monumental digits, and the ponderous architectural-heraldic hardware of garlands, shields, scrollwork, and Doric capitals: "stalwart heroes sheathing their swords before monetary units," the philosopher Walter Benjamin wrote of banknotes at the time of German hyperinflation—"ornamenting the façade of hell."[1]

These signatures of treasury officials and central bankers are part of the deliberate archaism of banknotes, present in the paper like wisdom teeth or a vermiform appendix, the relic of bills of exchange. Bills of exchange were vehicles for the intricate chains of credit that sustained European trade for centuries. It can be modish and misleading to describe earlier technologies and practices in terms of later ones, but bills of exchange constituted something akin to a social network platform, within which a set of relationships and schedules could be established.

A merchant in one city issues a bill to an agent, promising to pay a sum at some future point to another person. With this bill in hand, the person to be paid could endorse it and use it to pay someone else at a discounted rate, who could pass it again in their turn. Rates and values for these discounting trades were shaped by the larger picture of (in Rebecca Spang's words) "the volume of bills to be paid in a certain city and on the reputation of both the originally named payer *and* all those who had endorsed the bill as it traded hands."[2]

Between Antwerp and Genoa, Paris and Frankfurt, and Istanbul and Lisbon, each new arrangement added a link to a chain of signatures, and each signature invoked a specific person to be held accountable. As Spang put it, the written signatures "made it possible to imagine that even hitherto unknown individuals could be found and held responsible if necessary."[3] An individual bill was the expression of a unique arrangement of people and events and goods—furniture, brandy, Monsieur X, Dottore Y, Mijnheer Z, six months from now, at the fair in Leipzig—and was itself a unique object. If lost, the holder could advertise for it "as he might a lost dog or an umbrella gone astray." Since every person in the chain was liable for failure, it meant financial safety in numbers: the more signatures in place, the more people were affirming the probity of everyone else.

This mechanism for managing the flow of value maintained a balancing act between standardized reproducibility and the unique particulars of *these people, this deal, next year.* The delicacy of this balance was exposed in the crisis of signatures during the production of *assignats* during the French Revolution. Assignats were the currency of the new regime, tied, in theory and at first, to nationalized properties. They ended up in much wider production and circulation than bills of exchange, while still drawing on the authority of the particular signature, from the originating clerk through the links of endorsers passing it along. Sinister conspiracies of clerks were imagined with foreboding; the problem of bottlenecks on issuing new money appeared— limited by the flexibility and time of the hands and pens of signatories; engraved and printed signatures shifted the meaning of the objects themselves. Along with property, the assignats had been backed by an identity and a name. Some specific bureaucrat with his pens, his home address, the revolutionary tricolor pinned to his hat, could be found and held accountable. (The term "bureaucrat" itself was an invention of that period and came into its own in the Revolution: governance by a piece of office furniture that represented an information storage and processing system.)[4]

Spang's study of this period documents a profound and subtle shift: the adoption of new techniques and technologies in printing to confirm the identity of the note itself, rather than the person who endorsed it. These notes became "objects made in new ways," designed to confirm the identity of this piece of paper as money, rather than to confirm the identity of a particular person with assets.[5]

We can look to the United States for a comparable case. The paperwork of credit systems—payment orders issued to "factors," agents, jobbers, and brokers against commodities to be delivered, warehouse receipts, bills of lading, auction records—had a mutually sustaining relationship to the monetary notes issued by banks and bound to some particular building, some community of farmers or miners, some strongbox of bullion. Communal credit networks thrived: nineteenth-century Floridian orange farmers and pioneers took in Northern tourists, who often paid with checks that couldn't be cashed for considerable time. The checks themselves therefore moved up and down the water as money, bearing a growing list of endorsements expressing the social system of Indian River.[6] "The entire business of these waters," wrote the Irish visitor Thomas Ashe in 1808, "is conducted without the use of money."[7]

The mercantile life of North America, from the Atlantic piers to the slave empires of Southern cotton to the trappers and *voyageurs* in Canadian rivers to the wagon trains and eventual railroads of the West, was initially organized with systems that would have been familiar to a fifteenth-century Venetian merchant family.[8] It ran on kinship networks, tenuous foreign trade with double-entry bookkeeping denominated in "Adventure and Merchandise Accounts," occasional coins and paper, and signature-centric ways of managing people, records, and investments.

Into this polyglot monetary culture, with coins and specie (Bohemian thalers and "pieces of eight," pine-tree shillings, Spanish reales), bills of credit issued to soldiers returning from Quebec, bills of lading for future barges of coal or cotton, local banknotes, and "cash articles" like furs, beeswax, linen, tea, and gunpowder, the concept and practice of national notes came as a new vocabulary—with the same ontological twist Spang describes. Credit systems, from bills of lading to banknotes from a local institution, were networks of regional social trust and acquired experience. ("If a good bill, it must have, thickened here and there into the substance of the paper, little wavy spots of red," says a character in Melville's 1857 *The Confidence-Man*, examining a note from the Vicksburgh Trust and Insurance Banking Company.) Coins and cash articles were all matters of direct somatic knowledge—from being weighed in scales, to the fineness of a length of cloth, to the taste, feel, weight, pliability, and look of metal. National notes had to confirm *themselves* as a new form of monetary identity and to train their holders not just in new ideas but in new practices of assessing objects and understanding value.

You should be able to easily recognize a good bill without knowing how to produce one yourself: the challenge of *secure paper*. It should be trivial for the originator to create—after the initial engineering hurdles are crossed, it should have a marginal cost close to zero—while being enormously difficult for an adversary to reverse engineer and re-create. One party should be able to turn old blue jeans (mostly, in the case of US dollars) into stacks of crisp bills in such a way that no other party could either produce their own or replicate the bills that already exist. Lisa Gitelman opened a media history of the explosion of writing techniques and technologies in the nineteenth and twentieth centuries—the expansion of new ways of making documents—with a New York City death certificate: its multiple signatures, seals and borders, intaglio printing, barcode, watermark, thermochromic ink, microprinting, and expression of itself as "a true copy of a record on file."[9] With this elaborate armature in place, the kernel of fact—of an identity, a time, a death—could be used in specialized contexts, from public health to the disbursement of assets to the most melancholy kind of identity work.[10] Paper money must provide a similar level of security that it is what it appears to be and do so in contexts as varied as the market itself: everywhere a cash transaction might appear, and for everyone who might engage in one.

And, still more difficult, it must now do so in the larger context of digital technologies, the proliferation of "objects made in new ways" built on systems of perfect, bit-for-bit reproducibility.

LEARNING TO READ THE ONE-DOLLAR BILL

A one-dollar bill, US$1. It is one of the most ubiquitous industrially produced objects in existence, circulating in the tens of billions of units. It's hard to say exactly how many: we know how many the Federal Reserve has put into circulation each year (11,700,000,000 one-dollar notes in the year of 2016, for instance), but the bills have the life expectancy of a gerbil, between about one to five years. In a legal and an economic sense, as *money*, they are all precisely the same—fungible, interchangeably worth no more and no less than any other, and capable of acting as a measurement tool to compare the respective prices of different things. As objects and as currency, though, they are deliberately and circumstantially unique.

The particular bill we're discussing here carries a great deal of data in the numbers printed on it: where it was produced (St. Louis), the series and serial number of the run it is part of, the specific plate used to print it (FW A 81), and even its position in a sheet of thirty-two—in this case, the upper left-hand corner of the sheet (A1). It is creased, a little linty, torn on the border in two places. When I hold it in my hand—when we handle cash in general—I touch an object touched by more strangers than anything else I will encounter aside from the grab bars and straps of public transit: an act of collective, bacterial communion. Paper money carries populations of skin flora hand to hand across the world like cargo ships discharging ballast water in foreign ports.

The US one-dollar bill is an object designed to be *read*, in simple and complex senses. It is iconic and immediately recognizable, whether to a human or the bill validator in a vending machine. It is so visibly on-brand: the greenback, one volume in a uniform edition, its reverse featuring an eerie, bleak landscape with an unfinished and watchful pyramid standing alone like a Magritte painting, and twelve references, digital and numeral, to its cardinality—its *one*-ness—in relation to other numbers in the series of notes. I mean this idea, that the bill is to be read, very concretely: it is part of a larger genre of valuable paper, a potent symbol we know how to interpret in particular ways.

The design historian Frances Robertson has chronicled the close relationship between the development of the first modern banknotes and steel-engraved technical drawing and printing: the same technologies spurring the reproduction of the new industrial order—the precise and detailed renderings of mass-produced parts and intricate machines—were brought to bear on the production of notes at once easily recognized and inimitable.[11] The "self-acting tools," ancestors of sophisticated lathes, machine tools, and computer numerical control (CNC) mills and cutters, enabled geometrically precise production that could take the place of skilled handwork. These were used in producing the parts for still other machines like locomotives, ships, and bridges—and banknotes, with the looping, spiraling patterns of the rose engine lathe. Those exquisite guilloche patterns used on postage stamps, Fabergé eggs, watch movements, and stock certificates and other authenticable paperwork are also present on a dollar bill, the direct heritage of the challenge of making printed paper money.

The products of high-tech, industrial, mechanized reproduction needed also to be *authentic*, with their very authenticity rooted in the sophistication of their multiplication. They are identical, like the interchangeable parts of a rifle or a locomotive, and just as reliable. They are "true" in the philosophical sense (the real thing) and the mechanical sense: trued like a wheel, carefully engineered and checked. You can pass a banknote as you would ride over the trusses of an iron bridge.

The cultural historian Mary Poovey argued that this banknote is also part of a larger domain of *reading*, one that has become largely invisible to us. "It's not worth the paper it's printed on": a phrase applied to money and writing alike. For Poovey, the naturalization of widespread industrial banknote production and models of "literary merit" around the same place and time in eighteenth- and nineteenth-century Britain and Europe was not a coincidence; the note could carry worth as a page of prose or poetry carried worthiness, part of a related set of genres for defining value on printed paper. "Money," she wrote, "has become so familiar that its writing has seemed to disappear and it has seemed to lose its history as [various forms of] writing."[12] While too complex an argument to take up in its entirety here, it sets up another aspect of what this dollar is: a *document*, with a set of implicit and explicit concepts carried on it.

It is "legal tender for all debts, public and private," and every time we transact it, it acts as our allegiance to countries in general and the United States in particular. "The paper currency is a key specimen of the quality of the product of the federal government as it expresses itself on paper," wrote W. A. Dwiggins, the type designer and calligrapher from chapter 1 who proposed to redesign the notes. "The currency, and the federal stamps, are the most widely distributed *insignia* of state that anyone can adduce."[13] I take the insignia out of my wallet to participate in what the anthropologist and scholar of payment systems Lana Swartz calls a "transactional community."[14] In the case of US dollars, it's a community that extends far past the country's borders, from dollarized economies like Ecuador's to the cubes of shrink-wrapped bricks of hundred-dollar bills acting as cash reserves and settlement mechanisms for operations public and covert all over the planet.

As I smooth out this one-dollar bill, trying to get the laundromat's change machine to accept it and return quarters, I'm unfolding a living historical document, with a design approved by Franklin Delano Roosevelt, a territorial remit advanced by Lincoln, a value that oscillates with reference to the Nixon Shock and the judgment of the Federal Reserve responding to market activity, "a daily affirmation of the nation-state" (the phrase is geographer Emily Gilbert's), sixteen square inches and carried by most everyone in the country.[15] I'm holding a philosophical treatise on the concept of sovereignty—a treatise whose meaning is now being challenged.

THE UGLIEST T-SHIRT IN THE WORLD

Bearing in mind how much we can read in a one-dollar bill, let's look further up the ladder of value at a US twenty, which must meet a separate technical challenge. No one tries to counterfeit US$1s anymore; the era of small-time counterfeiters like "Old Mr. 880," the subject of the longest manhunt in the history of counterfeiting, is long past.[16] Many serious and sophisticated groups work on counterfeiting twenties. Along with everything it shares with the one-dollar bill, the twenty also must incorporate technologies to be readable but not digitally duplicable; it must police the analog-digital border by itself.

A US twenty-dollar bill is a very specific kind of object. It must be almost, but not exactly, like every other twenty-dollar bill in existence; if there is a single other bill *exactly* like it, one of them is counterfeit. There is no other bill like this one before me (serial number JB9557548B, 2009 series, Timothy Geithner's signature, a little blue ballpoint pen squiggle over the portico of the White House), as far as I know, but there are 6.4 billion others that are very close. They are in wallets and envelopes and the vaults of cash machines and banks and cash-in-transit vehicles and shrink-wrapped on pallets in warehouses and buried in backcountry lots in lengths of PVC pipe to escape metal detectors. The bill works as it does only because it is simultaneously specific and generic, recognizable but not reproducible; a great deal of work goes into keeping it that way.

This particular bill simultaneously does and does not have value in the way we are all familiar with: if we cut it into quarters, we still have the substance of the thing, but the meaning has changed and the value has gone (and we've committed a crime in our act of defacement—it's my note, but not really mine). It exists between now, when one holds it, and then, when it passes to someone else. It is only valuable to me because it can pass out of my hands. It is an abstract quantity, capable of becoming anything from an act of generosity to a fire extinguisher, but it exists in practice in terms of concrete qualities—it is variably earmarked and discounted by my personal circumstances, and I'll spend, save, or give it differently.[17] To all those simultaneities, we can add a new one: this bill is simultaneously analog and digital.

The friable edges between analog and digital were crumbling away in the 1990s, and the crisis for cash was imminent: the proliferation of high-resolution scanners, precise laser printers and color printers, and image editing software laid the groundwork for a counterfeiting emergency. The long, beautiful sequence of Willem Dafoe's counterfeiter at work in William Friedkin's 1985 *To Live and Die in L.A.* (one of the great montages of technique in movies, up there with the Charles Eames–directed construction of the airplane in Billy Wilder's *Spirit of St. Louis*) could be replaced with after-hours digital desktop publishing in any high-end design studio. Digitization broke the arrangement that made cash viable. New strategies were employed to deal with this problem: reactive inks and security threads, optical tricks, the feel of different textiles, watermarks, even denominations hidden in diffraction gratings that you could project on a wall with a laser pointer. The most telling of these was the EURion Constellation.

If you are reading this in much of the world, you likely carry this Constellation in your purse or pocket at this moment, alongside that set of signatures. If you are holding the Mexican twenty-peso note, it's the small yellow circles in the band by Benito Juárez's head; a UAE dirham note generally has the circles positioned near landmarks like stars in the background; on the ten euro note they're in the visual echoes of the arch; the US$20 hides them in small yellow "20"s. This dot pattern is recognized by the firmware in color copiers, scanners, printer drivers, and components deep in graphics editing software (like Photoshop), triggering currency recognition systems that refuse to digitize or reproduce the note.

In William Gibson's novel *Zero History*, he imagined an object he called "the ugliest t-shirt in the world": "There were huge features screened across it in dull black halftone, asymmetrical eyes at breast height, a grim mouth at crotch-level.... Diagonals at the edges continued around the sides, and across the short, loose sleeves."[18] It sounds like a cross between Shepard Fairey's *Obey* face and a QR code. This pattern acts as an instruction to the "deep architecture" of digital video surveillance. CCTV cameras will record a person wearing this pattern but will remove them from the recording on retrieval. "They forget the figure wearing the ugly T-shirt. Forget the head atop it, the legs below, feet, arms, hands."

In the novel, a "gentleman's agreement" has established that this cryptic symbol will work across the software of CCTV systems. It is effectively a magical object; Gibson's characters refer to it as a *sigil*, a symbol invested with supernatural power. Everyone paying in a major currency's cash has held and folded a symbol even more far-reaching: the Constellation, an expression of an international agreement that excludes particular objects from being digitized in particular ways. The ugliest T-shirt only works on CCTV systems; the Constellation only works on systems capable of high-resolution image capture, editing, and printing. (You can take a picture of it with your phone just fine.)

The Counterfeit Detection System software is freely available but closed source—meaning that its mechanisms cannot be reviewed, even by companies that have incorporated it.[19] There are other recognition mechanisms that still more obscurely apply. If you mask the Constellation, some digital optical systems still know not to capture or modify the object of money, using cues that researchers are still working on untangling. This is a body of symbols meant not for humans but for machines. They work to identify an object as money: not simply to make it valuable, but to keep it as one kind of object, on the analog borderline, and prevent cash from becoming digital.

What about cash that started digitally? How was it to be secured and authenticated—and read and understood?

CHAPTER 3

RECOGNIZABLE WITHOUT BEING KNOWN

We continue to explore what cash is, and how it is created and authenticated, by moving forward into the computational age. This chapter describes the development of public key cryptography, particularly the technologies of authentication used for "digital signatures," and looks at how they were assimilated into existing traditions of confirming documents—including the class of printed documents we call cash—and created, in the process, strange new hybrid forms.

THE AGONY OF CODING

Nancy Wake bicycled 250 miles in three days in 1944, more or less day and night. When she needed to sleep, she lay behind bushes or concealed in ditches. She brought makeup and toiletries, so she could freshen up as she went, always appearing to be out for a brief jaunt or some local errand. She needed to pass this way because she was the Allied agent the Gestapo dubbed "the White Mouse," in occupied France with a five-million-franc bounty on her head. A person of extraordinary grit and courage, Wake—who organized and supplied thousands of guerrilla fighters in the Auvergne and once killed an SS sentry with her bare hands—had to make the ride; otherwise she and her crew were trapped. Fearing capture during a retreat, the wireless operator Denis Rake had buried his radio equipment and destroyed their codebooks.[1]

Without codes there was no way to communicate with their support in the UK; to arrange drops of food, volunteers, arms, ammunition, and other matériel; and to coordinate their actions with other fighters. Wake knew the location of the nearest operator with a set of codes, so off she went, hoping to return before they ran out of food or were overwhelmed. By the time she got back, she could neither walk nor dismount her bicycle without assistance, but they had their ciphers.

Wake was part of an institution called the Special Operations Executive. The SOE trained, coordinated, and supported guerrilla fighters behind Axis lines. It was a chaotic, inventive, unorthodox, ad hoc organization. The SOE agents urgently needed secure communications tools and cipher systems that were reliable, portable, easy to conceal, and fast. The agents were people like Odd Starheim, a Norwegian who escaped to Aberdeen to get training in sabotage and secret messages—"the agony of coding"—so that he could parachute back into Norway and aid an SOE team in blowing up a Nazi heavy-water plant.[2] He couldn't be sent into the field (pushed out of a plane in the middle of the night over a glacier, for instance) with a twenty-five-pound cipher machine that would be grounds for immediate arrest and interrogation if found.

Their standard method was the "poem cipher." The poem, prearranged between sender and receiver, would be the basis for a set of words whose numbered letters acted as the transposition key for the message. This method had the advantage of requiring no equipment, since you could commit the poem to memory—but agents had the bad habit of choosing poems they knew well from the common stock of Keats, Molière, Shakespeare, and so on. Doing the ciphering in their heads led to slips and mistakes, making their messages confusing or even opaque to their recipients; using the same poems repeatedly, even original ones, made them less secure; SOE handlers often sent exactly the same text to many different agents, each in their personal code. If one of these identical messages were cracked, the adversary could test the text against all the others, breaking each of those ciphers in turn. Finally, if these ciphers were broken once, they would continue to be broken, since the codes themselves didn't change.

Leo Marks, the cryptographer who headed the SOE's code office, fought this practice. (Yes, the master cryptographer for the SOE was named Marks; in another Nabokovian detail, their offices were on Baker Street, not far from the chambers where Sherlock Holmes cracked ciphers like the "Dancing Men.") In the short term, he convinced many of the SOE agents to create their own original poems, or at least adopt uncommon ones— Nancy Wake, for instance, "used a pornographic poem which she'd made even more pornographic by her habit of misspelling it."[3] In the long term, he sought a more complete solution.

He found it in the "one-time pad," which he refined into the "letter one-time pad" (LOP) and printed in minute type on a sheet of silk. The LOP was a grid of randomly generated letters, used with a "substitution square": likewise a grid for ease of reference, twenty-six by twenty-six squares, for a set of substitution rules—for A plus A, write P, for I plus D, write U. Silk made the pads easy to conceal and to destroy, to sew into the lining of coats, wad into tiny balls, swallow, burn, flush down the toilet. (When the KGB used one-time pads, they printed them on flash paper to be immediately destroyed on use.)[4] Silk was expensive, but Marks presented the deal to his superiors as "silk or cyanide"—budget either for silks or for suicide pills for the agents inevitably compromised or captured.

AT MIDNIGHT, begins your message; OPXCA PLZDR, begins your pad of random letters. Check the substitution grid: for A plus O, write J; for T plus P, write X, and so on.[5] The first two words of your message will be JXFZD YXQZK. Once the ciphering is done, you can send your message and destroy the random letters used from the pad—it is "one time," never to be used again. (Reuse of the substitution square doesn't compromise security; without the original pad of random letters, nothing in the substitution square will tell you the text of the message—it serves only to make enciphering faster and less prone to errors.) The decipherer goes through the same process in reverse. As long as sender and receiver are using the same pad and substitution square, and starting at the same place in the string of random letters, the one-time pad can rapidly encrypt and decrypt messages in perfect security.[6]

"Perfect" meaning *perfect*: as pioneering information theorist Claude Shannon proved in 1945 (and Vladimir Kotelnikov, independently, in 1941), if the numbers are truly random and there is no reuse of keys, the one-time pad is absolutely secure.[7] No letter or string of letters in the ciphertext gives a clue to any of the corresponding letters, no matter how much ciphertext you have. All your adversary can determine is the length of the message; naturally, many users of one-time pads would add padding to their messages, to make even that unreliable.

All of these tools and techniques with their varying effectiveness—the wireless codebooks, silk handkerchiefs, memorized poems—shared a single, deeper problem: symmetry. Absolute as a one-time pad or vulnerable as a poem code based on a Shakespeare sonnet, all these methods relied on sender and receiver having the *same key*. The same poem, the same page of the same book, the same line of the same page of the one-time pad had to be used for encryption and decryption.

The key was also relied on to authenticate the communicants: that the message was properly ciphered was generally taken as proof that it was from the right person.

Symmetrical keys meant an enormous multiplication of points of compromise, in every step of storing, sharing, sending, and updating the keys. Intercept the luggage at customs, surreptitiously photograph all the cipher pages, and read the agent's traffic in your country at leisure—and communicate *as* them once they've been taken out of play. Symmetry made sender, receiver, and every point between vulnerable. The German naval code—which relied on the famous Enigma machine—included booklets for setting the device in sync with the rest of the organization (keeping the keys symmetrical) and using short codes to decrease chances of detection; these documents were printed in red ink on pink blotter paper, so they could be made immediately illegible with a splash of water to prevent capture. Nancy Wake bicycled hundreds of miles facing the possibility of capture, torture, and death for want of the codebooks.

This was the situation until one afternoon in computer scientist John McCarthy's house in Berkeley in the spring of 1975, in the mind of his housesitter.

TRAPDOOR

"The thing I remember distinctly is that I was sitting in the living room when I thought of it the first time and then I went downstairs to get a Coke and I almost lost it."

Whitfield Diffie was preoccupied with the problem of symmetric keys, which computers aggravate. If you don't want every signal between two computers "in clear," readable by anyone who can tap a phone line or tune a radio, then the computers need matching keys for encrypting and decrypting. But how are those keys to be transmitted? If the keys can also be picked up in transit, then any reliable computer-to-computer exchange—any possibility for digitally communicating in confidence so that we are not overheard and both are whom we claim to be—becomes almost impossibly difficult.

This story has been well told many times by the protagonist himself, in oral histories, and in several excellent books.[8] Diffie had been roaming the country in a Datsun 510, visiting libraries and meeting with researchers to answer two related questions: how to reliably verify ourselves and our machines (an issue in military equipment called *identification friend or foe*, IFF) and how to communicate with provable secrecy. He ended up housesitting for McCarthy, turning over, yet again, the problem of contemporary cryptography. That afternoon in May, he cracked a few different problems at the same moment with *asymmetric* key encryption; as he almost forgot, going to get a drink, history wobbled on a point of convergence in the living room.

Not that asymmetric—or, as it became more widely known, "public"—key encryption would never otherwise have been discovered. Many different people were attacking this question from different sides. Martin Hellman, Diffie's coauthor and collaborator, had already been studying it. So had Richard Schroeppel, who devoted his career to a mix of cryptography, elliptic curves, and the properties of magic squares. An undergraduate at UC Berkeley named Ralph Merkle was working on closely related ideas: a set of puzzles to establish a shared secret key between two parties with no shared secret beforehand, which he first proposed in 1974.[9] A prominent cryptographic mathematician, cryonics advocate, and Extropian, Merkle reappears many times in this book; his work on hashing paired data, the Merkle tree, underlies the "blocks" in the Bitcoin blockchain.

In fact, public key cryptography had already been independently discovered—as "non-secret encryption"—by James Ellis, Clifford Cocks, and Malcolm Williamson in the UK, with the initial breakthrough in 1969 ("Can we produce a secure encrypted message, readable by the authorised recipient without any prior secret exchange of the key?") and the mathematical solution, from number theory, in 1973.[10] But they worked for the Government Communications Headquarters (GCHQ), the UK's equivalent of the National Security Agency in the United States, and their work was and long remained secret.

What Diffie, Ellis, Cocks, Williamson, Hellman, Merkle, and others were all working toward was splitting the key. Symmetry means the same key is used for enciphering and deciphering; if you could separate those functions into different yet somehow related keys, then you could freely distribute one without compromising the other. This could solve the intractable problem of symmetrical key exchange in a single decisive stroke, like Alexander cutting the Gordian knot.

An asymmetrical arrangement means you can freely share your "public" key without endangering the security of your communications. Messages encrypted with that public key can only be read by using the "private" key, which is kept by the user. The keys correspond, but the first cannot be inferred from the second: you cannot extract the private key from the public. Instead of fretting over every weak link in the chain of custody of a symmetric key, and trusting in third-party repositories of matching keys to establish safe communications between computers, you can generate a keypair yourself and share the public key with whom you will and keep the private key as a secret for you alone. "The virtue of cryptography should be that you don't have to trust anybody directly involved with your communications," said Diffie.[11]

For this to work, the cryptographers had to find a set of "one-way functions." These had to make it very easy to compute a function and produce a result, and very difficult ("computationally infeasible") to work backward from that result—to invert the function. It only works one way, a door that permits entrance but not egress. We could sit down together with pen and paper and grade-school arithmetic and quickly multiply two very large prime numbers together. To factor out the resulting semiprime number, though, and determine which primes we multiplied to produce it, is an immensely difficult task: a protracted "brute force" search through an enormous space. With a sufficiently strong key, the solution process dwarfs not only our life spans but the history of written language, of human evolution, of geological time.

This function has one additional, vital component: a trapdoor. If you have semiprime factors for the number, you can quickly verify whether they are the correct ones. Possession of the trapdoor means that the function can be easily reversed by someone with the right information. "A trap-door cryptosystem," Diffie and Hellman wrote, "can be used to produce a public key distribution system."[12] What this means in practice, speaking at a high level: With the right set of functions, you can take a message and encrypt it without knowing the key necessary to decrypt it. The person with the key can do the decryption more or less instantly (with the aid of the "development of cheap digital hardware"), and an adversary can intercept the encrypted message, plus the public key, and still be unable to discover the private key and read the message. Diffie and Hellman were not certain of precisely the right function for this one-way operation, and many initial attempts proved too easy to solve with the aid of fast computation. The particular area of prime number factorization would wait a few years until the work of Ron Rivest, Adi Shamir, and Leonard Adleman in 1978 (for whom the landmark RSA algorithm and company were named), and set off what the scholar of computing infrastructure and cryptography Jean-François Blanchette described as "a gold rush for the discovery of additional suitable problems," each involving "different *computational assumptions*, distinct conjectures about the difficulty of calculating inverse functions for the scheme."[13]

Metaphors can mislead in this domain—there are properties particular to primes and semiprimes, and to different equivalent functions, that make certain numbers and operations much less suitable for this purpose than others. But the simple question remains: How was this number produced?

124620366781718784065835044608106590434820374651678880575481878888328966680118821085503603957027250874750986476843845862105486553797025393057189121768431828636284694840530161441643046806687569941524699318570418303051254959437137215902923609 9[14]

When Diffie and Hellman were working on the particulars of the system for splitting the key, they saw a second property the system would have. If such a split key existed, with a private and a public piece and the trapdoor between them, you could use the *private* key to encrypt a message so that the corresponding public key could decrypt it. This provided no secrecy: the public key should be widely distributed, and anyone with it could read a private-key-ciphered message. Instead, it gave *verification*. To decipher a message with the public key proved that it was ciphered with the private key. Assuming that the private key had been protected—still a secret, in possession of its creator alone—that meant you could verify the message had been produced by the holder of the private key and not altered in transit. The message could be given the equivalent of a written signature and a sealed envelope.

This was simultaneously a real thing—the system would enable just such a demonstrable outcome—and a powerful and somewhat vague metaphor. Diffie and Hellman talked about contracts and receipts; Rivest, Shamir, and Adleman about "signature," "proof," and "judge"—in quotes, as Blanchette points out, because "cryptographic algorithms are not transparently assimilable to the writing of one's name on paper."[15] For a start, they were constrained by the problem of copying. "Since any digital signal can be copied precisely," Diffie and Hellman wrote, "a true digital signature must be recognizable without being known."[16]

Recognizable without being known. This was a tall order, one that may seem familiar from the problems faced by banknotes. How do you create a reproducible object—a printed sheet of a currency, a signature—that can't be reproduced by the wrong parties? It must be verifiable but not replicable, easily created but not re-created, recognizable without being known, and provably reliable. (Bitcoin, decades in the future, will be almost entirely a system of digital, cryptographic signatures.) Diffie and Hellman wrote that "in order to develop a system capable of replacing the current written contract with some purely electronic form of communication, *we must discover a digital phenomenon with the same properties as a written signature.*"[17] "But what exactly," Blanchette asked in rejoinder, "*is* a written signature?"[18]

THE SAME PROPERTIES AS A WRITTEN SIGNATURE

When Sylvia Howland died in 1865, she left a will giving part of her enormous fortune in trust to her niece, Hetty Robinson. Robinson produced a second, secret will awarding herself the whole estate. The executor refused to accept it, and Robinson took him to court. The second will was in Robinson's handwriting; she had taken dictation from her elderly, infirm aunt. Only the signatures on the page were Howland's—or not. On this millions rested.[19]

Three words—"Sylvia Ann Howland"—would be among the most closely studied examples of handwriting in history. Quantified in terms of hours and expertise, few works of art could claim such critical focus: photographically enlarged and studied under microscopes and scrutinized by handwriting experts, bankers, scientists, and pioneering photographers and engravers.

The concern wasn't that the signatures on the different pages of the will were too different: it was that they were too similar. They were identical, stroke by stroke, and even their placement and distance from the margins on their respective pages was the same. This didn't look like authorship but like tracing. Dozens of examples of Howland's signature showed more variation, but those were over time. How much does your signature vary from day to day, hour to hour, document to document? Bankers and accountants—people with a professional background in approving signatures—testified to consistency and inconsistency.[20] Louis Agassiz used cutting-edge microscope technology to look for traces of pencil lead, providing testimony that sounded like an explorer traversing an alien landscape by balloon: he found deltas of ink distributed like mud on a silting riverbed, and none of the geological disturbances of scrambled strata that would be left by a rubber eraser.

The astronomer Benjamin Peirce and his son, the scientist, philosopher, and logician Charles Sanders Peirce, tried a very different approach, shifting to mathematics and probability and away from the sensory training of those skilled in signatures.

Father and son identified precisely thirty downstrokes characterizing Howland's signature and went through the dozens of examples, cataloging the variations and creating a statistical model of the likelihood of the signatures on the contested page precisely corresponding. It was to deliver the results of these calculations that Benjamin Peirce took the stand on that June day to describe a number—the chance of the signatures matching as well as they do—that "far transcends human experience."[21]

Charles Peirce would later cofound American pragmatist (or, as he preferred, "pragmaticist") philosophy, and the discipline of semiotics in the United States. His passion was symbolic logic, and of particular interest to him was how we distinguish signs that refer to things from signs that are things themselves: What does a zero or a dollar sign or a yardstick or a barometer's needle mean and how does it work? In the Howland Will case, he and his father had to distinguish a signature from a *picture* of a signature—to quantify and explain how to identify the moment of human presence and conscious assent in the written object, and to distinguish what it is from what it means.[22]

RECOGNIZABLE WITHOUT BEING KNOWN

A signature is known in a singular way: it is the index of an event, of a body in the act of writing. Charles Sanders Peirce, in his capacity as a semiotician, argued that there were three ways that a thing, a sign, could "convey knowledge of some other thing, which it is said to stand for or represent."[23] One way was the *index,* the sign that conveys knowledge by virtue of a physical connection to the thing for which it stands. Think "index" as in the pointing index finger: *it's over there,* you communicate without speaking. Distant smoke, the Pole Star, a bubble in a carpenter's level, a plumb bob, a map, a sailor's rolling gait on land, a fingerprint left on a glass: indices all, signs carrying information by physical connection. A signature is a set of written symbols based on shared convention and usage—as with seven arbitrary symbols: h, o, w, l, a, n, d—but also an *index*, the record of a hand, a second, a physical event linked to a body. "Taking the offered pen," writes Melville of Queequeg signing on as harpooner on the *Pequod*, he "copied upon the paper, in the proper place, an exact counterpart of a queer round figure which was tattooed upon his arm."

Signet rings, Chinese chops and Japanese *inkan* and Korean *dojang* and *guksae*, fingerprints, and the unique calligraphic *tughra* signature of an Ottoman sultan: the millennial and global history of human authentication objects rests on the paradox of an object that could be unique but repeatable, expressing a singular instant of presence each time. It had to be similar enough to itself that it could be confirmed without being precisely the same—recognizable without being known. The signature, the authenticating act, was intimately personal but could be delegated: from the presidential or prime-ministerial body to the Autopen or the rubber stamp. The cultural historian Hillel Schwartz argued that the signature only assumed its current cultural significance after the heyday of the European Romantic movement, focused as it was on the singular expression of personal genius and style. In a time of reproducible printed type, Schwartz wrote, the personal hand, "like a paraph spiralling off the end of a signature," had "a public flourish irreproducible by any printing press."[24] The paraph being a precaution against forgery: recognizable but not reproducible, a bit of unique human style.

The digital signature began as a superficially similar act of individual bodily presence, the authentication of a message with a private key corresponding to a public key—"a digital

phenomenon with the same properties as a written signature,"
as Diffie and Hellman had envisioned. But it did not have exactly
"the same properties." Written signatures involve similarity
without replication: what distinguishes an authentic signature is
precisely that infinitesimal bit of personal difference produced
each time that a Xerox machine does not possess.[25] Signatures
occupy a technically simple, socially complex role in the context
of witnesses, formalized positions like notaries and lawyers, and
systems of documents like checks, contracts, and forms.

The "digital phenomenon" of the cryptographic signature,
meanwhile, was a growing family of interesting mathematical
objects, software processes, and models. "Creatively assembled,"
in Blanchette's words, these elements yielded "mutations" in the
metaphor of the signature, a strange bestiary of new ways to confirm, authenticate, approve, or verify: chimeras with names like
one-time signature, multiproxy signature, ring signature, fair
blind signature, undeniable signature, forward-secure signature,
fail-stop signature, threshold signature, multisignature, desig-
nated confirmer signature.

There were occasional, obligatory paragraphs in the literature
where cryptographers would crank up the mainspring on the old
Victrola gramophone and drop the needle on convoluted analog metaphors and analogies: invisible inks, signed flaps, irrefutable stamps; locks and keys and safe-deposit boxes; cashier's
checks, bearer bonds, and banknotes. Imagine, wrote the cryptographer and entrepreneur David Chaum, a sealed envelope
lined with carbon paper, containing an unknown document,
stamped with a notary's embosser. Out of this strange notion,
implemented cryptographically, he would develop the first
functional digital cash scheme—one that he hoped could avert
a totalitarian future.

CHAPTER 4

BLINDING FACTOR

We begin with a nightmare of total surveillance and control from 1975 courtesy of electronic money. With predictions and fears of electronic transactions and computational commerce in mind, we turn to the work of David Chaum. His DigiCash project was a protocol for money that could be digitally issued and redeemed by existing banks in existing currencies with the anonymity of cash. Its failure left a design framework taken up by others who wanted to create, and not just transact, new kinds of digital cash.

ARRANGED ENERGY

First, the fantasies.

"BETTER THAN MONEY," trumpeted the subhead amid visions of "computerized communities," in Martin Greenberger's 1964 article "Computers of Tomorrow." He published it in the *Atlantic*, the same magazine that carried Vannevar Bush's landmark proto-hypertext vision "As We May Think" in 1945. Like Bush, Greenberger was extrapolating the "information utility" of the future and its applications: "medical-information systems," "automatic libraries," simulation services, "design consoles . . . editing consoles . . . computerized communities."[1] Key to all of these would be that "better than money" platform: "These cards, referred to by some as 'money keys,' together with the simple terminals and information exchange, can all but eliminate the need for currency, checks, cash registers, sales slips, and making change."

Greenberger meant something like the credit card infrastructure then being developed, relying on a highly centralized system of utility phone lines and existing banks and payment companies, plus a little futuristic magic. "Incidentally," he promised, "we can look forward in the process [of adopting electronic money] to displacing another class of manual labor: miscellaneous thieves who prey on money. The increased possibilities for embezzlement through fraudulent accounting may attract some of the resulting unemployed, but there are ways that the computer can be deputized to police its own operation, quietly and without danger of corruption." Do tell.

At a conference in Bordeaux six years later, the computer scientist John McCarthy was talking about something like those very "consoles" promised by Greenberger, with more rigor about putting them into practice.[2] (This is the same McCarthy for whom Whitfield Diffie was housesitting in Berkeley when he developed his part of public key cryptography.) Considering the future of "home information terminals," McCarthy was clear about the role "money" would play. Electronic money would enable new forms of digital commerce. He considered advertising, payments for information and articles—"the reader will have the system balk at what he considers overpriced material"—and as yet unrealized kinds of transactions. He anticipated "a profound effect on buying and selling." But how do you verify these transactions? Though it may seem simple in retrospect, digitally verifying a transaction contains subtleties of identity, authorization, receipt, and proof.

Five years after, Dee Hock, the CEO of Visa, was proposing an answer. Hock belonged in the company of people like Buckminster Fuller, architect of geodesic domes and global networks, and the bearded cybernetic sage and management consultant Stafford Beer: jet-set sales reps for the utopian infrastructure of the 1970s, publicists for the cosmos. Hock, fascinated by emergent order and self-organizing processes in nature, had little interest in merely building a business for "Electronic Funds Transfer" (EFT). His sights were set on the social transformation of "Electronic Value Exchange" (EVE). EVE was what money would be, he wrote: "guaranteed alphanumeric data" in "arranged energy" flowing seamlessly through computer networks around the Earth.[3]

For Hock, EVE would be a sister system to the nascent Internet, a global network machine with a related set of utopian fantasies. His design for the headquarters was a circular office, which symbolically contained the four corners of the planet, with sections devoted to each region's culture and booths for real-time translation across languages.[4] (He described his acrimonious departure from Visa as a search for "a life of anonymity and isolation ... with books, nature, and uninterrupted thought," as if he were a Taoist sage departing for the mountains.) EVE would be a part of the next epoch of cybernetic society.

But there was a catch. What "guaranteed" the alphanumeric data that money would soon become? What would direct and sluice those flows of energy constituting credit?

Surveillance.

THE BEST SURVEILLANCE SYSTEM
WE COULD IMAGINE

Now, the nightmare.

"Say you are about to buy a book," wrote the Stanford computer scientist Paul Armer in 1975 in an article for the journal *Computers and People*. He based his article on his testimony to Congress, for whom his recommended reading included

Orwell's *1984*, a Nixon administration memo on domestic intelligence gathering, and Dawidowicz's *The War Against the Jews, 1933–1945*. Armer's piece was startlingly prescient on the surveillance problem produced by authenticating electronic money. "You present your card (sometimes called a 'debit card'...)," he continued, "to a clerk who puts it into a terminal which reads it and then calls up your bank."[5] The bank either OK'd or declined the transaction—and there the trouble began.

When Armer bought a book with his debit card, the settlement system learned his location at that time, adding it to the log of his movements, and with it "a great deal of data about your financial transactions," and "a great deal of data about your life." What if you had already been flagged by the police for special attention? "I have no doubt that such systems have already been so abused." Given the task of building an ideal, discreet surveillance apparatus for the KGB in 1971, Armer and a group of computing and surveillance specialists came up with a version of an electronic funds transfer system: "Not only would it handle all the financial accounting and provide the statistics crucial to a centrally planned economy; it was the best surveillance system we could imagine within the constraint that it not be obtrusive."[6]

His choice of a book as the object of his notional purchase was deliberate: What if you were not yet flagged, but the purchase of a particular book put you "on a list," as part of a suspect population or pattern? If it is a book that authorities decided is not for you to read, will the system auto-decline your purchase attempt? Will your money be good for some things and not others?

Recall that Margaret Atwood's novel *The Handmaid's Tale*, written a decade after Armer's testimony, is partially a dystopian story about electronic money. Computerized accounts and credit identified as belonging to women are frozen—as Atwood said afterward, "now that we have credit cards, it's very easy to just cut off people's access to credit"—and she envisioned, among other systems of domination, a process of *monetary coercion*, with object-specific tokens to prevent independent choices and decisions: "I look at the oranges, longing for one," thinks her protagonist Offred. "But I haven't brought any coupons for oranges."[7] Real-world versions of this already existed or would come to exist: from the coupons and scrip of company towns, to color-coded state-issued food stamps, to welfare funds issued through electronic benefit transfer (EBT) in the United States—"money," in the case of food benefits, that will not permit itself to be spent on certain goods and that is subject to data collection and analysis.[8]

Electronic money could serve as a control apparatus for making the marketplace into a rapid response system for the police, a location log, and a Skinner box for rewarding and denying citizens into doing what corporations or governments wanted. In 1990, the philosopher Gilles Deleuze wrote a short piece called "Postscript on the Societies of Control." Deleuze started with the transition the theorist-historian Michel Foucault had identified—from sovereign societies to disciplinary societies, a transition in how power was expressed at every level of life— and then asked: Are people in postindustrial, networked, capitalist societies now living through a comparable transition to *control societies?* To explain what he meant, he turned to the exemplary technology of power: "Perhaps it is money that expresses the distinction between the two societies best."[9]

The previous disciplinary society operated as a series of enclosures, "interiors," with stabilizing and standardizing mechanisms at work to organize productive forces: to turn out biscuits, citizens, newspapers, soldiers, Model T's, healthy right-thinking bodies, and interchangeable parts. It did this, he wrote, in a framework of "minted money that locks gold in as numerical standard"—as a benchmark, a calibrating mechanism. The current and near future control society, he argued, models value with "floating rates of exchange, modulated according to a rate established by a set of standard currencies": a post-Nixon Shock system of as-good-as-instant telecommunications and continuous data collection, feedback, analysis, and adjustment.[10]

Knowing "the position of any element within an open environment at any given instant," the control system exerts power through a society that has become largely overseen and managed as "coded figures," as digital data, readily displayed, analyzed, and utilized. "Man is no longer man enclosed," Deleuze writes, as if delivering the voiceover narration of a dystopian sci-fi movie, "but man in debt."[11] Money on a card, money as data, can govern and control: payable here and not there, for this and not that, and producing real-time information about its user for further adjustment. In his speculative mode, Deleuze brings together house-arrest ankle bracelets and parole cuffs, just-in-time production and logistics chains, mobile phones and geolocation and what would become the quantified self, area and access denial technologies, and digital payment and electronic money platforms: a wide territory that defines the outlines of a new model of sovereignty, and of the expression and exercise of power.[12]

MAKE BIG BROTHER OBSOLETE

David Chaum, too, feared a future in which the ledgers of online credit and debit systems had become dossiers: "The granularity of information that's revealed about payments is going to explode," he warned.[13] In 1983, eight years after Armer's testimony, Chaum was also writing about buying books, along with many other transactions that "reveal a great deal about the individual's whereabouts, associations and lifestyle."[14] The same mechanisms that managed the trust in digital payment would produce a time-stamped and geocoded record from which much could be revealed—and that's before considering the ways in which digital ledger money could be actively manipulated for real-time redlining, price fixing and gouging, and other mechanisms of financial exclusion. Chaum talked about Panopticons, police states, Big Brother; speaking before Congress in 1995, he foresaw in the credit card and the networked point-of-sale terminal a human population of "electronically tagged animals in feedlots."[15] However, he had a solution to offer.

The alternative to the feedlot, he continued, would be "buyers and sellers in a town market square," with each party able to "protect its own interests." To "secure parity between individuals and organizations," he built on the technologies of public key cryptography and signatures, to make money that could identify itself while keeping its users secret. His Netherlands-based company DigiCash called the stuff "e-cash" (variously quoted as Ecash, eCash, and e-Cash). They created the first real and functional digital cash as an alternative to surveillance-based credit-and-debit systems; Chaum's approach, patents, and theories set the agenda for digital cash research for more than a decade.

Chaum was fascinated by "dead drops, document security, burglar alarms, safes and vaults, locks, flaps and seals." (His other patents included an electronic lock capable of recognizing different metal keys, and systems for ballots and voting.)[16] He developed an idea whose outline resembles old-school, analog document security. Imagine that you wanted to notarize a document without revealing what it was—to have proof of a discovery written down and deposited today, making a claim for precedence and priority without sharing the discovery with the world yet. The historian of science Mario Biagioli has described just such a problem in the practice of Renaissance science, with

Christiaan Huygens submitting an announcement of the discovery of the spring watch as an anagram ("4135373I2343242 abcefilmnorstux") and Galileo announcing the observation of Saturn's irregular shape as "smaismrmilmepoetaleumibunenugttauiras."[17] A paperwork solution evolved: sealed notes deposited with trusted institutions like the Academie des Sciences. This sealed-envelope approach could be taken one step further.

Slip your document into an envelope with a sheet of carbon paper, seal the flap, and then have a notary's stamp or a signature and date applied to the *outside* of the envelope. The person stamping or signing does not know what they are authenticating: a "blind signature," an indexical trace of time and proof that doesn't give its secrets away. The carbon paper envelope and the blind signature connect the proof to the *document* rather than its container, eliminating any possible accusation of envelope switching—of the steaming kettles, heat lamps, slender ivory spatulas, and other elegant tricks of predigital "flaps and seals" spy tradecraft. The document can prove facts about itself without revealing what it is: recognizable without being known.

Chaum developed an analogous procedure for digital cash. You would withdraw money from your bank account in digital form, just as you would by withdrawing a stack of euros, dollars, or yuan from an ATM—except that it would go to a dedicated transaction card, or a program running on your computer and connected to the Internet. Card in hand, or program open on computer, you could spend the digital money like cash: not as transactions reflected in a ledger, with the system checking in remotely to credit one account and debit another, but like tokens changing hands.

The money would be on, or in, the card or the digital wallet; if you lost your card, the money would be gone, just as if you had left an envelope of tip cash on the train after work. When you gave a card to a merchant or authorized an online transaction on your computer, their system could take the value off the card without needing to confirm your identity or check in with your bank; the "secured data representing value" (as Chaum put it) could prove itself, as cash in hand does.[18] Finally, and most important for Chaum, e-cash could not be connected to the person who withdrew and spent it: a technology of proof without identification that, Chaum hoped, would "make Big Brother obsolete."[19]

THE BLINDING FACTOR

This was not meant to be an autonomous digital store of value; Chaum was not proposing a new currency with his e-cash, but a mechanism for banks to turn existing currencies into digital cash and back again. The software developer Hal Finney— cypherpunk, Extropian, and eventually key Bitcoin contributor— made a good comparison when explaining the project in 1993: Before the last century-plus of national and territorial currencies, a local bank could issue money against their assets. A merchant would accept payment in those banknotes on the assumption that the note "could be redeemed at the issuing bank for its face value" in coin, bullion, or other stuff.[20] The bank held the "materials of value," and the notes circulated as their vehicles. Merchants in Chaum's system would likewise accept e-cash, knowing they could redeem it at the issuing bank for its face value in the national currency.

Let's break Chaum's mechanism into four parts, with each solution creating another problem to be solved in turn.

    1. How do you know the cash is real?
You want to make an online purchase. You request a twenty-dollar e-cash note from your bank. They withdraw

this money from your account—just as if you were withdrawing cash from the ATM—and generate a new e-cash
note, which they email to you or deposit on a smartcard.
The note carries a statement of value: the equivalent of
"This note is worth twenty dollars from Wells Fargo,
payable on demand." The bank encrypts the note with its
private key before they send it to you. Recall that anyone
with a public key can decrypt a message encrypted with a
corresponding private key, so a private key-encrypted
message acts as a kind of signature. Wells Fargo will
distribute copies of their public key to merchants far and
wide: your pub, *conbini*, taxi driver, bodega, and every
online storefront has a copy, so their transaction software
can instantly determine that e-cash notes are "signed" by
the bank, and how much they're worth.

2. *Why can't it be counterfeited?*

The use of public key cryptography here keeps no secrets.
The bank's private key signature authenticates the e-cash
note as a product of the bank and makes it impossible to
forge its value—a criminal can't create new notes that
appear to be from the bank. The signature can't protect
against *counterfeiting*, though: the duplication of e-cash
notes the bank actually produced. That "note" is just a
string of data, after all; it could be intercepted, copied and
pasted, and spent like someone writing a check for the
same two hundred dollars at every store on the block. The
bank therefore gives each note a unique serial number. At
the end of your cab driver's shift, she deposits the e-cash
notes accumulated on her smartcard at her bank branch.
The bank verifies that it signed the notes and their values,
and checks the unique serial numbers to make sure they

haven't been previously deposited—that is, that the same notes haven't been redeemed for dollars multiple times—and credits her account with these dollars. The unique serial number eliminates transactional privacy for the payer, though. When the merchant deposits it, the serial number corresponds to the one with which it was issued—to your particular account.

3. *Can't the serial number be used to track you?*
Chaum's solution was the *blinding factor*. The user—you—now generates a serial number for each note you want; you send these numbers to the bank with your request for e-cash; the bank signs these e-cash notes with their ten-bucks-payable-on-demand-from-us private key signature and debits your account for that amount. You can spend the e-cash where you will, as before. However, by an elegant trick of cryptographic mathematics, the serial numbers you sent have been multiplied by a random number known to you—the blinding factor—that you can divide out once the bank provides your e-cash notes, before you spend them. The bank has accounted for the money and created banknotes that you can spend, which it will redeem for national currency, but it no longer knows, nor needs to know, that they were from your account. Neither does the merchant who accepts them. The bank will check the serial numbers of the notes that merchants give them to redeem, to make sure they weren't spent before, but the numbers no longer correspond to any other data and do not connect your transactions to your identity. They have stamped a sealed carbon-copy envelope to confirm that what it contains can be redeemed for ten dollars, without having a record of the document within.

4. What about fraudulent offline spending, though? With offline transactions, using a "cold processor" wallet—in our notional taxicab, for instance—it would still be possible to spend the same note several times, before the bank could compare the serial numbers, in the digital equivalent of a bounced check. The bank would then refuse to honor all the e-cash notes after the lucky first merchant deposited theirs, and, with the blinding factor in place, would have no way to connect the fraudulent spending to you. This would obviously discourage merchants from adopting this new system and would cause trouble with many areas of payment, from offline contexts (like food carts and flea markets) to systems that need very rapid settlement (like an electronic tollbooth scanning a tag as your car drives through). (DigiCash worked on the payment system for an early electronic tollbooth infrastructure for the Netherlands.) In a final stroke of great elegance, Chaum, Gilles Brassard, and Claude Cripeau developed a mathematical mechanism by which each e-cash transaction would involve a question—a numerical challenge the spender's software would have to answer about each note.[21] One such answer would be meaningless, and would not compromise the anonymity of a given e-cash note, but *two* answers—which you would only give if you tried to spend the same note twice—would reveal the account to which the note was issued, deanonymizing the spender.

With the whole system before us, notice that the merchant—whoever redeems e-cash they've been paid—is not anonymous. Bribes and black market activity would have no easier time of it with e-cash than they would with hard currency. In fact, their activities would be further constrained by how much more difficult e-cash would be to launder compared to paper money and coins. Chaum had found a way to produce a kind of digital cash that broke with the all-or-nothing model of electronic money and surveillance—a technology that protected the privacy of individual customers and clients without further empowering drug deals, ransom demands, and the rest. Spending it was untraceable unless the spender tried to cheat the system, at which point they'd reveal themselves through the very act of abuse.

On a technical level, e-cash still had complex problems to resolve—like making change, getting refunds, and reversing charges—and many subsequent refinements would be developed by others. But the whole structure was functional and coherent: anonymous digital cash secured against surveillance, forgery, and counterfeiting by the same mechanisms as "the most sophisticated codes used to protect nuclear materials, military secrets and large-value wire transfers," as Chaum said to Congress. It met many of the challenges in his model of privacy's future crises, and without building infrastructure for potential malefactors.

His promise also had an implicit threat. "If we don't get the national currencies in electronic form properly," he warned, "then the market will route around them and make other currencies."[22] It was a prediction whose consequences we are now living out.

A CERTAIN DESIGN SPACE

By the mid-1990s, the Netherlands-based DigiCash had a pilot program under way at a bank in St. Louis. They issued unbacked, playful "CyberBucks" for publicity, which were good for buying T-shirts, *Encyclopaedia Britannica* articles, transcripts of old

Monty Python routines, and reprints of Chaum's past work.[23] Chaum was putting a deal together with Deutsche Bank, and studies of similar technologies were under way from Singapore to the UK. DigiCash software existed for all the common operating systems and was integrated into the web browser Mosaic. ING, Visa, Microsoft, and a string of banks came calling at Digi-Cash's offices in Eindhoven.

Before the end of the decade, DigiCash was bankrupt.

The reasons are complex and still argued, but the legacy of DigiCash and its technology for those making digital currencies and speculative monies was clear: as an inspiration and as a warning. Jean-François Blanchette puts it perfectly: Chaum's work "opened up not only durable research avenues but also—more importantly—a certain design space. That space suggested that computers need not necessarily be linked with images of surveillance and social control and that coherent and creative scientific research programs could be driven by explicitly social goals—in this case, privacy protection, anonymity, and their implications for democratic participation."[24] That design space and its social goals opened a terrain that would fill with further experiments: people seeking all-sides anonymity, or seeking money with new kinds of properties, or seeking permanently digital e-cash without banks—or nations—at all.[25]

The work of Chaum and his colleagues, and DigiCash's rise and fall, provided a reference point for many other proposals. After e-cash would come "smart contracts," "digital bearer certificates," and monetary mechanisms suited not just to protecting privacy and preserving parity between people and corporations, but as the basis for more extreme projects: off-the-books transaction systems operating in international waters and the ciphered interstices of the network itself, and active conspiracies against the legitimacy of central banks and territorial currencies.[26] Chaum and e-cash provided an example and an aspiration: a concrete research and development initiative in the service of anticipating and averting a malign future. Hal Finney described what cryptography and e-cash meant for him in 1992. The avenue Chaum had opened, Finney wrote, "balances power between individuals and organizations. . . . If things work out well, we may be able to look back and see that it was the most important work we have ever done."[27]

E-cash was also a cautionary tale. "I was asking the world to change the way it did things so that there would be perfect privacy," Chaum said, in retrospect.[28] There was so much inertia to overcome to get these tools adopted. The computer scientist Arvind Narayanan used the phrase "societal buy-in" to explain one of the challenges faced by "ambitious ideas such as Chaum's": "a critical mass of potential users unhappy with the status quo" who must take up the new system completely and immediately for it to work.[29] Tools like email encryption can be incrementally adopted by individuals and small groups, but Chaum's system needed wholesale transformation. The technology alone is not enough, in other words. Even with good math, scientific discoveries, the free circulation of ideas, reliable hardware, and running code, you need a desire, a vision, a dissatisfaction, a fantasy, a story. The glow of a utopia just over the horizon, and a cosmogram for getting there.

What if, to meet that challenge, you could create the society first and the platform afterward? What if you could build a world in which the technology became inevitable?

CHAPTER 5

COLLAPSE OF GOVERNMENTS

We discover the cypherpunk model of radical money in the 1980s and 1990s, with crypto anarchists, the American Information Exchange, and the Xanadu project all trying to make digital data valuable in itself—and laying the foundations of subsequent marketplaces. Creating truly autonomous digital cash meant solving three fundamental problems: coordination, duplication, and adoption. This chapter explains the first two problems, introducing visions of what a digital cash future could look like.

BLACK HOLE

In 1992, on Friday, September 25, at a club called the Black Hole in San Francisco, StJude met ambassadors from the future.[1]

She knew they were figures from a world to come, members of "the revolution which is, heh, already in progress," because they were opaque and anonymous. They wore chadors and "three-eyed" goggles; when they talked, it was through vocoders that filtered and synthesized their voices into saxophones and cellos, Kraftwerk croaks and sawtooth speech, rendered unrecognizable and broadcast through head-mounted speakers. And not only their voices: other people spoke through their speakers as theremins and rushing water. The third-eye goggle was a lens transmitting to a networked community. "People are ringing in and out." When she told a joke, the chadors echoed with "orchestral chuckles" from many time zones. "Was I an international hit?" she wondered.

The ambassadors towered over her, both exactly the same height: they wore *cothurni,* thick-soled weighted shoes with concealed lifts. They lurched around like deep-sea divers in their lead boots, their costume interfering with any distinctive gait or gesture. As they loomed out of the smoke in the Black Hole— a club from which not even a photon of information could escape—she had them pegged: "I think you're crypto anarchists—what I'd call cypherpunks! . . . You want to take over the world." A cello with a Dutch accent, nettled, disagreed: "We don't believe in takeovers. In fact, we are working to make things UNTAKEOVERABLE."

The two chadors and the "many overlapping voices" that talked through them—who knows which voices in particular belonged to the bodies under the yards of black cloth—outlined their project: pseudonymous economies, with "encrypted EVERYTHING," online reputations and a distributed credit rating system, secure digital money in "Swiss bank accounts for the millions." It added up, said a theremin, to a "global monetary system that makes governments obsolete."

"No, I'm not quite delusional," StJude wrote. She *had* met the cypherpunks; in fact, she'd given them that name. It took place in lucid coastal California light in Berkeley the previous Saturday, in a private home, not the smoky "near dark" of the Black Hole club. But she got the reality of the situation across with her fictional account of polyphonic network-attached silhouettes, blank inkblots with spiked gloves, stun guns, and encryption schemes. "A definitely false rumor," she said in her closing line: "the revolutionists can be contacted via cypherpunks@toad. com"—a real address for a real mailing list, started that very week, on which she was circulating the first draft of her story.

Decades previously, Jude "StJude" Milhon cofounded Community Memory, a very early digital social network, with teletype keyboards set up in the back of a record store and a public library.[2] Community Memory hosted a thriving scene of pseudonymous characters like "Dr. Benway," who hammered out Burroughsian riffs, live broadcasts from the Interzone. The bare-bones system didn't have anything like a login, so anybody could write as Benway—or as anyone else. "Certain nefarious pirates have spoken of cloning the Benway Logo," said the original author. "Go right ahead . . . it's public domain."[3] What difference does it make who's talking through those speakers, under that name? "One of Jude's philosophies," wrote a friend after Milhon passed away in 2003, "was that you shouldn't have to tell the world who you were."[4]

"So you're protecting your meat identity, right?" asked StJude of one of the chadors in the Black Hole, and, simultaneously, of her actual audience: her newly christened "cypherpunks."[5] "Clarifications, expansions, corrections are welcome. Also abuse and threats, for that matter." She was writing the story, "The Cypherpunk Movement," for "Irresponsible Journalism," her column in the cyberculture magazine *Mondo 2000*. (*Mondo* was *Wired*'s anarchic older sister, with hoaxes, band interviews, and fashion shoots running alongside pieces on virtual reality, psychedelics, encryption, and experimental fiction.) She addressed the draft to the people who inspired it, the earliest members of the "cypherpunks@toad.com" mailing list, the group who had physically assembled in Eric Hughes's house the week before at the inaugural meeting. Milhon had been there, taking notes on the ideas, and now was "concerned only that they be correct and clearly stated"—and that she captured the *feel* of the future being explored there, an order built on cryptography, pseudonymity, and "secure digital money." "Down come the governments," whooped the theremin from the looming, opaque shadow.

COLLAPSE OF GOVERNMENTS

Timothy C. May had been at that Saturday meeting in Berkeley with StJude, where a loose crew of engineers, programmers, and cryptographic enthusiasts became cypherpunks.

He was a retired engineer—retired at 34, after careful calculation of how much money he would need to remain independent for the rest of his life. At Intel he had solved a famously subtle problem involving errors in microchips produced by the alpha particle emissions of their ceramic casings. He had a physicist's sense of the stubborn facticity of the universe— radioactivity is radioactivity, whether or not humans are aware of it in a pile of sand or a piece of quartz—and a sardonic contempt for the flakiness that characterized humans and their machines alike. In the alpha particle paper, after pages of precise evidence and argument about chip design and radioactive decay, the last sentence was, "From the human engineering point of view, it is somewhat gratifying to note that the microcomputer controlled robots of the twenty-first Century may be plagued by some of the same ills that befall human beings; robots may be as fallible as mortals."[6]

Like most people who spent time online in those days, May had a signature block, a .sig file: a chunk of text that would be automatically appended to his emails and posts to forums and threads. Signature blocks were a place for phone numbers, affiliations, in-jokes, and bits of ASCII art. (Another participant in the cypherpunks mailing list, Julian Assange, included a sardonic Nixon quote in his sig.[7]) May's sig had a Talking Heads lyric, a math pun involving the then-largest known prime number, and a timeline of the future, a science fiction story in miniature: "Crypto Anarchy: encryption, digital money, anonymous networks, digital pseudonyms, zero knowledge, reputations, information markets, black markets, collapse of governments."

It was an inventory of components, a list of interests, and a chronicle of an imagined future—things to come, credited in order of appearance. We can rewrite it as the story of the dawn of the prospective Crypto Anarchist Age: a set of fundamental breakthroughs in encryption and decades of engineering and research funded by the government now enables its destruction. Experiments with anonymous networks and digital pseudonyms, zero-knowledge systems, and reputations provide the infrastructure for digital cash. What is needed is a proof-of-concept information marketplace that can demonstrate these components at work, attracting and educating new users. This would enable the creation of global, networked black markets of untraceable, untaxable commerce, after which governments, of necessity, would collapse.

His job was to make this story come true. He could not do it by himself. He needed partners, a movement, a vanguard conspiracy of mathematicians. "A specter is haunting the modern world, the specter of crypto anarchy," he read to the group that had assembled that Saturday in September, Jude Milhon among them: this was the opening line of his "Crypto Anarchist Manifesto."

From their first meeting, the cypherpunk community existed in several kinds of overlapping time. They made reasonable guesses: "As soon as there is money flowing through the networks which is tied only to pseudonyms and not to physical people, then you'll see a lot more virtual-only identities."[8] They speculated about things like "Spatial VR" as a kind of residence on the "Permanent Frontier." They looked for signals of the future in their own adoption of the techniques and technologies that would, one day, scale to the millions and billions on the network. "What we are discussing are long-range implications of these ideas."[9]

The subtlest and most significant historical condition of the cypherpunk project was its untimeliness. It was untimely not only in the classic Nietzschean sense, making a project in advance of its own historical context, but also in the sense of being *too slow*. There was a distinct lag between the proof of cryptographic primitives (low-level, reliable algorithms) and their implementation into a working system. "Why have most of the things Cypherpunks talk about *not* happened?" asked May.[10] The very manifesto he read at the first cypherpunk meeting that Saturday was four years old, having been circulated among "like-minded techno-anarchists" in 1988, 1989, and 1990. "For historical reasons I'll just leave it as is."[11] We are "on the verge of providing the ability for individuals and groups to communicate and interact with each other in a totally anonymous manner"; why was it taking so long?[12]

Progress could be made in areas like email, with a set of widely accepted common protocols, but "the situation becomes much murkier for things like digital money, which are not standalone objects and are often multi-party protocols involving time delays, offline processing, etc."[13] Building digital cash was both technically complex and semantically confusing. "While it's fairly clear what 'encrypting' or 'remailing' means," wrote May, "just what is a 'digital bank'?"[14] It's one thing to discuss—say—the vulnerabilities of email or the strengths and weaknesses of different cryptosystems, but *money* is an implicit set of assertions about value, time, history, and social structure. What you mean by a "digital bank" is part of a cosmogram, a way of knowing, organizing, and explaining the world. Defining it is a project of consensus building that precedes the consensus on programming languages, databases, formats, collaboration tools, and versioning systems that you need to actually start getting code together.

Building a digital bank is a deep problem of *coordination*, one commonly solved—in Yochai Benkler's terms about the work of making free and open source software—by price systems or managerial structure.[15] You can have a marketplace that rewards and incentivizes certain kinds of activities, or you can have firms or institutions that pay salaries, assemble teams, and give orders: two different but compatible ways of getting a bunch of people heading in more or less the same direction. Building a digital banking platform would normally take place within the command architecture of Visa or the Federal Reserve or some other large institution with a mandate, office space, and a tier of project managers or executives to resolve internal conflicts. The cypherpunks, by contrast, had an informal double-digit gang of very smart people and a mailing list. "We on this list are not being paid to develop anything, are not assisted by anyone, and don't have the financial backing of corporations to assist us."[16]

The story of free and open source software is the story of new technological communities overcoming exactly those odds to build everything from operating systems to the server platforms on which much of the Internet relies. While all of those projects featured the endless, internecine bickering that open source efforts generate like sawdust from a lumber mill, the complexity of the conversation required to create something like a digital bank was of a different order. It didn't start from fun technical questions but from philosophical and social commitments on authority, sovereignty, and the nature of value.

The situation was far too urgent for that long, slow dialogue, out of which consensus might never emerge. Perhaps you could pull together a critical mass of contributors, users, and participants to push one of these schemes along? If you could get to the stage Hughes identified—"money flowing through the networks . . . tied only to pseudonyms and not to physical people"—the system would be self-sustaining, with a population incentivized by a new kind of price system to support and build it.[17] They would have achieved a state of being *passing current*. With enough people, you could build that kind of literal and figurative buy-in, which was not just a matter of building technologies, but of telling stories.

A chapter in the story May wanted to tell—the story of the victory of digital cash and the collapse of governments—was the rise of the "information markets," which would create a platform for valuable data and an economic context for digital cash. How could the online information marketplace get off the ground? Two closely related companies in May's orbit tried to answer this question, and their systems, promises, and partners would shape what became digital cash. The first of the two was the American Information Exchange, founded by Phillip Salin. May's first discussion of the crypto anarchy project with a like-minded group, in 1988, happened in Salin's living room.[18]

AMERICAN ROCKET COMPANY

Phillip Salin lived at one end of a road a hundred miles long: it ran straight up from anywhere he stood to outside the planet's atmosphere. He mapped out a trajectory from Palo Alto to low Earth orbit. His team at Arc Technologies—later Starstruck, as in "a truck to the stars," and finally the American Rocket Company under new management—experimented with sugar-based "rocket candy" fuel for less expensive launch vehicles and lived off funds invested by Michael Scott, the first CEO of Apple

Computer. Salin wasn't an aerospace engineer, though; he was an economics wonk with an MBA, a devotee of the market-centric Austrian School economist Friedrich Hayek, a believer in the power of market operations alone to drive change. Salin thought the greatest challenge the space future faced was a force more powerful than gravity or the strain tolerance of metals: misallocated money.

The Shuttle was too cheap, he argued before a congressional committee: its costs were subsidized and artificially depressed, discouraging the entrepreneurial rocket industry.[19] The movement of money alone could get us out of the gravity well: "The next great breakthroughs in space will be economic breakthroughs," he testified.[20] Salin was fascinated by marketplaces for information, by the circulation of money and knowledge—money as information, and information as money.

In 1984, as the business of space was running into trouble, Salin started a project he had been contemplating since the 1970s, when he was reading Hayek and Karl Popper and working on time-sharing computer systems: a digital marketplace for intellectual property. He called it the American Information Exchange, AMIX, envisioning it as a place to retail all kinds of brainwork. It would provide you not merely with information but with answers: surveys, market analysis, patents, floor plans, CAD renderings, solutions to problems, formulas. "We're just trying," Salin said, "to reduce the friction and transaction costs that keep people from trading their knowledge for gain."[21]

To do this, they had to build an auction and sales system with profiles and ratings and comments and market managers for the new profession of "information broker." They needed a platform to handle accounting and billing and transactions and payments. They needed personal computers across the United States running the custom AMIX software (which even a puff piece described as "cumbersome") so every customer could dial into Unix servers storing an array of topics, subtopics, and items encompassing the whole specialized world of potential information products and services.[22] The team at AMIX, as the technology journalist Doc Searls recalled, was "trying to create an online service from scratch," a bespoke version of the whole infrastructure the Internet itself would later provide. "Phil had to create his own Internet."[23] Prior even to solving those problems, though, AMIX had to explain why digital information was *valuable*.

Esther Dyson put the objection simply in 1990: "The law of supply and demand can't work for a product, such as information, that can be replicated at almost no cost."[24] Dyson was then primarily an industry journalist for the computing boom and an advocate for the development of digital information marketplaces. There was a problem with these potentially perfect cyberlibertarian markets, and it lay at the heart of Salin's business plan. Dyson wrote repeatedly about AMIX, trying to answer the recurring objection about the value of digital media: "Once it is created, it can be replicated almost costlessly."[25]

Back in 1972, the peripatetic writer and artist-activist Stewart Brand—of the Whole Earth Access Catalog, among other ventures—spent time with the subculture of "computer bums" writing code and playing an early video game called *Spacewar!*[26] He laid out the implications of digitizing analog media with the clarity of dawn: "Since huge quantities of information can be computer-digitalized and transmitted, music researchers could, for example, swap records over the Net with 'essentially perfect fidelity.' So much for record stores (in present form)."[27] His phrasing is inapt in an important way, a mistake of semantics we continue to commonly make today. His musicologists aren't "swapping" records, trading them back and forth—they're *making* records, since each copy (on my computer, on yours, stored on the server, in local cache storage, on a music-playing device) is a perfect bit-for-bit copy unless we do something deliberate to filter, compress, or alter it.[28]

Much of the technical history of computing and telecommunications in the twentieth century is the history of the challenge of *fidelity*, of accuracy and error correction: to store and transmit perfect copies using imperfect media and noisy channels, from telephone lines to radio waves to the wiring between a single computer's storage, processing, and display.[29] The work of computing, especially networked computing, can be told as the creation of a global era of copying machines whose capacity for replication far exceeds printing and photography.[30] The facing page of Dyson's column on AMIX in *Forbes* was a full-page ad for Xerox, celebrating a "National Quality Award" in its role as "The Document Company": like Konrad Zuse's earliest computer programs, which used digital instructions punched into old 35 mm movie film, here two different media systems were neatly juxtaposed.[31]

This was another step in the ongoing, multicentury crisis of the concept of "intellectual property"; the digital turn enabled new answers to the old questions of how and why and in what ways information is valuable.[32] Salin's answer, in the framework of AMIX, had a deceptive, market-driven simplicity: digital information is valuable because people will pay for it. Who knows which information and why? "Juan's common knowledge is Alice's electrifying discovery," Dyson wrote in one of her essays on the AMIX idea. "Let the market decide."[33] But this answer included a deeper question. AMIX was indeed a marketplace: a transaction and payment platform for digital information. "Digital information" was coming to include money itself, the thing paid. What made the digital money of the digital marketplace valuable?[34]

The same mechanisms that enabled the transmission and storage of information as a swiftly verifiable string of bits, moving from account to account, put the money thus transacted on the thinnest ontological ice. Tim May pointed out that you could use steganographic techniques (concealing some data within other data) to hide a fortune in digital cash in the file of a song or a high-resolution image. A banal digital photo could hold a whole armored car full of cash. But the cash was of the same stuff as the photo and had the same fundamental problem of duplication. Dyson had argued for AMIX on two grounds: digital information was free to replicate in general but costly to find in particular, and the most valuable data tends not to be widely available. How would that work for the kind of digital media that we call money?

Salin did not live to see what became of these projects, dying in December 1991 of liver cancer at 41, shortly after AMIX was acquired by the computer-aided design (CAD) company Autodesk. He became the fifty-ninth person to undergo controlled cryonic suspension, having a "neuro" procedure—his head removed and frozen to be recovered by the society he anticipated, with his brain revived or digitally reconstructed and his body cloned or prosthetically replaced. He discussed one of the problems this raised with May: how to move your assets forward through time with you to immortality. If it was challenging to accurately price the Space Shuttle, and difficult to securely transact payments between people on the American Information Exchange, imagine transmitting money into an unknown and unrecognizable future in which you yourself have been "deanimated," frozen in a cask in Arizona, and recovered in some posthuman format.

May's notes from 1993 on "timed-release cryptographic protocols," theoretical methods for encrypting a message so it can only be read after some length of time or a specific event, presented the first use case from a discussion with Salin years before: "Foremost, to send money into the future, while protecting it in the meantime from seizure, taxation, etc.," a matter of interest "to cryonics folks who want to arrange for their own revival/reanimation at some time in the future."[35] (A decade later, Julian Assange would take up the same question on the cypherpunks list, but for securing the release of secrets.[36]) It would be a future-proofed bank account and could offer a reward for resurrectionists: the first group to bring the account holder back to life gets a promised prize once the data is decrypted. It would be the ultimate score for the information brokers of the future Salin wanted to create: a pricing system for bringing its own creator back from the dead.

HYPER-WARPING INTO THE TECHNO-HUBRIS ZONE

Salin's eccentric orbit took him and his collaborator, cofounder, and spouse, the nanotechnology advocate Gayle Pergamit, around the speculative edges of a series of near-future industries: from time-sharing computers, to writing economic analysis that fed into the breakup of the Bell Telephone monopoly, to a private space program and a digital information marketplace—but his oddest job title appeared on the employee roster for a business called the Xanadu Operating Company (XOR): "Accelerator." (Pergamit's title on the roster was "Hidden Variable.")[37] Xanadu was a sister project to AMIX, an initiative to digitize all human knowledge and weave money into it at the most fundamental level.[38] For the Xanadu team, as for Salin, money was the best rocket fuel, the propellant into the future: Xanadu's Theodor "Ted" Nelson (XOR employee title: "Director") described himself and the "final implementation squad" he assembled in Pennsylvania in an effort to finish the project as "Devoted capitalists all . . . I from hatred of committees, blunted creativity and the dilution of thought; they from desire for their own space shuttle."[39] Digital information and digital money, properly implemented, would carry them from their chairs in front of a PDP-11 computer in King of Prussia, Pennsylvania, to the stars.

It was through investing in Xanadu that the computer-aided design software company Autodesk came to invest in AMIX. The two companies fit together, and not just by virtue of sharing several people, including Salin. They were both about finding, navigating, and, above all, *pricing* digital information: "To accept that in our age," as Autodesk founder John Walker put it in a memo to his executives, "information is a commodity as tangible as wheat, live hogs, Swiss francs, or the S&P500 index."[40] Information was somehow *money,* or could be, and the network that used it could offer utility "as self-evident as the function of currency futures in the post-Bretton Woods era."[41] In Xanadu and AMIX, Walker saw a way to develop information marketplaces whose operation and pricing could speed the growth of a new kind of research and development suited to digital systems— a kind of accelerator for technological society as a whole.

AMIX's mechanism involved building a straightforward (if sweepingly ambitious) marketplace for information. Xanadu's system was far more extreme, a model for all human culture, past and future, in which digital information and money would be inseparable and indistinguishable. It was effectively a reinvention of *everything* as digital money, forever. From the position of trying to keep a company afloat in the quotidian present, Walker described surreal conversations with the Xanadu team who planned to "design, in its entirety, a system which can store all the information in every form, present and future, for quadrillions of individuals over billions of years."[42] The whole project, he wrote, had "hyper-warped into the techno-hubris zone."

Hyper- was a good choice of prefix. Nelson had coined the term "hypertext," first publishing it in 1965 in a paper "A File Structure for the Complex, the Changing and the Indeterminate." He had been intermittently evangelizing and arguing for a system to realize his vision for decades. This system, named Xanadu, promised to become a global network of terminals providing authoring and access tools to *all* text that had ever been or would ever be written, plus relations within and between texts, audio, video, "n-dimensional graphics," things, people, places, and "DNA/RNA."

Xanadu would be a kind of cosmic ampersand, linking everything to everything else and refusing any form of conclusion, closure, or endpoint for everything *except* Xanadu itself, whose design would be definitive. "The reason it has taken so long is that all of its ultimate features are part of the design," Nelson wrote. "Others begin by designing systems to do less, and then add features; we have designed this as a unified structure to handle it all."[43]

A system with such cosmic ambition and scale meant that design choices had metaphysical implications. The design reflected the revelation, Nelson argued repeatedly, of "the true structure of the ideas."[44] The true structure was one of property, ownership, and the circulation of digital money. Much has been made of Nelson's novel ideas about the navigation and display of digital text, and the trainwreck glamor of the unfinished and unfinishable four-decade project that Xanadu became, but at the deepest technical level Xanadu was a payment system—a marketplace infrastructure—on which new textual practices would be built. Nelson described the system as "a technical structure and an ownership convention."[45] Knowledge existed in terms of fixed authorship, ownership, and payment. The future user of Xanadu, one of those quadrillions of individuals over billions of years using the perfect knowledge system, was the "rightful copyright holder, or someone who has permission from the copyright holder and pays for storage." The basis of the Xanadu network of many Xanadu terminals hooked together would be "a royalty on every byte transmitted."[46]

One of the most important developers on the project, Mark Miller (XOR employee title: "Hacker") led the development of an addressing system to make this possible—the "tumbler" system, based on the properties of transfinite numbers—which could specify the location and owner of any particular byte. "In the literary tradition, it has an owner, and may be quoted and linked-to by other documents—within certain rules intended to be fair," wrote Nelson (making one wonder to which "literary tradition" he was referring, copyright and authorship being comparatively recent developments).[47] Miller, who spelled his middle name $amuel to express his allegiance to money as a force, kept an aphorism on his homepage: "If it's not allocated by a market, then it's *more expensive than money*."[48] He would go on to develop "agorics," market-like computational systems, and espouse smart contracts; he reappears later in this book among the Extropians.[49]

A particular structure of property, authorship, and payment was built into the deepest structure of the system; to write, in Xanadu, is to *own* in relation to other owners—and to pay for time on the server. This "unified structure," with absolute conditions and "all of the ultimate features" set in advance, would by fiat make all digital "complex clusterings of text (i.e., thought)"[50] into scarce and controlled commodities, impossible to duplicate. (Quoting text in Xanadu would not copy it, but "transclude" it from its location in memory and the account of the person who created it—a chain of attribution and royalties.) It would "monetize" thought not just in the sense of making it pay, but making it *into money itself.* All exchanges of information would also be transactions of funds. To write and read would be to pay and be paid.

How Xanadu would implement the movement of money— the aggregation of all those micropayments, far below a cent, grouped and settled—remained still more vague than many other aspects of the system. The demand was clear, though: digital information needed to become a market in itself, at once priced and the metric of price. The future demanded nothing less of us. Miller returned from a hiatus to work on Xanadu in 1988, he wrote, "because of fear about the dangers of nanotechnology, coupled with incredible excitement about the promises. . . . By creating better media for the process of societal discourse and societal decision-making, we stand a much better chance of surviving the dangers posed by new technologies."[51] The path to the future lay through the information market and the decisions it drove. Working for them as a consultant, the libertarian economist Robin Hanson created a prediction market internal to Xanadu where employees could bet on future events, including the claim "Xanadu will deliver its product before Premier Deng of China dies."[52] Hanson explained: "They hoped that their product could help China through a post Deng-transition to democracy." (Hanson also reappears in this book among the Extropians, developing a currency of "idea futures.")

Xanadu existed in a permanent future tense, from the "final implementation squad" in Pennsylvania in 1979 to the promise from Walker in 1988 that the new team would "bring an initial Xanadu system to the market within 18 months."[53] Receding always into the future, Xanadu would operate for millions of years starting six months from now. AMIX had to build their "own Internet," and Xanadu, operating from deep within the techno-hubris zone, had to ship a single unified structure capable of scaling to all expressions of all forms of thought forever. Two years after the investment, Autodesk was in the process of selling its 80 percent stake in AMIX and Xanadu and the business of figuring out how to make digital information quantifiably valuable.

Both AMIX and Xanadu were *public* systems, built around explicit authorship connected to every word, document, and link, and bound to bank accounts and persistent identities. Tim May was well aware of the ways such a system would be used if identity could instead be concealed, encrypted, or obfuscated. Several key Xanadu programmers were on the cypherpunks mailing list that began after that first meeting in 1992, the people Jude Milhon transformed into her visitors from the future. Talking with Salin about AMIX, May pointed out how quickly it would either provide the model for a black market for information or become a black market itself. Someone has a very specific technical question for AMIX, May hypothesized, about microchip design and fabrication—effectively a trade secret. "How long before a guy who works for a chip firm offers to sell his company's tens of millions of dollars in research for a hundred thousand dollars?"[54]

That was a way to make digital information valuable, and a step toward the genesis of crypto anarchy. It was a different version of the marketplace that would alter the world, and it too had its roots in a story, May wrote. "My thinking was already heavily influenced by Vinge's 'True Names.'"[55]

CHAPTER 6

PERMANENT FRONTIERS

Along with coordination (agreeing about what to build) and duplication (making easily copied data scarce), the cypherpunk digital bank faced a third problem: adoption, or getting enough people to start using it. The cypherpunks set out to build markets and transaction systems—and the social prototypes to go with them—that would destroy every government standing in the way of a new encrypted society. They needed experimental communities, stories of marketplaces, and myths of the future to create the societal buy-in for their envisioned systems: the Other Plane, the permanent frontier, the Xth Column, BlackNet.

MR. SLIPPERY

"He's shown some interest in crypto things," Timothy May wrote of Ted Nelson, a year after Autodesk spun Xanadu off, "and talked to some of us at a recent Hackers Conference about the implications."[1] The Hackers Conference was a "network forum," a phrase the communications scholar Fred Turner used, in his history of countercultural computing, for gatherings where separate technical communities could collaborate, find ideas in common, and discover new shared projects.[2] May gave talks and distributed papers about crypto anarchy at the Conference; Walker met the key figures from Xanadu there, which led to funding Xanadu and AMIX; John Gilmore discussed cryptography; Eric Hughes spoke about digital money; Rudy

Rucker, a mathematician-writer who worked for Autodesk and bylined with Jude Milhon at *Mondo 2000*, presented on artificial life. Programmers and electrical engineers met "legal hackers"—lawyers, often connected with the Electronic Frontier Foundation—and "prose hackers" who wrote science fiction.[3] One of these prose hackers was a mathematics professor from San Diego named Vernor Vinge.

Vinge wrote about thresholds. His theme was irrevocable lines in time or space, on the other side of which things are different. He wrote about "bobbles," fields of stasis in which time is suspended; you step into one of them and then step out, a subjective moment later, indefinitely and irrevocably far in the future. He introduced the contemporary, popular version of "the Singularity" at a NASA workshop in 1993: a series of accelerating self-reinforcing technological breakthroughs, particularly in artificial intelligence, which immediately supersede all prior models and systems. "The imminent creation by technology of entities with greater than human intelligence," he explained, would lead to a sudden, consequent cascade of further breakthroughs, "an exponential runaway beyond any hope of control. . . . It is a point where our models must be discarded and a new reality rules."[4] It was a barrier in the history of technological development, beyond which the world would swiftly outstrip human comprehension: a borderline beyond which lay the unimaginable.

Writing about telecommunications networks in his 1981 novella *True Names,* he envisioned computers acting as a threshold to another world, a virtual environment called the Other Plane. The goal of the hackers who operate there is to conceal their real identities, their "true names," to protect themselves from dangers posed by the government, gangsters, and one another. Vinge's protagonist goes by the handle "Mr. Slippery" as he tangles with the enigmatic and possibly nonhuman entity called the Mailman. The awkward locutions in Vinge's dialogue around the Other Plane presage decades of attempts to police the border between online and off: "He has had no notoriety in the, uh, real world as yet."[5]

Folktales and myths are full of mysterious thresholds, liminal spaces, and other realms with different rules: cross over into fairyland, east of the sun and west of the moon, for a night and return centuries later. Vinge drew on that narrative style, with his computer hackers taking up an adopted language of sorcerous metaphors (as some actual hackers did in fact do). Vinge's hacker warlocks understood that—as in fairy tales and demonology—access to the real name of another gives you power over them. This is a classic folklore element (Aarne-Thompson-Uther folktale type number 500, "Name of the Helper"), but it is also the practical experience of modern-day identity attacks and "doxxing," blackmail, and strategies of identification and disclosure taken up by and against organizations like Anonymous. In such a world, names are power.

As a theremin-voiced unknown in a chador said to StJude in that loud, smoky club in 1992: "Actually, unmasking your real identity could be the ultimate collateral—your killable, *torturable* body." When the prolific and inventive cryptographer and software developer Wei Dai introduced a digital cash project called *b-money* in 1998, he opened his proposal with "I am fascinated by Tim May's crypto-anarchy . . . a community where the threat of violence is impotent because violence is impossible, and violence is impossible because its participants cannot be linked to their true names or physical locations."[6]

Vinge's future in *True Names* is lively with the possibilities of digital cryptography—with one notable omission. The Coven, Vinge's hacker cabal, can operate online without fear of identification and the "True Death" that could result (as opposed to the symbolic death of being dumped offline), free to prank and trifle with nations, companies, mafias—and financial services, who are particularly vulnerable. Toward the end of the story, when Mr. Slippery integrates his nervous system with the global communications network, he feels the movement of money itself as part of his omniscient surveillance: "No check could be cashed without his noticing over the bank communication net."[7] In Vinge's future, disembodied minds roam through virtual reality Tolkien landscapes and see in ultraviolet through satellite sensors, but money is still money, checks are still deposited, funds laundered through account surpluses, and banks are still banks. There is no digital cash.

RELICS OF THE PRE-CYBERSPACE ERA

One night in 1993, before a discussion about nanotechnology, May wrote a brief piece of speculative fiction himself—one that took a step beyond *True Names*. In the style of Edgar Allan Poe presenting a Vernean sci-fi ballooning adventure as a real newspaper story—the doughty Monck Mason crossing the Atlantic in three days, published as *ASTOUNDING NEWS!* in the *New York Sun* in 1844—May wrote a straight-faced invitation to a secret organization called BlackNet. It began: "Your name has come to our attention."

He had been pondering the idea, and the evocative name, since that conversation about AMIX with Phillip Salin in 1987. "I played the Devil's Advocate and explained why I thought corporate America—his main target for customers—would shun such a system."[8] An information market implies an information black market, and by the early 1990s all the technological pieces but one were in place to realize it.

May's fantasy of such an organization filled out the details of his invitation. BlackNet's operators would never know their users, and their users would never know them. BlackNet would make a public key available, with which messages to them could be encrypted so that only they could read it—but there was nowhere to directly send such messages. Instead, the would-be client would post the encrypted message to a newsgroup or mailing list online, using an anonymous remailer to avoid being identified as the poster. (Newsgroups were public message-boards particular to the pre-Internet system called Usenet.) The BlackNet crew would monitor a handful of such newsgroups.[9] The invite requested a description of the material to be sold, the potential value, a special public key for the reply, and "your payment terms."

When the BlackNet group spotted a message encrypted for them, they would decrypt and read it. Since it was shared in public, there would be no way to directly connect the potential clients to the BlackNet market administrators. If they were interested, the BlackNet group would respond in kind, with an encrypted message posted through anonymous remailers to a public newsgroup or mailing list—an approach Miron Cuperman called the "message pool." (At the time, Cuperman was a computer engineering student at Simon Fraser University with an AMIX account and an interest in "immortalcybercomput-inglaissezfaire"; he would go on to adapt Bitcoin technology for institutional finance.) If the encryption and anonymous remailer systems held, this system could enable an untraceable two-way channel for the business of BlackNet.

It would be like a digital version of the cryptic back-and-forth of confidential personal advertisements in Victorian and Edwardian newspapers, when a single issue of the *Times* of London contained a message in alphabetic cipher ("Zanoni Yboko z jo wn m?") and another in numeric code ("30 282 5284 8 53"), both published so the writer and their intended reader could not be linked by a third party.[10] In the papers the codes were generally simple prearranged substitutions—readers solved "ozye wpe ud dpp jzf wzzv le logpcefdpxpye" almost as soon as it was published in the *Daily Telegraph*—but BlackNet was using a public key cryptosystem that was, if properly implemented, provably unbreakable.[11]

All the technology, all the tools, really existed to make Black-Net a reality—all but one. "BlackNet," May promised, "can make anonymous deposits to the bank account of your choice, where local banking laws permit, can mail cash directly (you assume the risk of theft or seizure), or can credit you in 'CryptoCredits,' the internal currency of BlackNet."[12] This was an idea inspired by AMIX: CryptoCredits could be saved and spent on other secret information from other users on Black-Net. The CryptoCredits were a leap into complete fantasy, like the part of another Poe balloon-hoax story where Hans Pfaall's fairly realistic balloon takes him to the moon.

Like Vinge, like Poe's hoaxes, like the deeper shelves of speculative and utopian literature, May's invite to a nonexistent organization was a story about a threshold that could be crossed into another kind of *space*. The other space was, deliberately, nowhere—announced, as Thomas Rid put it, by "an anonymous voice out of the emptiness of cyberspace."[13] This was not the accidental nowhere of Thomas More's *Utopia*, which is situated somewhere specific in the world, off a cape and in a warm current. (More's traveler Hythloday tells us *exactly* where Utopia is to be found, but someone coughs and More doesn't hear all the words.[14]) The "Galt's Gulch" of libertarian fantasy from Ayn Rand's *Atlas Shrugged,* stashed away in the Rockies with sci-fi gadgets to camouflage its existence, is based on the real town of Ouray, Colorado. BlackNet, by contrast, is a purpose-built nonplace: the only fixed point is an address associated with its public key: "nowhere@cyberspace.nil."

The production designer Ken Adam created the War Room in *Dr. Strangelove* and a string of secret bases for James Bond movies, with their shark tanks, vast cartographic displays and control panels, gantries and missiles. In conversation with Adam in 2008, the critic Christopher Frayling raised the question of what the contemporary design of a Bond-villain set would look like. It wouldn't look like a headquarters at all, he suggested; it would be a cell phone, perhaps a briefcase—not a fixed fortress, but an access point for a pervasive invisible network. Adam's designs are a technological fantasy of mid-twentieth-century power expressed as modernist bunkers filled with employees in jumpsuits. May's BlackNet invitation was just such a design for the 1990s: productive of paranoia rather than megalomania, it promised a population of potential spies working not through command-and-control hierarchies but ongoing double-blind relationships sustained by computer networks, encrypted data, and anonymous digital cash.

Working out of no place in particular, using preexisting networks, without base or territory, BlackNet could flow through the infrastructure of existing institutions like rainwater trickling down inside the walls of a decaying house. BlackNet, May wrote, "considers nation-states, export laws, patent laws, national security considerations and the like to be relics of the pre-cyberspace era."[15] BlackNet operated only in the future: in a new kind of nowhere.

THE SOCIAL PROTOTYPE

Though written with tongue somewhat in cheek, with in-jokes for the nanotechnology crew he was about to address, May's BlackNet invitation persisted. Forwarded and posted to other groups, it attained a brief notoriety and a lasting resonance, re-appearing during the upheaval following the "Cablegate" disclosures on WikiLeaks almost twenty years later.[16] It prefigured parts of the model of Julian Assange's plan for WikiLeaks in his paper "Conspiracy as Governance": to create a cryptographic framework for anonymous leaking that discloses information to the public while making organizations dysfunctional by turning every employee into a potential leaker.[17]

The cypherpunks were at once developers and users, living in and testing out a version of the future they anticipated—projecting themselves forward. Their mailing list itself was a prototype: not of a mailing list alone but of cypherpunk practices, including digital cash. The regulars on the list saw the flakiness of their own platform as something that had to be resolved for digital cash to be viable: a distant early warning signal about robust hardware. So were the meetings, the discussions, the games they played and scenarios they presented and fiction they wrote. The gathering of the cypherpunks was a launch apron for probes into future time. Together they could elicit, document, and explore "interesting emergent behaviors" that would arise in the future and work on the technologies themselves: "to experiment with them, see what kind of emergent behavior appears, see what kind of flaws and obstacles arise, see how they break, etc."[18]

In the open source community, this has taken the form of what the science and technology scholar Chris Kelty calls "recursive publics." Recursive publics work in constant reference to and modification of the very technologies that make them a public, hacking on the same tools by which they collectively hack. Lana Swartz has a related idea from studying cryptocurrency developers, the next step of the recursive public: "infrastructural mutualism," groups who "value the ability to mutually build and support a collaborative platform upon which to transact, free from the prying eyes and inference of corporate intermediaries"— fertile environments for social prototypes.[19]

"Social prototype" is Fred Turner's term. "These modes of gathering," he wrote of Silicon Valley design practices, from start-up office space to Burning Man, "have technologies at their center, but they are also prototypes in their own right—of an idealized form of society."[20] Turner studied the prototyping practices of software engineering and argued that they didn't just show off technical possibilities but pulled new groups of people together. They produced not just a thing but the kind of community that would make use of that thing. "These stakeholders can help bring the technology to market, but they also represent new social possibilities in their own right."[21] Indeed, part of Silicon Valley's business in the early twenty-first century lay in identifying, cultivating, and packaging new kinds of societies, which happened to incorporate a product or a platform or a service: coworking and coliving, ephemeral photo messaging, holacracy, gamified fitness metric competitions, walking around in the evening looking for geotagged Pokémon creatures. The prototype builds on the past, on what is available, but it acts as a zone for modeling and performing a potential future: a kind of self-reflexive cosmogram. The space where people are working on computers was a distributed version of a neutrino-detecting bubble chamber, looking for tangible traces of intangible things, measurements of the immeasurable future.

PERMANENT FRONTIER

"Cyberspace," said John Perry Barlow, "is where you are when you're talking on the telephone"—when you are "here" but absorbed in a somewhere-else mediated through a device. William

Gibson coined the term "cyberspace" as a future technological condition. (Asked about it in an interview in 1985, he said "Cyberspace is where the bank keeps your money."[22]) Barlow imported the term to the present in the summer of 1990, on the very early West Coast social network the WELL—which had been created by Stewart Brand, previously seen watching people play *Spacewar!* Barlow was announcing the launch of the Electronic Frontier Foundation, a legal organization in the service of digital civil liberties. "In this silent world," he wrote, "all conversation is typed. To enter it, one forsakes both body and place and becomes a thing of words alone. . . . It extends across that immense region of electron states, microwaves, magnetic fields, light pulses and thought which sci-fi writer William Gibson named Cyberspace."[23] "That immense region" was the frontier of the Electronic Frontier Foundation.

Gibson's cyberspace was a civic-infrastructural dreamtime dominated by megacorporations, public utilities, and (high above the grid) the remote galaxies of military systems. Barlow reimagined it as the promise of an enormous *outside* that was present and accessible from this world—the blank flip side of the map, open country for self-reliant homesteaders. Anywhere you could plug in a modem or get a packet radio signal, you could "light out for the Territory ahead of the rest" like Huckleberry Finn. It was a crucial moment in what Fred Turner calls "one of the Internet's founding misunderstandings": that "the Internet was somehow a *place*"—and specifically an American place—rather than a set of interoperating global infrastructures.[24]

Part of the fantasy of this nonplace place, the network's vast outside, lay in encrypted anonymity and the values it would produce. Tim May wrote that it would act as a "pressure relief valve: knowing one can flee or head for the frontier and not be burdened with a past." It would cultivate a community (of sorts) that maintained the "frontier and Calvinist spirit of keeping one's business to one's self."[25] The program, instead of rural electrification, would be *ruralizing electronic society* into a lawless wide-open space, with reputations and nicknames, banditry, DIY technological self-reliance and self-defense, and sacks of untraceable money with no conventional banks in sight.

The intellectual high country was there to be claimed from the big ranchers, May said, as he read the manifesto Jude Milhon heard in Berkeley in 1992. "Just as a seemingly minor invention like barbed wire made possible the fencing-off of vast ranches and farms, thus altering forever the concepts of land and property rights in the frontier West, so too will the seemingly minor discovery out of an arcane branch of mathematics come to be the wire clippers which dismantle the barbed wire around intellectual property." In the BlackNet proposal, he put the mission in more extreme terms, citing two kinds of intellectual property that had been used to slow the spread of cryptographic technology: "Export and patent laws are often used to explicity [*sic*] project national power and imperialist, colonialist state fascism."[26]

In 1996, Barlow published the "Declaration of the Independence of Cyberspace." Written at the global power gathering in Davos, Switzerland, the prose was styled to be orated from horseback, suited to the windswept plateau of May's open country: "Governments of the Industrial World, you weary giants of flesh and steel, I come from Cyberspace, the new home of Mind. On behalf of the future, I ask you of the past to leave us alone. You are not welcome among us. You have no sovereignty where we gather.... You are trying to ward off the virus of liberty by erecting guard posts at the frontiers of Cyberspace."[27]

This chain of metaphors, analogies, and references had nothing more to do with the factual history of the American West than Gibson's cyberspace did with actual servers, telecom deals, or web browsers: they were historical fiction to complement the science fiction of near-future platforms like BlackNet. Settler frontiers, like that of westward expansion, were the product of state power, not an escape from it: made with legal frameworks and military deployment, naval and mercantile shipping, maps and political promises, and investment schemes and subsidies.[28] They were in the service of expanding sovereignty rather than redistributing it. Mere accuracy was not the point, however. The stories the cypherpunks told were not true, but they were not wrong, either—because their task was not to make a historical argument but to convey a feeling.

The comparison juxtaposes two very different fantasies, the Wild West and Cyberspace, made stronger by the fact that they weren't *real* but rather expressed a potential future mode of being. The imagined historical "frontier" could be all the more compelling because it was being put forward in the 1990s by engineers with PhDs who went to Sunday brunch at the Thai Buddhist Temple in Berkeley to discuss cryptography before a visit to the rifle range. (Barlow was an actual rancher on the Bar Cross Ranch in Wyoming, founded by his great uncle, so he came by his high-plains-drifter ways honestly.) "A new frontier, untouchable by outside, coercive governments," May wrote. "Vinge's 'True Names' made real."[29]

That the digital frontier was a fantasy made it easier to map onto a dematerialized experience they predicted, the shared outside of the bodiless network interpenetrated with everyday life. "Ours is a world that is both everywhere and nowhere, but it is not where bodies live," wrote Barlow, sounding like a Gnostic prophet: "Our identities have no bodies, so, unlike you, we cannot obtain order by physical coercion."[30]

Who would join the wagon train of bodiless settlers heading for the frontier of everywhere and nowhere, to build their economy on digital cash? "These are the areas often pioneered by early adopters, by those motivated by risk-reward trade-offs to adopt new technologies."[31] Present rewards were needed to draw people in, and places where experimental communities could provide cover for the genesis of the kind of groups that would thrive in this future space: people who had reasons for building out an unreliable, occasionally disastrous, sometimes dangerous network of covert money and value exchange.

INFORMATION LIBERATION

May dubbed the shock troops of crypto anarchy, the currency holders of digital cash, the "Xth Column." This was a mathematical play on the term "fifth column," for a subversive community undermining a country from within in the service of an enemy power: his saboteurs and spies were represented by a variable, working on behalf of an unknown element. To recruit people into the Xth Column, he wrote, you needed outside pressure. The demand for restricted goods like illegal drugs would provide one of the drivers: cells of dealers, customers, and administrators, dead drops, and secret arrangements for vetting quality and reputation. (Decades later, Ross Ulbricht would directly credit this idea for inspiring his darknet market, the Silk Road.) But the appetite that really interested May was for suppressed *information*—for valuable digital data.

The cypherpunk community—whether on board with the whole crypto anarchy project or not—were all already in the "information liberation" business because their shared area of interest and research was heavily classified and policed. Gilmore, who started the mailing list, devoted himself to library research and Freedom of Information Act requests to declassify, digitize, and share the work of the cryptographer and cryptanalyst couple Elizebeth and William Friedman and the work of Ralph Merkle—last seen in this book as a Berkeley undergraduate working on cryptography in the 1970s, whose study of hashing systems would one day undergird Bitcoin. Relevant papers published in specialized academic journals had to be borrowed and photographed or scanned or, if it came to it, typed out by hand to share on the network.

"Cypherpunks write code," said Eric Hughes, and they did so with the mind-set of people who knew about the history of secretly vulnerable cryptographic products being released without public review. They had the shared background, too, of Unix hackers who had circulated multigenerational photocopies of guides to the proprietary operating system, and phone phreaks writing out the lists of control tones published in Bell Telephone technical journals. Many of the cypherpunks were closely involved in the free/open source software movement, which took as a fundamental aim that software must necessarily be *open*—available for review, study, sharing, debugging, and improvement—and free: "as in 'free speech,'" as Richard Stallman's remark put it, "a matter of liberty, not price."[32] (In 1997, when May was speaking at digital privacy conferences about the importance of untraceable transactions, Stallman published a sci-fi story, "The Road to Tycho," set in a dystopian society where the act of reading someone else's book is theft, easily detected since all books are digital.)

There were other audiences for covert information: the overseas researcher without access to major libraries or publications, or the broker looking to engage in insider trading. The cheating student ("Back Issues of Tests and Libraries of Term Papers—already extant," wrote May, "but imagine with an

AMIX-like frontend?"). Lenders looking for illegal credit reports, insurers for health records, employers for criminal histories. Employees, quitting or fired, building a golden parachute from filched data and violations of NDAs. People interested in the how-to for overclocking a computer, growing hydroponic weed or producing methamphetamine, making free long-distance calls or fixing a refrigerator with a warranty-violating modification. Every cinephile was a potential recruit, every gamer, fan-subbing anime devotee, collector of old comics or reader of out-of-print books, every crate-digging record collector, jazz aficionado, bootleg-swapping curator of the Grateful Dead, every opera cultist (to whose illegal phonograph recordings we owe the only documentation of many early live performances)—to say nothing of pornographers and their customers.

Political activists, dissidents, leakers, and whistle-blowers were a natural fit, needing both access to suppressed information and the means to communicate secretly. Early anonymous online remailers saw their heaviest use by ex-Scientologists and anti–Church of Scientology activists swapping documents from the higher levels of thetan-hood. A landmark raid on an anonymizing Usenet system in Finland, anon.penet.fi, was conducted by Interpol at the behest of the Church seeking the identity of a particular leaker. The Finnish Internet technologist Johan Helsingius, who ran the remailer, warned at the outset of his project: "Well, if the police or the local Secret Service comes knocking at my door, with a court order to hand over the database, I might comply."[33] But what was the alternative?

"Short of having everyone run a public-key cryptosystem such as PGP," he warned, "there is no way to protect users from malicious administrators."[34] PGP stood for "pretty good privacy," software for encrypting and signing messages. It had been created in the context of the Nuclear Weapons Freeze Campaign, whose members were often under domestic surveillance. Helsingius's advice sounded like an argument in favor of "everyone" adopting just such a system—laying the groundwork for crypto anarchy through political protest. The cypherpunk technology entrepreneur Sameer Parekh, who would work on digital cash and financial cryptography, got his start transcribing Thoreau's *On the Duty of Civil Disobedience* into an Apple IIGS as a high school student in Illinois in 1991, digitizing a landmark in the history of American dissidence to share online. (To this day, stumbling across a copy of Thoreau's essay online you might find a note at the end: "Typed by Sameer Parekh.") He turns up later on in this book at the launch of an offshore data haven on a theoretically sovereign gun emplacement in the North Sea.

All of these groups also had commonsense reasons to need something like a digital cash transaction system. Drug dealers, pornographers, piratical file sharers, and retailers of secret or illegal knowledge and their customers and supporters all needed tools for surreptitious commerce. Activists and dissidents needed ways to support the tools that made their work possible, and to take care of each other when circumstances turned against them. These concerns were not theoretical, as events in the years since have shown, from credit card companies blocking donations to WikiLeaks, to payment processors and donor platforms like PayPal and Patreon freezing the assets and blocking the transactions of "adult content" and sex workers.

There was one other community whose need for secret knowledge and digital cash was less apparent but would become more consequential—the immortalists. May discussed them at length: the students of bootleg medical research, seeking personal posthumanity, who were devoted to hoarding, sharing, and putting into practice life-extension and anti-aging techniques. Such a group would seek anonymous reputational systems for publishing forbidden scientific results and studies, and tools for rating secret clinics. They would need marketplaces for experimental pharmacology, offshore medical tourism, and support communities for illegal or unproven practices.

This community would require specialized financial tools: bizarre insurance schemes, investment tontines for groups whose members expected to either perish experimentally or live for centuries, and wills, investments, and the set-aside asset vehicles for people preparing for a temporary "metabolic coma"— that is, cryonically frozen to be revived in the future. They would need forms of money that could fund their experiments and bodily preservation, and enable savings, transactions, and payouts over the long, long term.

May's description of them was partially fictional, but this contemporary group did in fact exist; the experimental money they planned and designed would be a step toward living forever. But digital cash still faced a set of fundamental problems that had not yet been overcome.

CHAPTER 7

NANOSECOND SUITCASE

What if the cypherpunks actually won? How would an anonymous digital infrastructure not be overwhelmed with spam, fraud, and forged digital cash? Some of the problems their cipher utopia was facing could be solved by a computational tool called *proof of work*. Exploring how this technology functions reveals a menagerie of experimental digital tokens and currencies— hashcash, RPOW, bit gold, b-money, and other Bitcoin precursors—and introduces the challenge of building secret banks.

WHAT IF WE WIN?

Adam Back made the T-shirts for the revolution. They featured blocks of white text on black cotton, including a warning, text of relevant laws and documents, four lines of code, and a big square of machine-readable barcode. The shirts were legally classified as munitions in the United States: you could not let a foreign national *see* the shirts, much less photograph or export one. Wearing one of Back's shirts on an international flight was a complex kind of crime. In France, wearing the shirt could accrue a massive fine and jail time. The code on the shirt was the RSA encryption algorithm—a working implementation of public key cryptography—rendered in the brutally laconic programming language Perl.

The shirts mocked the structure of the regulations by their very existence. So did the people who got RSA-in-Perl tattoos: able to say, along with martial artists in 1980s action movies, that their very bodies were classified as deadly weapons. Putting a shirt on, being photographed for a magazine or—worse still— appearing on television, was to suggest the impossibility of containing the cypherpunk toolkit and keeping it from widespread use. The garment implied victory.

Adam Back was then faced with the question implicit in May's Xth Column scheme: What if, in fact, the cypherpunks won?

Crypto for the millions! Public key encryption software becomes so widespread, reliable, and convenient that there is no reason to communicate insecurely. Your most casual online exchanges are authenticated by public key signatures, transacted over anonymous remailers, and wholly enciphered from outsiders. Governments effectively abandon cyberspace and the cypherpunk dream is realized.

It is immediately rendered useless by *spam*. The new crypto anarchist order blows out on the launch pad, overwhelmed with penis-enlargement promises, ads for counterfeit watches and home refinancing and deadstock appliances, porn-site hustles, phishing scams, and "Hello dear friend in Christ. I have Eighteen million five hundred thousand united states dollars fortune . . . ."

The most effective tools for keeping email spam traffic at manageable levels used identities and addresses (whitelisting) or the content of the messages themselves (filtering, whether based on keywords or ongoing machine learning). Wide adoption of encryption by individuals made the messages opaque to everyone but their intended recipients, so even the crudest filter— one that just looked for "porn" or "only $" to discard messages— became useless. The addition of tools like anonymous remailers, passing messages along without disclosing their original sender, wiped out the utility of blocking mail from suspicious or known-bad addresses. What an inglorious fate for the cypherpunk dream: to succeed against the black glass monolith of the NSA and its army of top-tier mathematics PhDs only to be beaten by the small-time hucksters, pill touts, and con artists of the spam world, as though NASA somehow lost Mission Control to a Floridian time-share scam. Would the Other Plane be an endless wave of rip-offs, phishing messages, spoofs, spam, and hoaxes—an economy of messages flooded with worthless paper?

On March 28, 1997, Back presented his first draft of a postage system that could address this embarrassing scenario. What if the very computational work used to create and send an encrypted message—work that had become steadily more efficient for decades—could be turned against abuse of the encrypted network? To understand what Back built—and its consequences for digital cash—we must first understand what "computational work" meant.

NANOSECOND SUITCASE

Grace Hopper used to travel with a suitcase full of nanoseconds.

Meeting with students and generals, speaking with Congress, with engineers, or on television, she brought luggage filled with units of computational time for her audience to take home.[1] A computer scientist and one of the very first programmers, Hopper liked physical analogies: when she developed the first compiler, a program for transforming instructions written in programming language into machine language to be executed by a computer, she thought about the passing rules from when she'd played basketball—ways of "jumping" between the steps of a program.[2] She knew how hard it was to understand the *time* of computation and telecommunications, especially the wasted time. It was difficult for humans to think in terms of tenths or hundredths of a second, much less millionths (micro) and billionths (nano). Men gleaming with military brass would ask, Why does a satellite transmission take so long? How can we build faster computers? And Hopper would reach into her bag.

Her nanosecond was a length of wire almost thirty centimeters long, 11.8 inches—the distance light travels in a vacuum in that time, the upper bound on any movement of information in the universe.[3] There are many nanoseconds, she would tell the admirals, between a ship at sea and a satellite in orbit; hence the delay. A computer with inches of wire between components was racking up the nanoseconds with each instruction and each result—a pulse of electricity, passing back and forth. (The Harvard Mark I, the first computer she worked on, had 530 miles of wiring.[4]) A badly designed or poorly programmed computer was wasting comparatively glacial microseconds, as Hopper would illustrate by holding one up: a massive coil of wire, 984 feet long. "I sometimes think we ought to hang one over every programmer's desk, or around their neck—so they know what they're throwing away when they throw away microseconds."[5]

This perspective can be dizzying: one clock tick of a high-end modern computer's processor (at three gigahertz) takes about a third of a nanosecond, during which it can execute some amount of work. If we imagine that tick as a full second—*one-Mississippi*—then the time it takes to send a packet of data one way from New York to San Francisco over a fiber optic cable, twenty-one microseconds, is the equivalent of about two years. Wagon trains waiting out the winter in Iowa or clipper ships sailing around Cape Horn and up the Chilean coast could beat that schedule—and twenty microseconds is a duration still very far below the human ability to detect. That's the temporal scale of computing, the scale where Hopper worked, and where Back's proposal was set.

When you send an email to me, Back proposed, your email program generates a "hash" of the message—a small piece of data corresponding to the data of the whole of the email. The hashed data includes components like the date and time the message was sent and the receiver's address, so each hash is good for one and only one message. Making this hash takes some very small amount of computational work on your part. Because of the properties of a particular set of tools called *partial hash collision algorithms*, we can turn the dial on how much work it will take your computer to produce this valid hash.

Then, on the receiving end, my email program checks that the hash is correct. If the hash indeed corresponds to the message sent, I receive the message; if not, the message is discarded. The deep ingenuity of the notion kicks in with the fact that you and I, writing back and forth—even writing to mailing lists and the like—never notice that this is happening. The computational work happens too fast to matter.

However, if you start emailing people in very large numbers, in the hundreds of thousands, the work becomes onerous. Producing the correct hash for every single message becomes a problem only in aggregate, with your computer slowing to a grind as the fans whir to cool the overheating chips. Since most spammers only operate profitably at a scale of tens to hundreds of millions of messages, this creates a built-in brake on their ability to do business, bumping them down from wholesale to retail. In the long term, as the performance of new computers improves, the ability to dial up the difficulty of the hashing problems will let this system keep pace.

The hash accompanying the message therefore functions as a kind of metered postage—a small token of effort, an expenditure, which inhibits mass mailing while leaving personal correspondence effectively untouched. A little "proof of work," if you will. Prior to Back's announcement, proposals had been made advocating some kind of micropayment stamp, some small financial gesture or quantity of computing work, using a digital cash system.[6] This is why, despite this token bearing seemingly little relationship to what we might think of as money, Back called his concept *hashcash*.

He continued to refine the idea in the following years. What else could you do with this hash that operates as a small token of effort, as a proof of work, easy to do little and hard to do big? In a 2002 paper about hashcash, Back lists potential applications for the idea, concluding with: "hashcash as a minting mechanism for Wei Dai's b-money electronic cash proposal, an electronic cash scheme without a banking interface." In fact, hashing tools would be useful for minting money and creating banks in more ways than one.

DESTROY EVERY VESTIGE OF STRUCTURE

"Thus the concept of hashing finds wider application than just in computing addresses," wrote G. D. Knott in a survey of hashing functions in 1975. "It is a basic concept which can be useful in many circumstances."[7] Indeed it can. A *hash*, as in the random jumble of ingredients produced by hashing, cutting or chopping, began as the solution for a seemingly simple question with profound implications: What is the fastest way for a computer to look something up?

The data a program needs may be scattered across the space of available memory—those magnetic stripes laid on the spinning platter of a hard disk, or on a reel of tape spooling and unspooling. Even a simple program will be making many small changes to whatever churns in its working memory. How does it find those places, redirect when it copies one part to another location, and return to a thing it has altered? As fast as the machinery can move, there is still travel time for the read/write head to find its place on disk, and as Grace Hopper would remind us, that time adds up. Either you update the whole table that lists the location of every item in memory, every time it changes, or you add to the table unsystematically and go through the whole thing again every time you need something.

A solution to this problem was "scatter storage," a way of making a key that could correspond to any given entry in storage—to where that data lives on the disk or the reel of tape—with a transformation that evenly distributes keys through the table of things to look up.[8] You are as likely to find what you need anywhere you land, if the distribution is really equal. This approach, pioneered by Hans Peter Luhn at IBM Poughkeepsie, works poorly for humans but wonderfully for computers. As Matthew Kirschenbaum summarizes it, in his study of the applications of hashing to computer memory and digital forensics, "structure—and with it predictable access routines for the drive's mechanical read head—emerged from normal patterns of statistical distribution among the numeric indices rather than from any kind of semantic correlation between index and key."[9] Or, in the beautiful phrase of a history of IBM's early computers: "[Luhn's] fundamental insight was to see merit in deliberately abusing keys, thereby attempting to destroy every vestige of structure."[10]

To do this, you need something rather magical: a way of transforming data that will always give the same result for the same data, and a different result for different data, so the same key

won't correspond to different inputs. (The term for this accidental correspondence—giving the same hashed key for different
data—is a *collision*.) The magical transformation has become a
commonplace matter in computer science: a *hash*, a function that
takes data of any size and returns data of fixed size, usually much
shorter, which corresponds to the original data. Any change to
the original will produce a different hash. You can select a particular hashing algorithm and tune it to different parameters,
producing brief units of gibberish that directly correspond to
what that data is.

Hashing schemes and algorithms multiplied, as did the uses
for hashing itself. Hashes could be used to confirm that two digital objects—texts, files of code, pieces of media—were precisely the same and had not been altered by corruption or an
adversary's deliberate action. Furthermore, you could confirm
that identity without having to compare whole objects, or even
to reveal precisely what the objects are; instead you could just
compare their hashes. You don't need to know the original texts
to know that one is different. Finally, you cannot figure out the
original data from the hash of the data. It is—at least in theory,
if not always in practice—not *reversible*. The hash of the thing
tells you nothing about the thing, except that the hash corresponds to it, and to it alone. If you run an online service that
requires passwords, when your user logs in, their system can send
the hash of their password to you, rather than the password itself. You can confirm that they have the secret, verified by the
hash, without having it yourself—recognizable without being
known.

We will take this technology further, to explain how it came
to be built into the heart of digital cash, with two unorthodox
applications of hashing tools. First, hashes can also be used to

create irrefutable chains of linked, time-stamped events—blocks of linked events, chained together (blockchains, if you will). Second, and bringing us back to Back and hashcash, hashes can be used to demand and verify an exact amount of work from a computer.

ENTROPY ARCHIVE

Consider an esoteric but vitally important problem: the challenge of distributing verifiable, reliable random numbers. We need and use reliable randomness for doing quality assurance checks on new cars and pharmaceuticals, for recounting ballots to ensure the integrity of a vote, for conducting medical screenings, even for generating the secret keys needed for encryption or making financial or military decisions that can't be predicted. With fake randomness you could manipulate a market, fix a lottery, produce an illusion of security with secret codes you know how to break, and hide all kinds of malfeasance. To meet this challenge, some organizations generate their randomness in-house. The network security firm Cloudflare keeps a wall of one hundred lava lamps in their San Francisco office. The fluid movement in the lamps is a high-contrast source of entropy, an estimated 16,384 bits worth, perfect for capture by a digital camera (with changes to the ambient light) whose images can be the seed for generating random numbers. (Cloudflare also uses the spinning of dual pendulums, the decay of a chunk of uranium, and other less entertaining industry-standard randomness sources.) But that's private, and subject to potential manipulation.

What about a public, shared, reliable source of randomness? How could you be sure you could trust the information? Imagine an adversary wants to falsify a set of random numbers to their advantage. Our enemy means to plant the "random" factor that determines where we do a ballot review so it will be conducted in a preselected district to conceal a rigged election. This challenge, and its solution, will loom large for digital cash.

The National Institute for Standards and Technology (NIST) in the United States maintains a randomness beacon, a "public randomness service": a new string of random characters, 512 bits of entropy, generated every minute and broadcast on the Internet. They have been doing this since a little before noon on September 5, 2013; the first message began "17070B49D . . . ." If you are incorporating randomness into life-and-death decisions and processes, how can you be sure the latest string of random characters from NIST has not been inserted into their system by an enemy hacking into their website? Each new unit of entropy is signed with NIST's private key, just like the digital cash withdrawn from a bank using David Chaum's system—but perhaps your adversary has also stolen that key.

Each of NIST's initial random numbers are combined with some related information (a time stamp, a status code, and so on)—including the value of the *previous* randomness broadcast. This collection of data is then hashed all together. NIST signs that hash with its private key, hashes the whole thing again, and broadcasts the resulting string: "63C4B71D51 . . . ." The results of the hashing process are easy to verify as corresponding to the input data but impossible to predict in advance. It's here that the significance of including the previous broadcast comes in. Your enemy can steal NIST's key, and they can figure out how you'll use the randomness so they can cook up factors that will produce the outcome they want. But the randomness broadcast from NIST will have to include the prior broadcast, which anyone can check, making the results of the enemy's hashing impossible for them to control. That prior broadcast's hash incorporates the broadcast before it, in turn, which incorporates the one before it, link by link in the chain, four years back, sixty seconds at a time. The hashes using previous hashes makes the latest broadcast reliable by connecting it to a public archive, with each event cryptographically incorporating previous events, so that attempts to change the past are immediately apparent—breaks in the chain.

COSTLY BITS

Consider one last thing you could do with hashes. Recall that different hashes generated by the same data are called *collisions*. Collisions are to be avoided if you're using hashes to look something up or verify passwords: a hashing algorithm that gives you a bunch of different hashes for the same input would be disastrous.

However, with such a system you could demand a particular hash out of the many possible hashes the algorithm can generate from some given data. If the algorithm can generate a lot of possible hashes from the input, you can request a hash with certain properties—that some number of its initial bits sum up to zero, for instance. You could make this request knowing precisely how hard it will be to find the correct hash output, the hash that meets your requirement and corresponds with the data, without knowing what the output itself would be in advance. With a particular hashing algorithm like SHA-1—used by Adam Back, Hal Finney, and the earliest drafts of Bitcoin—there are no shortcuts to producing the right hash. "Because of SHA-1's properties," Finney wrote, "the only way to find a string with a large collision size is by exhaustive search: trying one variation after

another, until you get lucky."[11] Here is an example of a hashcash
token for one of Finney's emails:

"1:28:040727:halmail1@finney.org::1c6a5o2of5ef5c75:63cca52"

The SHA-1 hash of this string looks like this: "ooooooooa86d41
df172f177f4e7ec3907d4634b58"—with seven zeros. Someone's
computer will have to produce and discard many hashes from
the email Finney wrote before it finds that string with seven zeros
at the beginning: about a million tries for a 20-bit collision, a billion for 30. (The Finney example is a 28-bit collision.) As with
other kinds of hashes, it takes some work to produce each one,
but it is trivial to verify that one is correct once you have it in
hand.[12] By changing the properties you require from the hash
of your data, you can make it *arbitrarily difficult* to compute the
correct hash for something.

What use could we get from such an absurd machine? You
could build a mechanism, like the Sphinx, that asks a riddle.
There is only one right answer to the riddle. As the creator of
the mechanism, you do not know the answer, but you know
exactly how hard, and how time consuming, it will be to guess
successfully. If people guess too quickly, you can crank the
ratchet a few teeth forward into greater difficulty, demanding
more "proof of work." With such a device, you could set the
amount of work that was of interest to Adam Back: the computational time it would take to produce a hash of a particular
email. A collision could be demanded that would be invisible
to the everyday email correspondent but an impassable threshold for someone trying to mass-mail millions of people. Call
this quantity of demonstrable work "postage," a digital object
that was hard to make, and easily verified as having been hard
to make.

The historian Anson Rabinbach's *The Human Motor* documented the search for quantifiable metrics for the expenditure of human force, and the "ergographic" instruments that served to measure and represent human bodily work and muscular energy. These instruments (special gloves, arrangements of dumbbells) were in the service of a larger project—to understand the nature of fatigue and find "nerve whips" that could overcome exhaustion and the diminution of bodily power—but reading Rabinbach's history now it's easy to imagine these systems as prototypes of minting mechanisms for a currency based on units of human effort. The project he documented was constantly undermined by the problem of confounding factors of measuring effort and fatigue: Was it muscles, or nerves, or keeping a fixed position, tedium, diet, or temperature?

With partial hash collision algorithms, this fantasy was realized—but for machines, not humans. The algorithms are an exquisitely precise way to demand and demonstrate quantities of computational work: cycles of a central processing unit, expressing watts of power consumed. Furthermore, being hashes of particular data, this work is connected with a specific digital object. With a partial hash collision system, you have a device that can demand a precise quantity of computing work—a number of guesses—that anyone can verify as having been done, based on data you specify: hashcash.

BIT GOLD

Postage stamps, like mobile phone minutes, easily became currency. In the United States around the time of the Civil War, for instance, the dearth of small change led to a formal order for postmasters to no longer honor stamps that were "soiled or defaced," to prevent their monetary circulation.[13] "They would have just as much value, and would answer precisely the same purpose, so long as the community chose to take them," said the 1862 *New York Times* of the stamps, as they might of hashcash strings a hundred and thirty years later. But platforms would be needed to circulate these chunks of proof of work, "P.O.W. tokens," so that they could be reused—rather than the one-and-done of the hashcash postage for sending mail—and function not as metered postage but as something closer to money.

Hal Finney jumped into this expansion of Back's idea. He designed a system where a hashcash token could be sent to a special server, which would return a *reusable* proof of work (RPOW) token. You could spend this, redeem it, or otherwise transact it with someone, who would send it to the server in turn for another such token. "In this way," Finney wrote, "a single POW token is the foundation for a chain of RPOW tokens. The effect is the same as if the POW token could be handed from person to person and retain its value at each step," like cash. It would—at least in theory—retain its value, and the one-time transactions meant you could not copy-paste the same chunk of difficult hashcash to spend it repeatedly. It would rely on a "transparent server" system he was developing: a way for everyone to verify that the proof-of-work renewal system was working properly—neither duplicating nor deleting—without making the server itself vulnerable.

Finney sketched out applications for this strange vehicle of work and value. He described a kind of poker with RPOW tokens functioning as chips, and envisioned a version of the peer-to-peer file-sharing protocol BitTorrent that rewarded people with RPOW tokens for making their downloaded files available to others, and the tokens could in turn be used to pay for a faster spot in the download queue next time—a bit like the

"CryptoCredits" Tim May proposed as the internal currency of BlackNet. With such a device, in other words, you could build systems akin to metered postage, credit card reward points, and a casino's system for redeeming chips.

Nick Szabo discussed how proofs of work might function as something more akin to gold, a scarce commodity. Szabo had worked with David Chaum on the digital cash system at Eindhoven and corresponded on the cypherpunk list. (He appears among the Extropians in the next chapter, and is one of several people proposed as the identity behind the Satoshi Nakamoto pseudonym as the creator of Bitcoin.) In the late 1990s, in conversation with Finney and others, he toyed with the idea of using a hashcash-style technology to create a store of value he called *bit gold*. In a 2001 paper, Szabo referred to Finney's RPOW as an implementation of "a version of bit gold" (and he thanks Mark Miller, the Xanadu programmer, for his comments and encouragement).[14] "Unforgeably costly bits," he argued, "could be created online with minimal dependence on trusted third parties, and then securely stored, transferred, and assayed with similar minimal trust."[15] The costly bits would be the result of a proof-of-work computation on a set input—the "challenge string"—which is derived from the most recent verified bit gold proof of work, linking them together.

The new bit gold proof of work would be time-stamped and signed into another system of Szabo's, a "distributed property title registry"—an "unforgeable . . . chain of digital signatures" granting control over pieces of bit gold to their owners. As they were sold and exchanged—their ownership signed for and reassigned—these proofs, unique and variably valuable, would be grouped together into useful chunks, akin "to what many commodity dealers do today." It is a mechanism that prefigures aspects of the Bitcoin blockchain, a distributed ledger whose "coins" consist of nothing but ownership assigned through proof of work and a chain of digital signatures.

Something like a casino, something like a postal system, something like the gold desk at a commodities broker. What if you could take this technology a step further: to build something like a bank—with a kind of money that was not just on the network's hardware, but *of* it? What would a hashcash-based bank look like?

THE IMPOSSIBILITY OF VIOLENCE

The standard mental model of the secret cypherpunk bank— a model inherited from physical banks—went like this: There is a central server, a computer that stores a list of accounts and the amounts of some kind of "digital coin" assigned to each account. I have five coins, and you have ten. In exchange for services rendered, you log in to the bank and send three of your coins to my account. The "coins," some string of letters and numbers, never leave the bank's server; they get reassigned to one or another account. These "coins" may be issued with reference to grains of physical gold stored in a safe-deposit box—a lemonade-stand version of the New York Federal Reserve's gold storage, where ownership transfers involve moving marked bars between compartments or shelves in compartments without ever leaving the facility. The bank is "encrypted" in the sense that our transactions and accounts are anonymized, and the computer on which all this activity takes place is likewise encrypted.

This presents two problems.

First, what happens if the server goes away, temporarily or permanently? The server on which the bank lives must physically sit somewhere: in the closet of some Gadsden-flag-flying libertarian who's already on a police list for their cannabis legalization activities, or in an office park that's just lost its lease, or a hurricane-prone Caribbean jurisdiction. Can it be defended?

Second, and worse, how sure are you about the person in charge of the server, which is also the bank? How are you sure that the digital "coins" in your account at the covert bank are really backed by anything? Can the administrator make and sell as many as they want? Is that gold ingot on the digital scale next to the day's newspaper in the photograph real or not? Is their security absolutely airtight, or could hackers empty out accounts or make copies of the same "coin" and spend it as often as they like?

How to secure the virtual bank? Sustaining the fantasy of intangible, untouchable cyberspace required the metaphorical "'solidity,'" May wrote, of "walls, doors, permanent structures" provided by encryption—but as a practical matter that other space was defined by a constantly leaking permeable membrane.[16] Signals pass through walls, people keep passwords and addresses on sticky notes for reference, and computers and servers and digital media are physically seized, bagged, and put in the vans of Interpol or the FBI. Someone with a powerful electromagnet—or just access to the fuse box—could damage or destroy a covert messageboard or secret bank, for any reason, from deleting accumulated debts to making mayhem for its own sake (never an impulse in short supply on the Internet). "Physical security is needed," May argued; you could not—yet—really run a network wholly apart from the planet on which it was embedded.[17]

Some of the machines involved needed "controlled access" and protection—one of the longer-term strategies was to run crypto anarchist networks on satellites, which would be much more difficult to shoot down. Some of the cypherpunks anticipated potential reprisals or dangers from extortionists or criminal cartels. The work of securing the network was not just a matter of mathematics after all, but required hardware, facilities, and tradecraft. "For much the same reason no 'digital coin' exists," May concluded: you couldn't rely on the security of the machinery to secure the transaction records and the mint. Without control of a built environment, the systems of exchange and accumulation would never escape the suspicion of vulnerability. The Other Plane, disembodied cyberspace, needed physical spaces. It needed zones, sovereign territories, spaces of exception—a trajectory that would one day lead to an abandoned artillery platform in the North Sea.

Tim May and Ryan Lackey—a technologist who would later turn up on that North Sea platform, hoping to build an anonymous bank—argued the merits of scopes on Dragunov guns and the relative utility of the AR-15 assault rifle, generally in the context of fighting a government raid. Armed resistance against such a physical assertion of state sovereignty was, they conceded, a terrible idea. "I figure that if I'm ever in a situation where I have to engage multiple targets quickly," Tim May wrote in response to a detailed analysis of "Soviet-style weapons" in raid defense, "I'm probably a goner."[18]

"I don't understand why there is so much talk about guns here lately," Dai wrote on the mailing list in January 1998. "Unless someone comes up with a weapon that has some very unusual economic properties, individuals cannot hope to compete with governments in the domain of deadly force."[19] (Economic weapons: One thinks of the rays developed by the scientific vigilantes in Technocratic sci-fi, which blank banknotes and turn gold into tin to soften the human terrain for their rational coup.) "Think about it," he continued: "if we can defend ourselves with guns, why would we need crypto?"

On November 27, 1998, Wei Dai posted a proposal to the cypherpunk mailing list for "a new protocol for monetary exchange and contract enforcement for pseudonyms," which he called "b-money."[20] The idea would, in retrospect, loom large, but he mentioned it in passing. The link appeared at the end of a note about PipeNet, a project to shuffle messages using encrypted communications on the network to make it difficult for an adversary to figure out who is speaking to whom. (It was akin to the Onion Routing system that became Tor.) His b-money text file began, "I am fascinated by Tim May's crypto-anarchy. . . . It's a community where the threat of violence is impotent because violence is impossible, and violence is impossible because its participants cannot be linked to their true names or physical locations."

What Dai was proposing was something different, though, from May's envisioned "digital coin" that needed physical protection for the machinery, like a bank. It was a form of cash that was built on the very mechanisms it also used for transactions. It was a currency that was itself wholly *cryptographic* in its mechanisms, and not just encrypted in its transactions. It was the first mint that belonged natively to the permanent frontier. "It's almost too simple to describe," wrote Hal Finney about b-money: "In principle, it is just a matter of everyone keeping track of how much money everyone else has."[21] That's part one, and brings us back to the second problem with the fantasy of the cypherpunk bank: How do you know you can trust the banker?

MONEY IS NOT ABOUT ATOMS

Dai's solution was to deconstruct the bank into distributed components: a set of accounts that can hold money, a mechanism for transacting the money between accounts, and a means of issuing that money in the first place. Then, rather than the bank being some central location (literally and metaphorically) to which all its clients would refer, every client working together would constitute the bank collectively. Dai exploded "the bank" outward, into a decentralized network composed of all of its participants.

All the accounts on Dai's network are pseudonyms, in the now-familiar public-private key arrangement, and each pseudonym keeps a copy of the ledger of the whole bank: "everyone keeping track of how much money everyone else has." Finney continued his description: "Whenever there is a transfer of money, this fact gets broadcast and everyone updates their databases."[22] When you spend some money, that act is announced to the whole network (signed with your private key); everyone checks their ledgers, and, if you have the money to spend, they update accordingly: you debit three, I credit three.

Finally, and most ingeniously, anyone on the network can produce new money according to a set of collectively agreed-upon rules. In the case of Dai's first version, new money can be added to the system by broadcasting "the solution to a previously unsolved computational problem." It must be easy to determine that the solution is true, and likewise to measure exactly how hard the problem was to solve, so that the difficulty can be calibrated in terms of "a standard basket of commodities." Minting would therefore be challenging and moderately expensive, but not impossible, and pegged to the price of some mix of barrels of oil, bushels of grain, feet of lumber: as money became scarce and more valuable, it would be worthwhile to expend computational work on minting more of it; as more was produced, the supply inflating and dropping in value, fewer people would spend the computing energy—the work, the money—to mint, and the money would become more valuable again.[23]

The heart of the project lay in rebuilding money on computational, and specifically cryptographic, lines: public and private keys for identity and authentication, untraceable networks for transaction, and some well-established way of setting computational problems to be solved. (Dai also discussed how the same tools used to reconcile transactions could be used to set and validate contracts.) For the problem-setting, as Back pointed out, partial hash collision systems were an ideal fit; he gave public feedback within days to Dai's original proposal. Abstracted from an institution or an established group of people, b-money was *of* the network rather than on it, built of cryptographic tools rather than simply concealed by them, native to the Other Plane.

A decade later, Satoshi Nakamoto, Bitcoin's pseudonymous creator, wrote to Dai: "I was very interested to read your b-money page. I'm getting ready to release a paper that expands on your ideas into a complete working system"—the "complete working system" that would be Bitcoin.[24] "Adam Back (hashcash.org) noticed the similarities and pointed me to your site." In January of the next year, Nakamoto followed up: "I just released the full implementation of the paper I sent you a few months ago, Bitcoin v0.1. . . . I think it achieves nearly all the goals you set out to solve in your b-money paper."[25]

In 2002, Finney ended his summary of b-money by putting the matter into a larger context: "The important point in these conceptions of money is that it is fundamentally a form of information. B-money shows that most clearly. Money is not about atoms, it is about bits. Extropians should shun old-fashioned views of money as based on material goods."[26]

CHAPTER 8

HAYEK IN BIOSTASIS

We follow all of these technologies, and many of the same people, into the hard-core utopianism of the Extropian movement. Extropians fused Austrian economic theories with new technologies and Bay Area techno-optimism to produce a model of transformation through speculative monies—from idea coupons to anonymous digital cash—that could be cryptographically authenticated, with their value backed by the very future they promised to bring about. They tried to accelerate the arrival of their utopia with a financial project to overclock human civilization.

THE VANGUARD OF THE FUTURE

"Most persons claiming to be futurists have social and economic views at odds with the principle of spontaneous order," wrote Max More (né O'Connor) in the journal/zine *Extropy* in the summer of 1995. "We continue to explore a different kind of future."[1]

The Extropians created a way of explicitly thinking about the historical and temporal condition of their time *expressed as money*, which would be at once proposal, prototype, and mechanism for bringing their future to pass. "In place of most futurists' ideals of world government, technocracy, and monetary supranationalism," More wrote of this movement, "we can examine the alternatives of polycentric/privately-produced law and competing digital private currencies"—the latter including "electronic money," "free banking or competing currencies," and "anonymous digital money."[2] "If we are to remain the vanguard of the future," he continued, "let's see what we can do to hasten these crucial developments."

They built their vision on the theories of a group of Austrian economists—particularly the work of Friedrich Hayek. "I deeply regret Hayek's death," wrote More. "Not having been placed into biostasis, Hayek will never return to see the days of electronic cash and competing private currencies that his thinking may help bring about."[3] "Biostasis": cryonically frozen in a vault in Arizona, awaiting revival as a body or a brain in a future of posthuman abundance and stellar ambition. The first version of Bitcoin would in some ways be the retrospective artifact of the new cosmogram fashioned by the Extropians—their model of the future, of the world as it could be.

Some utopias become purer, harder, and harsher as they diminish, like an evaporating lake growing more saline every year in its shores of crystalline salt: think of the theorist-revolutionary Guy Debord, ostracizing and expelling people from the Situationist International movement until you could fit the future of artsy council communism around the back table of a Parisian bar. Some utopias dilute into the surrounding society that gives them context—the well-lit, spare, clean, glass-and-steel spaces of the Bauhaus are now the default setting for expensive apartments and bank lobbies, their mystic-visionary content reduced to homeopathic doses. Some die all at once with their founder or settle into a second act as businesses: silverware from the Oneida Perfectionists, hammocks from the Skinnerian behaviorist community Twin Oaks, or wind chimes from Arcosanti, which was once to be the germ of anthill arcologies honeycombing the planet.

Of all these ways to end, a handful of utopian projects—perhaps the most successful—evaporate in practice but produce a persistent icon of the future for a group or subculture, a shared arrangement of visions, a magnetic field by which other people unknowingly set their compasses. Extropy was one of these.

The Extropians—an email list, a string of conferences and events, a magazine and a foundation, a handful of prominent organizers—seem penny-ante, especially given the cosmic scale of their ambitions. Even at the most generous estimate, there were never more than a few thousand Extropians, fellow travelers, and interested bystanders, and they dissolved into a millennial haze of posthuman, transhuman, and Singularity projects after scarcely more than a decade and a half of existence. Within those numbers, though, a remarkable mix of people gathered, including almost every key figure in the eventual genesis of Bitcoin. Szabo prognosticated about the adoption of digital cash in the pages of *Extropy*. Finney and Merkle and Mark \$amuel Miller (the Xanadu developer and prophet of market-based "agoric" computing systems) wrote articles for the magazine and discussed ideas on the Extropian mailing list with Wei Dai, Tim May, and other cypherpunks; the list had been set up and hosted by Perry Metzger, who would go on to run the cryptography list where Nakamoto would post the Bitcoin paper on Halloween in 2008 and the first Bitcoin code the following January. (One of the newsgroups May's BlackNet thought experiment proposed to monitor for encrypted messages was alt.extropian.)

To go back and read the agenda set in the first issue of *Extropy* is to experience déjà vu: it is a near-comprehensive litany of subjects of interest to a specific coherent slice of online culture to this day. "Artificial intelligence, cognitive science and neuroscience, intelligence-increase technologies," the list begins, written by Tom Bell and Max O'Connor before they reinvented themselves as T. O. Morrow and Max More. It continues with "life extension, cryonics and biostasis, nanotechnology, spontaneous orders, space colonization, economics and politics (especially libertarian), science fiction," studying and producing memes, "morality and amorality," psychedelics, and "mind-fucking" (by which they meant prankish weirdness and highbrow trolling). That list is from 1988.[4] With a little updating of terminology and references, most of the material would not be out of place in threads on Hacker News, Less Wrong, subsections of Reddit, and other redoubts of the contemporary Anglophone rationalist-utopian geek scene, amidst the Soylent, Martian colonization schemes, regimens of "nootropic" smart-drug supplements— and Bitcoin drama.

Of course the Extropians were not, as they dubbed themselves, "the vanguard of the future" (notice the singular—one future, one vanguard). But they were a benchmark of unalloyed purity against which the spirit of a very particular time, place, and subculture could be judged: the exemplary expression of 1990s West Coast digital optimism. They were the computational equivalent of "air-mindedness" in early aviation, promising comprehensive social change through the advent of new technology.[5] The archive of their journals and other publications and ephemera radiates glaring, hammered-gold sunlight when opened. Max More framed their tenets early on: "(1) Boundless Expansion; (2) Dynamic Optimism; (3) Self-Transformation; (4) Intelligent Technology"; and later added a fifth, "Spontaneous Order."[6] Their project was to move time's arrow of cumulative thermodynamic and informational entropy in the opposite direction, toward "extropy": increasing intelligence, longevity, energy, information, life, growth. Hence More's new name. Renaming was a practice of the Extropian inner circle, who took on identities like MP-Infinity, Simon! D. Levy, T. O. Morrow, Skye D'Aureous, Max's partner Natasha Vita-More, and their forebear and inspiration FM-2030 (previously Fereidoun M. Esfandiary).

They hybridized American libertarianism, Austrian economics, recent technological advances (and prospective fantasies), a science-fictional sensibility, and modish theories of emergence. To this they added a coastal Californian culture of experimental diets, self-help psychology, exercise, high-end gadgets, and gleaming-smile positivity. They operated inside a custom-built model of history, seeking a set of different techniques to "hasten" it, as More said, into full bloom. They worked on new kinds of money, especially digital cash, as a speculative tool and accelerant. This was a subject about which Extropians had a unique, self-reflexive position.

THE FIFTEEN-HAYEK NOTE

The playful mock-up of a future currency on the cover of *Extropy* was issued by the "Virtual Bank of Extropolis" over the "Distributed Networks of Extropia," dated 2030 and denominated in "hayeks." Hayek himself appeared in the oval portrait, looking owlish and remote. On the reverse—where a US$5 features the Lincoln Memorial—Max More and T. O. Morrow appear, waving in sunglasses with the posture of rock stars doing a curtain call: their future's so bright they need to wear shades. What brought the subjects on the face and the back of the Extropian fifteen-hayek note together? The Extropian project drew conceptual strength from the counterintuitive marriage of the "Austrian School" of Viennese economics with Silicon Valley futurism: Friedrich Hayek being sealed in the cryonic tube to be revived later, like Ripley in the escape pod in *Aliens*.

The Austrian conversation extends from the present day back to the 1870s; the core of the Austrian economist community was in the same milieu, and in some cases the same cliques and salons, as people like Gödel, Wittgenstein, Carnap, Mach, Boltzmann, Otto Neurath, Freud, Musil, and Karl Kraus. They were part of the long generation for whom the question of how and in what ways something could be known and communicated was of the utmost importance, exemplified by the *Wiener Kreis*, the Vienna Circle, with whom Hayek and Karl Popper, among others, were close.[7] The ranks of the Austrian economists and their interlocutors were varied. Ludwig von Mises, for instance, created an eccentric, convoluted theoretical framework called *praxeology*, which deduced all subjective human actions and desires from logical, axiomatic first principles, "not subject to verification or falsification on the ground of experience and facts."[8] Karl Popper was best known as a philosopher of science and the cosmopolitan author of *The Open Society and Its Enemies*. Mises's student, Murray Rothbard, was an anarcho-capitalist radical, one-note ideologue, racist "paleolibertarian," and an inspiration to Ross Ulbricht's Silk Road drugs-for-Bitcoin marketplace. Hayek was an erudite, self-identified classical liberal who shared a Nobel Prize in Economics in 1974 and supported and endorsed the Pinochet dictatorship in Chile. For our purposes, the central question uniting these disparate characters was an epistemological problem—a problem of knowledge, closely related to the problem of the future itself: How do we know how much something should cost?[9]

Prices are a form of information. They signal subjective needs, desires, circumstances, and expectations of the future in the form of what buyers are willing to pay. But how do we know that this information, expressed as prices, is accurate? What if the way things are priced is incorrect, or a misallocation of resources, or unjust, or otherwise in need of adjustment—how would we even know? I need an insulin shot, you want a liner for a truck bed, and a semiconductor company must eventually update a billion-dollar microchip fabrication line: the Austrian argument is that allocating and pricing resources appropriately to this varied tapestry exceeds the capacity of any form of planning. Prices are an information transmission system for subjective needs and desires, and the market is an ongoing, undecidable calculation of the worth of all things relative to each other. The worth—the price—comes not from some great framework within which value can be assigned, but from what particular people are willing to pay: price signals, which in turn drive other forms of action. Any attempt to control this system, however slight, would diminish the efficiency and subjective utility of the market at work.

The revolution promised by Technocracy Inc. would start, in Howard Scott's words, by "smashing the Price System": the Technocrats with whom this book began planned to solve the chaos of subjective value by subtracting variables from their command economy, including any human activity that did not have a spot preassigned in their energy budget—spreadsheet totalitarianism. For Popper, Hayek's colleague, friend, and correspondent, such movements exemplified the tendency to "utopian engineering" that emerged from a particular understanding of history.[10] The Austrian alternative (in Popper's argument) was trial and error and open-ended uncertainty, driven by the subjective guesses, assumptions, and impulses of individuals. Such an approach would respect the subjectivity and desires of the individual while producing a more fluid and dynamic economy—in Hayek's potent and problematic phrase, a "spontaneous order." (Hayek and Mises preferred the obscure term "catallactics" to "economics," since it focused etymologically on exchanges—"the order brought about by the mutual adjustment of many individual economies in a market"—rather than the "household" of economics, which implied collective goals by the members of the marketplace.[11])

There would be no control, no planning, no centralized foresight; they sought a universal solvent capable of dissolving any structure that might try to crystallize the fluidity of markets. Price moves on, creating new regimes of value and disruptive breakthroughs as it goes, not memorializing crypts of past labor and invention but pricing them cheap and accelerating into the future, toward the next thing, and carrying society in its wake.[12]

The Austrian School's theories offered something dizzying and anarchic—especially to noneconomists, like most of the Extropians, who read and misread their documents creatively. The Austrians spoke not to a science-fictional subject but to a science-fictional *sensibility*: the economy as a machine directed to unknowable ends, ungovernable and computationally irreducible, beyond human ability to steer or outguess, a machine made of whole populations of desires, impulses, fantasies, hungers, and other subjective drives that consumes and transforms everything set before it. In their most extreme form, they become apostles of "a general, absolute, and apparently transcendent faith in the market" with a corresponding set of magical practices, rituals, and prohibitions for getting good results. These began with the production of money.[13]

For these ideas to hold, money itself must be free from any governmental or institutional interference. If not, how can we be sure that any prices, any signals, are accurate—that anything costs what it should? Money is the epistemological bedrock on which the Austrian machine is seated. If money becomes uncertain, the system trembles on the verge of ontological collapse.

The economists offered two principal solutions to this problem.

The first was that money must possess "intrinsic value," an approach championed by Mises. He argued that economic equilibrium was effectively impossible, but the promise of it would lead to efforts to interfere with the market doing whatever it's going to do; therefore, money must be removed from the ability of the state to adjust. (The Austrian theory of business cycles— which was partially responsible for Hayek winning his Nobel— argues that recessions and crashes are the result of central banks setting interest rates too low and creating too much easy credit; interference with the money supply produces misleading signals for the market, fueling investment frenzies and bubbles leading to inevitable crashes.) The challenge of finding *intrinsically* valuable money turns, of course, to precious metals and stories of barter economies, bolstered by the elaborate armature of praxeology with its logical portrait of all human motivation and valuing.

Hayek's alternative was a world of competing private currencies, a proliferation of new ways in which things could be banks, could be money, and could be exchangeable. Their churn, their flux of subjective value, operating in the same flows of the free price system, would produce nothing less than "spontaneous order": a product of human action but not human planning, as Hayek loved to phrase it—a price system emerging from the "collective brain" as a new informational platform, like the development of language itself.

The relentless process of profit, surplus capture, pricing, and competition that structures a theoretical Austrian economy is a revaluation without end, a steadily accelerating expansion into *more*. It expresses with singular purity Marx's description of the essence of capital as a force: "tearing down all the barriers which hem in the development of the forces of production, the expansion of needs, the all-sided development of production, and the exploitation and exchange of natural and mental forces."[14]

Within that accelerating, expanding system, the Extropians planned to issue their own digital currency: denominated after their inspiration and authenticated with cryptography, an interwar Viennese epistemology reinvented by Californian superoptimists in the heart of an information processing boom. Along with the all-seeing eye, the notes are decorated with an Extropian symbol that belongs equally to the Austrian tradition: a ring of curving arrows all expanding outward, a system exploding into every direction at once.

IDEA FUTURES AND GEODESIC SCHEMES

"Who invented language? Who thought up money? Who is responsible for our society's customs?"[15] All products of spontaneous order, the superior source of developments to planning, the Extropians argued (in the spirit of Hayek). They didn't want to indulge in mere foolishness—"wasting money needlessly is entropic"—but to proliferate the mechanisms by which the unknown route to the known future might present itself, the abrupt efficient walk manifesting across the multiplying nodes.[16] The Extropians found themselves in a monetary-historical paradox: to reach the known future moment of abundance and transformation, lying somewhere up on the hockey-stick curve of exponential growth and innovation, they had to relinquish as much control to the *unknown* in the present as possible, and arrange their affairs for maximum "spontaneous order." Creating their own money was the first step.

They made reputation currencies, like the Hawthorne Exchange or "HEx" market, trading in "thornes" to buy and sell shares in the reputations of particular Extropians, favorite concepts, and speculations on the future—a game of almost pure confidence. The stock ticker symbols were a roll call of Extropian interests and luminaries: HFINN (for Hal Finney), EXI, CYPHP, HEINLN, LEARY, RAND, MORE. Timothy May (TMAY) used the thornes issued to bid up his own shares and then—in the largest foreign-exchange transaction in the history of the market—bought fifteen dollars' worth of thornes from someone else, so he could continue driving up his personal share price.

They made sketches, essays, and playful prototypes of new monies, many of which tried to reinvent Chaum's DigiCash or work around his patents to produce an open source equivalent. Some just promised that, while the "Chaum-style blind signature" is patented, using it "for experimental purposes only" should keep you under the radar.[17] Finney himself wrote a thorough overview of David Chaum's papers in the pages of *Extropy*: it was true "digital cash," he explained in detail, albeit still reliant on existing banks and their governmentally endorsed money.[18] Chaum wanted digital cash because of straightforward privacy concerns ("Computerization is robbing individuals of the ability to monitor and control the ways information about them is used"), but Extropians were able to fold it into the timeline of their cosmic project without much difficulty.[19]

"Magic Money" was one of these Chaumian offshoots, developed by the awesomely pseudonymous Extropian "Pr0duct Cypher." After outlining their implementation of Chaum's ideas and the command line interface for running transactions, Cypher provided a four-paragraph explanation of money itself: "Now, if you're still awake, comes the fun part: how do you introduce real value into your digicash system?" She or he understood how Magic Money, as well as being more or less working software, was *speculative currency*, a performance of a certain subculture and their model of futurity, and should be treated with an appropriate theatricality. "You can make your cash more interesting by giving your server a provocative name. Running it through a remailer could give it an 'underground' feel, which would attract people. Your digicash should be scarce."

Matt Thomlinson experimented with "Ghostmarks," from the (provocatively named) "Phantom Exchange." Mike Duvos issued "Tacky Tokens"—a hundred free each "to the first 10 people who mail my server." Hal Finney adopted the tokens for an existing model and tried to drum up interest on the cypherpunk list for kicking the tires on a digital cash system and getting some transactions going—you could buy a GIF with them, or a list of state requirements for ID cards. Black Unicorn's "DigiFrancs" were backed by and redeemable for ten cases of warm Diet Coke in Washington, DC, and exchangeable at floating rates for Ghostmarks—an agreement bannered with sarcastic sobriety, as if in a press release to the *Financial Times*.

There were "idea futures," coupon-like currencies issued against future events by date: if some given number of humans were living on Mars by the first day of a given year, the notes would mature. One issue of *Extropy* came with a stapled-in coupon betting on a "Nanocomputer in 2020," at "$U.S. +5% from 1990," payable following research by a designated judge into the claim made by its issuer, the libertarian economist Robin Hanson (or his estate) in 2025. (Hanson was last seen in this book developing an internal prediction market at Xanadu in 1990; he went on to create Overcoming Bias, a blog on which Singularity theorists, the rationalist vanguard, and various neoreactionaries all cut their teeth as commenters.[20])

Hanson explained his goal with the coupon issue: to produce a market price for a long-range future outcome, as a picture of likelihood—a bettor's odds—and an incentive for realization.

Matters on which to buy coupons ranged from guesses about unknown physical constants, sea-level rise, and human migration into outer space. It was another way to tilt the solar panels to catch the light from the day that has not yet broken: "Like cryonics, idea futures are another way to take advantage now of the fact that the future should be rich with power and knowledge."[21] (There were also monetary projects and proposals suited to the ultra-long-term financial planning and wealth management needed by those pursuing immortality through cryonic storage.)

"Money. It's everywhere," wrote Richard Potvin just after the millennium. "But not enough of it flows through the coffers of transhuman oriented organisms' bank accounts to accelerate the changes we need to see happen." Potvin was a transhumanist, a member of the Bay Area Cryonics Society (among others), and early in the first month of the new millennium he extended "A Solicitation to Extropians to Buy Virtual Shares."[22] Extropians, Potvin wrote, should become "players" in StockGeneration (SG), a virtual stock-trading game played with real money. The stocks paid dividends, also in real money, as the market grew, with some shares guaranteed to rise in value at a fixed rate. The source of this income was steady waves of new players recruited by those already in the game. The whole operation was run by a European company, banking in Estonia (among other places) but registered and operating servers on the Caribbean island of Dominica.[23] The complete virtuality of the scheme was a selling point—"a totally stable financial system" completely insulated from the outside world, "virtually autonomous" in its "game format." No political upheaval or economic downturn could hit the SG, any more than friction could take energy from a perpetual motion machine. It was a straight-up pyramid scheme, of course, but Potvin embraced that. "This is no 'ordinary' pyramid," he wrote. "It's more like a geodesic dome."[24]

Seen in the right light, the property of being a pyramid scheme was a *positive* thing: a way to deliberately produce a bubble and move enough money into transhuman projects that you could boost right out of the conventional scarcity economy entirely before the bubble popped. What does the usual human ruin of boom-bust *matter*, after all, in a posthuman era? Turn the ludicrous dot-com frenzy into your booster rocket with a self-supporting geodesic scheme and cut it loose to burn up in the atmosphere once you're out of the gravity well.

OVERCLOCKING HUMAN CIVILIZATION

Chaum sought digital cash for privacy, and May for a particular, narrow form of liberty ("the real choice is between a total state and crypto anarchy"). The Extropians wanted it for these reasons, too, but also as a spur to utopian transformation.[25] Where Chaum worked on digital cash that permitted the withdrawal, circulation, and deposit of anonymous tokens, but still relied on banks to produce and manage the money supply and deanonymize double-spenders, the Extropians wanted to multiply the mints—a flowering of multifarious, competing private currencies and payment systems.

In Rebecca Spang's aphorism, reflecting on the monetary projects of Revolutionary France, "Trust is habit congealed through repetition into faith."[26] The paradoxical strategy of the Extropian model was to transform empirical trust in particular technologies, like applied cryptography, and in the repetitive experience of technological shock in the computer business (every day, it seemed, brought some new improvement) into faith in a logically inevitable future. The trust in demonstrable things could be translated into faith in the spontaneous operation of a system in a state of permanent disruption, seeking an equilibrium that would never be found. This faith could then work *backward*, a self-reinforcing expression of "dynamic optimism." The model turned causality inside out, with the known future rendering the present unknowable in order to secure its own advent.

It worked like this: we are on the verge of inevitable breakthroughs (computing, cognition, longevity, biotechnology, automation), a proliferation of singularities on the far side of which the human condition ends in an abundance of time, space, and energy. However, we cannot deliberately bring this about: planning, centralized control, resource allocation, the whole toolkit of human decision making will fail to deliver us to that inevitable transhuman event, because that future exceeds our mediocre, bureaucratic, institutional intelligence. It can only spontaneously emerge from the operation of a frictionless market.

Anything that gets in the way of this market is going to slow, or possibly stall, the emergence of new, spontaneous, unforeseeable social and technological orders: FDA regulations on "smart drugs," or work visas and labor laws, or surveillance of information traffic, or models of limited personal identity, or control of currency to manage the economy. Unrestrained Austrian-style capitalism is thus a kind of time machine, but not in the classically capitalist sense of investment in future outcomes whose delivery expands the present economy and closes the loop of credit. Rather, it is a mechanism out of which spills a future of total, near-metaphysical disruption—the end of death, the advent of abundant posthuman intelligence, anatomical and biological transformation, the resurrection of the "biostatic" dead, expansion into interplanetary and interstellar space. It is a "hole into the future," as a character described the futuristic Zone left behind by aliens in *Roadside Picnic*, the science fiction novel that became the Tarkovsky movie *Stalker*: "Knowledge comes through this hole. And when we have the knowledge, we'll make everyone rich, and we'll fly to the stars, and go anywhere we want."

The Extropians provided intermediate sketches of this process, starting with establishing the Extropy Institute (ExI) as a permanent foundation. The ExI would raise money for Free Oceana, a "seasteading" project—an initiative to create a sovereign colony in international waters—that would build on research from Biosphere II. (The anti-aging advocate Roy Walford, the chief medic in Biosphere II, was a favorite interview subject; seasteading schemes proliferate later in this book.) At sea, Free Oceana would act as "Sociosphere II," a testbed for new social and political systems. Those models would become the human prototyping lab for the move to space, to "Extropolis"—from which those hayek-denominated notes would be issued.[27]

This is, in other words, a cosmogram vision of the world as it could be and its trajectory. But it could only come to pass by creating the appropriate context and mechanisms that make it impossible to control—so the spontaneous orders can freely evolve—and then stepping out of the way. For all their starry-eyed West Coast hedonic optimism, the Extropians were well aware of the current technological limits—the performance envelope of the entire industrial world—which had to be surpassed for their visions to be realized. New kinds of money, new exchange systems and marketplaces and investments were needed to drive this transformation. "What you spend now shapes your future self," as Extropian muse Romana Machado put it.[28]

One last consequence of this line of thinking: If we *know* this future is coming, and we know how to arrange the propitious circumstances for its genesis, could we not accelerate the process somehow and force the hand of chance? We can't out-predict the market, no more than we could determine the output of the computational halting problem, but we can build faster computers. Why can't we effectively overclock human civilization?

Money could do this—not just by sluicing "through the coffers of transhuman oriented organisms' bank accounts" but through the creation of new flows of incentives, covert markets, innovation-seeking pricing schemes, and models of prosperity that would exploit the energy of spontaneous order. Nick Szabo made thoughtful predictions at Extropian events about the coming of this new money.[29] Though many of Szabo's forecasts were conservative by the standards of the Extropian community—he put "uploaded minds" (human consciousness running on computational hardware) much farther in the future than many of the others—he was bullish on the very near-term adoption of digital cash and encryption technologies, given the "economic or cultural barriers to overcome."

In 1995, he predicted the benchmark of more than a million people using anonymous electronic cash would be reached by 1999, and an untaxable anonymous digital cash economy exceeding a billion dollars annually by 2005. The point of highlighting this is not to mock—forecasting is not a forgiving art—but to capture the urgency they felt, the need to "hasten these crucial developments," as More wrote. Because here's the rub of living in the Extropian model of history: we are on the verge of transformations of which we can scarcely conceive, but what if they finally begin just after we die?

CHAPTER 9

FUTURE DESIRES

With their plan, the Extropians built a historical trap they could only escape by being cryonically frozen for future revival, a practice intimately connected with their currencies—and one that plays into the creation of Bitcoin. We follow their ideas into the financial arrangements demanded by the extreme investment of immortality, further connections with the theories of Friedrich Hayek, and the economic implications of both the fantasies and reality of frozen human bodies, from the Bolshevik Revolution to the turn of the millennium.

THE HISTORIOGRAPHY OF COLD

With this paradox of futurism, the Extropians had created a singularly poignant and—despite all their relentless cheerfulness and dynamic optimism—very melancholy model of history, a cosmogram of singular cruelty for those who lived in it. They knew a future of glory awaited them, one that so exceeded modern expectations that it would torch through the structure of the "future present" like a beam of coherent light. With reputation currencies, virtual finance schemes, and, more seriously, idea futures and digital cash experiments, they could bank on this future and underwrite its production at the same time. But they could neither predict its precise advent nor control *how,* much less when, it would take shape. For a group of can-do hyperrationalists, this was a very painful state of affairs. What if you, yourself, laid all the economic and financial groundwork for generating an emergent posthuman paradise and then did not live to see it?

What if you, in your untimeliness, are one of the last generation to perish prior to posthuman existence? If you can make it a few more years—with the "Walford high-low life extension diet," the bottles and pillboxes of supplements, the cold showers for thermogenesis, the calibrated fitness regimen (Hal Finney's spouse, Fran Finney, wrote about this for *Extropy*[1])—you could live forever.

Hence biostasis and cryonics—a stopgap, an emergency better-than-nothing strategy to cross that historical border that is somewhere near us, sometime soon, but not quite yet. You arranged a payout from your life insurance—and, in some cases, set up far more complex and strange financial vehicles. You put on a bracelet with medical instructions, or even got a tattoo on your chest for the paramedics: the emergency phone number, the offered reward, and "PUSH 50,000 U HEPARIN BY IV AND DO CPR WHILE COOLING WITH ICE TO 10C . . . NO EMBALMING NO AUTOPSY."[2] In case of misadventure, you won't miss out on the billion-year spree to come—with the unfortunate hurdle of still having to die.

Cryonics was the ultimate idea future. It expressed the spirit of Extropian money in a form purer, and more successful, than the money itself: no one transacts in thornes, hayeks, or Ghostmarks, or waits to redeem a stack of idea future coupons, but more than a hundred people are currently frozen, and more than a thousand are signed up with their affairs in order. Alongside the development of digital cash in the 1990s and into the millennium, we find debates on how to move your consciousness into the future that these speculative, utopian currencies will help create: "a biomedically mediated form of investing in the self," as the anthropologist Tiffany Romain put it in her study of cryonicists.[3] Cryonics made it possible to develop new forms of digital money in what Romain calls the "long, long term," transforming the nearly inconceivable Extropian future into a present-day form of *extreme investment.*

The "long, long-term" time frame of investment and financial speculation is no longer a matter of planning your retirement and senescence but of arranging assets to transcend your life and, ultimately, money entirely. Aschwin de Wolf, editor of *Cryonics,* an industry magazine for the life extension and preservation nonprofit Alcor (whose current CEO is Max More) speaks to the challenge of reintegrating the "patient" from their storage at metabolic zero into some unknown future condition: "If proper thought is given to this issue, the person should at least have access to a modern home and money in the prevailing currency of the time (if 'money' as we know it has something like the same significance then)."[4] In the meantime, rather than scattering your assets to heirs, you can construct a dynasty trust, which will hold your capital and earn interest until you reclaim it post-posthumously.

In this context, digital cash had to walk a knife's edge between money as a store of value—an inherently conservative position, particularly for those followers of Austrianism demanding money with "inherent value" and the preservation of social and technical structure that would sustain it—and money as a solvent and agent of chaos, with speculative profit melting every obstacle in the path of transcendence. It would wipe out established industries, create and destroy markets, render laws irrelevant, make existing social practices and commitments meaningless, and ultimately vaporize humanity itself into something else entirely. Until then it would be as stable as a Treasury bond and solid as real estate.

This put digital cash work into a paradoxical bind. It needed to be robust, suitable for denominating and holding in the ultralong-term financial architecture of the deep future, which put an emphasis on the reliability of natural and mathematical constants like the key systems and hashing schemes of cryptography. But it could also ultimately be disposable, as rickety as the "geodesic scheme," if the goal was to get to a society of radical abundance, cosmic proliferation, and immortality. Like many imagined machines of the Singularity, all digital cash had to do was run well enough to make itself obsolete, and then vanish from the scene.

Cryonics made it possible to imagine a nearly inconceivable future and build instances of it now as an extreme investment vehicle. The specialized "dewers"—the massive stainless steel flasks holding liquid nitrogen and the bodies or heads of cryonics patients—are effectively broken time machines, assembled with crude components in the hope that future engineers will be able to activate their cargo successfully and bring the passenger out of the past. Lined up in the Alcor facility, they are the biomedical versions of the runways and bamboo radios of millenarian religions in post–World War II Melanesia—what outsiders dubbed "cargo cults"—which, among other more immediate social goals, meant to *summon* the requisite technologies: clearing and grading landing strips for the planes to come, trying to use an effect to act on a cause.

Charles Platt, a science fiction author, technical writer, and cryonics technician (with patents on "liquid ventilation" systems for rapid cooling of the body, as well as other medical applications) described the attitude necessary for advancing the goals of cryonics: "In science and medicine, *first* you prove that a technique works, and *then* you apply it. If you invert this sequence, you're not involved in orthodox science anymore; you're working speculatively, gambling on the future."[5] And while a certain gambling spirit is necessary, even vital, you have to be able to deliver "a product that works." The challenge inherent in that working product is that it's not only a body successfully returned to functional order, a mind piecing itself together (remembering the last moments on the hospital bed or the hospice porch), but also a corresponding future required to bring it back in full: a brilliant, healthy, gloriously posthuman age. Banking the body for revival means having a future that can be banked *on*. And that is the future that digital cash, the disruption machine, the motor of innovation, had to be able to deliver.

In 1996, two announcements were made on facing pages of the same issue of *Extropy*. The first was the launch of Chaum's dollar-denominated e-cash through a St. Louis–based bank—"perhaps of particular interest to Extropians is the pending acceptance of ecash by Laissez Faire Books." The second was a public vow, an example to encourage others: to donate a thousand dollars a year, for ten years, to an initiative called the Prometheus Project. This would start a business to do the research that could "convincingly demonstrate and publish" a successful "fully reversible brain cryopreservation."[6]

To live at the intersection of these technologies meant "living largely in the framework of possibility," in Romain's phrase, rather than current conditions. Extropian life was conducted by combining empirical, rational, biomedical, and computational research with the "dream work" of science fiction, imaginative extrapolation, and fantasies of innovation. (Dream work: In 1990, aerospace engineer Rand Simberg proposed to make cryonics and space tourism cost-effective by putting the remains in space, lowering the price of launching and cold storage at a stroke; one of the interested parties was the then-president of Phillip Salin's American Rocket Company.[7]) Idea coupons and digital cash, and dewers in the Arizona desert (holding the heads of a few people discussed in this book) are the preeminent artifacts where this particular framework of possibility, and the model of history on which it relied, was manifested. Two alternate accounts of economics and cold sleep put the Extropian project into proper perspective.

MY LAST EVENING IN THE TWENTIETH CENTURY

"You don't have to know what the future may bring," wrote the physicist Leo Szilard. "All you have to do is understand what the future may bring one day before most of the others do." He left Berlin soon after the Reichstag fire, the day before the order to halt and interrogate those departing went into effect; he had kept two suitcases always packed by the door as the Nazis took power, and he walked out with his life savings hidden in his shoes. He seemed in general to have lived always a day or a few years ahead, like a traveler at relativistic speeds (he and Einstein were friends), in a string of unimaginable futures.

Before the first nuclear chain reaction test at Stagg Field in Chicago—the validation of a theory he had developed walking around London years before—he had a second dinner, "just in case" the experiment worked too well and some portion of the University of Chicago's campus and many of its best physicists, himself included, were annihilated.[8] As they pushed the chain reaction toward criticality, repeatedly changing the scale on the recording equipment to accommodate the new levels of neutron intensity, Szilard could feel past and future split apart. (That afternoon, at the shores of a new age, the physicists drank Chianti from paper cups in subdued celebration.) He envisioned societies collapsing under the effects of scientific and technical progress, the nuclear extinction of humans on Earth, societies of machines, world governments to contain the threat. He spent most of the rest of his life in hotels, living out of two suitcases—"to be able to move at a moment's notice came to be important to me"—thinking about potential futures and how to reach them, and writing patents, petitions, and science fiction.[9]

In July 1948, he opened a story with a scene of a rabbit brought back to life. It returned from days at 1°C without "appreciable metabolic activity." With injections of "dorminol" and "metaboline," the bunny could be cooled safely to just above freezing: "we could keep the rabbit 'asleep' for a week, a year, or one hundred years, just as well as for one day. . . . If this worked for the rabbit it would work for the dog . . . if it worked for the dog, it would work for man." In the 1920s, Szilard and Einstein had collaborated on the design of an experimental refrigerator without moving parts (in lean years, Szilard would live, if meagerly, off income from his refrigeration patents), and he made the refrigerator into a time machine for his narrator.

Szilard's story shared this narrative device of long sleep with R. C. W. Ettinger's fantasy of cold storage from the same year, "The Penultimate Trump." Ettinger, a physics teacher, devoted the rest of his life and career to popularizing the idea of practical cryonics, directly inspiring the Extropians with speculative nonfiction books like *The Prospect of Immortality* and *Man into Superman*.[10] (Ironically, Ettinger's Extropian-influencing story ends with a twist for his rapacious, Randian arch-capitalist protagonist: he is revived into a future society that evaluates his past crimes and dumps him on a penal colony on Mars.) Ettinger argued for the arbitrage of money now into unlimited time to come, a thousandfold return on the investment of your days: the "open-ended future," he wrote.[11]

Szilard's narrator explained his plan. "I intended to 'withdraw from life' (as we proposed to call the process) as soon as we had perfected the method, and to arrange for being returned to life in 2260." In cold sleep, the narrator can skip through centuries into the future that fascinates him (but: "I would not have dared, though, to go much beyond three hundred years," fearing a world too alien, leaving him literally "too much behind the times").

After a legal battle about his status is resolved, the narrator throws a temporally fractured party at the chamber for his hibernation, celebrating "my last evening in the twentieth century." The historiographic dislocation between the narrator and his guests is severe: "Most of them seemed to have had the feeling that they were sort of attending my funeral, since they would not see me again alive; whereas, to me, it seemed that it was I who was attending their funeral since none of them would be alive when I woke up."[12]

Pulled out of his refrigerated limbo after only ninety years, rather than the three centuries originally planned, he finds himself in a society stricken with the possibility of hibernation: tens of millions of people had "withdrawn from life." When the next Great Depression hit, millions went into federally subsidized hibernation until things picked up again, authorized to be revived when the labor market had likewise come back to life. ("Operating the refrigerator plants of the public dormitories for twenty-five million sleepers is part of our Public Works Program," a politician mentions in passing.) Szilard fills his tale with satirical economic strategies—like plates that chew food into slurry for diners, who must chronically overeat to consume the food surplus generated by so much of the population time-shifting decades or centuries into the future.

The heart of this story about accelerated history is a project to decelerate it: the narrator, dreading the more extreme dislocations of the future to come, becomes part of a cabal to *slow science down*—to orchestrate centuries of little real scientific and technological progress, giving "the Art of Living a chance to catch up." With techno-scientific progress artificially throttled under the pretense of support, the narrator considers whether to leave with his packed suitcases for another few centuries hence and cross the border into the future. If change is stalled, he says, then "Two hundred years hence, the world should be a liveable place." In other words, he bought himself some time.

WORKSHOP OF HUMAN RESURRECTION

At the end of the nineteenth century in Sofia, Bulgaria, the physicist-biologist Porfirii Bakhmet'ev became curious: How is it that insects do not freeze to death during the winter?[13] How are they able to revive in spring? He discovered and painstakingly documented a state of hibernation into which his moths and butterflies could go, a temperature range where they were seemingly frozen—and capable of remaining so indefinitely—and yet not actually dead, and able to be returned to life. He called this state *anabiosis*, not dead nor alive. Naturally, he became curious if mammals such as humans could go into an anabiotic state. We can successfully freeze sperm and eggs for future use, and many animals can go into a kind of cold metabolic standstill and come back out of it again. If humans could do so, for how long? A season? A decade? A thousand years?

Bakhmet'ev's applications for this state between life and death were straightforward and practical, as though he planned to install wind power turbines on the stormy bluffs of Purgatory. You could transport cattle and horses by rail in an anabiotic state, reviving them at their destination, to save on feed, cleaning, and misery. You could ship sturgeon and caviar "live." If tuberculosis bacteria die at −6°C, and a human can be revived from −8°C, you could freeze TB victims for a week and bring them back to life cured. Perhaps creatures from other ages—relics of the historiography of cold—were still anabiotically preserved in Siberia; expeditions should be made to find and revive them. (As I write this now, the human species has, with admirable initiative, taken up that last notion of Bakhmet'ev's by collectively warming the Earth's atmosphere a few degrees and melting the permafrost, to see if we could find unknown ancient viruses and bacteria we can foster in the growth medium of human biomass.)

During the Russian Revolution, the temporality of anabiosis changed: no longer a way to access the past or aid in short-term economic and medical projects in the present, it became a way to interact indirectly with the future. It was a time for experiments: "We will remake life anew," promised the futurist-Soviet poet Vladimir Mayakovsky, "right down to the last button of your vest." As with the economic reinvention of the world, the goal was never mere health but superhumanity and immortality, the anatomical equivalents to the unlocking of as yet unknown sluices of abundance, efficiency, and organization—as on Alexander Bogdanov's science fiction of Soviet Mars, with fully automated factories managed by proto-computers and data transmission tools in a "moving equilibrium" of labor, supply, and production demand. Bogdanov celebrated and engaged in blood transfusions, the prelude to a future society where human vitality itself was the ultimate store of value and medium of exchange—a "physiological collectivism," where the storage and circulation of comradely life was an act of almost telepathic intimacy in an economy that was a self-regulating organism, a homeostatic machine. (Bogdanov himself died of renal and liver failure following a botched exchange with a visiting student in 1928.)

Others, in the midst of developing the modern command economy, turned to fountain-of-youth endocrine therapies, injections of "glandular secretions" and goat hormones, and "Steinach" vasectomies to restore energy: posthuman potency, on demand, as a corrective to the "revolutionary exhaustion" and "nervous disorders" claiming the lives of the vanguard of the future. Ettinger's capitalist captain-of-industry protagonist, prior to his cryonic interment, underwent a similar battery of technologies—part of the popular biomedical imagination of the first half of the twentieth century: "They gave him gland extracts, they gave him vitamins, they gave him blood transfusions."

In this spirit, what if you could enter anabiosis during the wretched years of multifront civil war and terror, trauma, paranoia, the relentless grind of "revolution from above," malnutrition, and "war communism," and wake up in some summer hence, when the promised future has arrived at last? The idea of turning the crank on Marxist historical inevitability was everywhere. Popular Russian sci-fi stories concerned exactly the notion played with decades later by Leo Szilard: evil capitalists putting their workforce on ice during downturns, to prevent labor unrest and keep "full employment," and thawing them out when the boom part of the capitalist economic cycle kicked in again. In the Kremlin, immediately after Lenin's death, the faction arguing that he should be frozen almost carried the debate with the promise that perhaps he could be recovered, one day, in what Mayakovsky called "the workshop of human resurrection." The poet was addressing scientists of the future, pleading with them to bring him back in an age of abundance and peace, when no one needed money anymore. He and his muse Lili Brik would return in the "thirtieth century," into "future nights" of "countless stars," with their bodies restored to the fullest life:

"Put a heart in me," he requests, "transfuse blood / to the uttermost vein."

Other stories, though, concerned the violent temporal dislocation experienced by the cryonically saved, with "comrades-in-anabiosis" thawed into a future in which they had become alien—as alien as Bogdanov felt, who called himself "a Martian stranded on Earth." They were marooned in history, the world around them rendered incomprehensible, sick with "the disjunction of time." The revived comrades-in-anabiosis expressed the experience of *untimeliness*—being too early or too late. They had launched out of history into new kinds of time from which they could not return, rendered "alien to everything and everybody."

The Extropians couldn't wait for this shock, though—indeed, they eagerly anticipated it—not least because they saw themselves in the role of the prefiguration, the prototype, of the order to come. They had faith in the particular dynamics of the technologies, the attitudes, and the optimal outcomes for which they were the social prototypes. If they could create the right social, monetary, and technical framework, they would be brought back to life, prepared to be astonished and transformed—but not surprised. They knew it would happen, and they knew they *could not know* how to get there, only how to create the initial conditions from which would come the transfiguration of the world. They would not be left behind.

FUTURE WANTS AND DESIRES

The Extropians drew strength as a utopian movement by combining the predictable and the unpredictable. They fused the starry-eyed certainty of dynamic optimism in great things to come—the dawn already visible on the horizon of expectation, the exponential curve of growth and improvement going vertical against the y-axis on the graph—with a contemptuous skepticism about the capacity of human planning and existing social structures to reach those goals. We would get there, certainly, but not all of us: only the daring, the brave, the angel investors, and the early adopters. This is perfectly captured by their iconic image of Hayek in biostasis: launched like a pharaoh in his sarcophagus into the unknown and unknowable future that was his abiding obsession, and theirs.

Hayek meant something very specific—and surprising, given the way many of his acolytes took up his banner—by his idea of "liberty": it has not to do with us but with some future person who is as yet unknown. "What is important is not what freedom I personally would like to exercise but what freedom some person may need *in order to do things beneficial to society*. This freedom we can assure to the unknown person only by giving it to all."[14] This is the historical model at work in the Extropian cosmogram and in the Extropians' version of digital cash: a propitious arrangement of society whereby the "unknown person" may come to transform the world. Hayek's conclusion to the third volume of *Law, Legislation, and Liberty*—the abstract summary of his philosophical model and ideas, in 1979—is a single sentence, entirely italicized in the original: "Man is not and never will be the master of his fate: his very reason always progresses by leading him into the unknown and unforeseen where he learns new things."[15]

That sentence concludes his indictment of the empiricism, scientific socialism, and psychological insight that characterized the Viennese milieu of his youth. Individually, we are mysteries to ourselves; collectively, we are at the mercy of forces and circumstances that are complex beyond our ken. Hayek was the most broadly influential of the Austrian economists; he was also the most tragic in the classical sense. This does not excuse his choices or his arguments—most notably his admiration of dictatorships that privatize public institutions and maintain "free" markets, like Pinochet's—but it explains his framing sensibility. We operate in a universe in which humans are mostly ignorant, when not actively misguided; the gods are capricious; death awaits us all; and the best things available to us come from spontaneous emergence out of clashing needs, impulses, and desires, rather than foresightful planning.

The heart of his argument in *Law, Legislation, and Liberty* is to distinguish (in his terms) *taxis* from *kosmos*: order that is "made," constructed by organizations, and order that spontaneously "grows," emerging from conditions. "Its degree of complexity," he wrote of *kosmos*, "is not limited to what a human mind can master."[16] He compared it to crystal lattices and organic compounds; *kosmos* comes of itself out of the operation of a set of rules that describe the behavior of the elements—with the question then becoming how to properly organize the rules for the spontaneous generation of the world for which we hope. Inevitably, Hayek returned to his ideal model: "The market order in particular will regularly secure only a certain probability that the expected relations will prevail, but it is, nevertheless, the only way in which so many activities depending on dispersed knowledge can be effectively integrated into a single order."[17] This is the *kosmos* mechanism at the center of Hayek's cosmogram, and, strangely transplanted, that of the Extropians.

As Corey Robin has argued in detail, this is all very Nietzschean—aside from the obsession with markets, economics, and money, which Nietzsche generally despised. Likewise Nietzschean is Hayek's impulse to look to mysterious successors, the "Philosopher of the Future," Hayek's "unknown person," revealed as an *Übermensch* who will come next and justify what has been before—making something of it that we cannot.[18] So is Hayek's elitism, the desire for a superior aristocracy of taste, refinement, and wealth who can exploit and create "the next range of desires and possibilities" when the time comes, as well as the "uncompromising rejection of the political structure of every modern democratic society" (as Robert Drinan put it).[19]

In Hayek's version of a future without oligarchic industrial dynasties and permanent, capital-holding elites, the world will continue to toil along with people merely satisfying existing needs, settling for less, and asking—to take the famous phrase of Henry Ford's—for better horses rather than developing automobiles. Piketty's income inequality gap, with return on capital outpacing wages except for the occasional redistributive initiative, is for Hayek not a bug but a feature. The ultrarich can feed appetites and afford luxuries that will spur new technologies, drive prices down, and keep avant-garde culture alive. This last detail is perhaps the most Viennese of all: Hayek writes of magnates and heirs in ways that recall the great Ringstrasse families of his own youth, like the Wittgensteins, who supported poets, painters, composers, and architects.

Holding all that money, he argued, sensitizes the very rich to the price signals of the future to come, the impulses and desires on which they can act. "What today may seem extravagance or even waste, because it is enjoyed by the few and even undreamed of by the masses, is payment for the experimentation with a style of living that will eventually be available to many."[20] Hayek's aristocrats are not *investing* in these systems, necessarily, but merely indulging in them: it's a trickle-down theory of vanguard technologies as luxury goods, which Hayek credits with everything from inexpensive refrigerators and radios to airplane flights. None of this is historically true for technologies, in particular or in general. It's a fairy tale of the superior shopping habits of the very rich. But that should not distract us from the larger significance of these mythic characters for those who came in the Austrian wake, like the Extropians: money gives access to the future as an experimental zone where those whom Hayek called "scouts" could find "new goals."[21]

Hayek even outlines how a socialist country should take advantage of this concept, in one of the most peculiar recommendations in the history of economics: "It would be necessary in a planned economy . . . to designate individuals whose duty it would be to try out the latest advances long before they were made available to the rest. . . . In order to know which of the various new possibilities should be developed at each stage, how and when particular improvements ought to be fitted into the general advance, a planned society would have to provide for a whole class . . . which would always move some steps ahead of the rest." This was precisely the role the Extropians sought to seize for themselves: to be, returning to Max More's words, "the vanguard of the future." This was the project woven into their digital cash and the free market for which it was built: speculative currency would be the fuel of unrestrained, spontaneous order, and its makers would be the experimental pack who got to live in the future already, "some steps ahead of the rest," in the country of new desires and new possibilities. This was currency and utopia at once, Austria and California, the 1920s and the 1990s: Hayek in biostasis.

Another thing unites the late 1920s and 1990s: they were boom years that preceded global financial calamity. Projects, ideas, technologies, and people in the Extropian community were adapted into the new context of the crash—first in the early 2000s and then, with Bitcoin, the global financial crisis in 2008. Instead of idea coupons and geodesic schemes, the new money would be identified with precious metals and coinage, forms of currency closely connected with the libertarian politics of catastrophe, and a theory of the near future where things fall apart. Digital cash was yet again being repurposed: not to bring about the demise of governments for a wild utopia of ciphers, nor to protect privacy against a future of ubiquitous surveillance, nor to power relentless innovation toward an emergent utopia of abundance and immortality, but as a dystopian currency established to speculate on imminent collapse—a bet on an emergency.

The technologies of digital cash spliced easily into a dystopian speculative monetary tradition belonging to groups, schools, and subcultures the next chapters explain: agorists, goldbugs and silverbugs, Objectivist followers of Ayn Rand (who took her name from her typewriter but coincidentally shared it with the compound name of the South African gold coins), seasteaders and builders of libertarian enclaves and micronations, "sovereign individuals," proprietors of digital gold currencies (DGCs), and moneyers who struck their own coins. Their money, like all money, was built on the promise of a future. Their anticipated future was one in which the collapse of existing systems into some combination of tyranny, decadence, and anarchy would force a return to sources of "objective value" and the validation of their philosophy—a collapse that could be accelerated if things were moving too slowly.

It is only fitting, for a story of how Extropian ideas became unrecognizably transformed, to close this chapter on a note of Hayekian melancholy rather than "dynamic optimism." After that final sentence of his epilogue to the final volume of *Law, Legislation, and Liberty*—his last significant book and summation of his thought—Hayek skipped a line and added a short paragraph: "In concluding this epilogue I am becoming increasingly aware that it ought not to be that but rather a new beginning. But I hardly dare hope that for me it can be so." His work was only tangentially for his contemporaries; the hope—and his model of history—was to create something that would provide new circumstances for those about whom he could predict nothing. It would be a new beginning, he believed, but not for him.

CHAPTER 10

EMERGENCY MONEY

We come to Bitcoin's announcement at the nadir of a global financial crisis. Many people and technologies met previously in this book now reappear, as this chapter explains how what came before in the history of digital cash was incorporated in the Bitcoin proposal, its ideas, and its code. Following those pieces as they come together helps to explain precisely how the initial version of Bitcoin itself worked and some of the paradoxes and problems created by the system in action—from the world's most valuable garbage to trust as a by-product of heat.

HALLOWEEN NIGHT

Early in October 2008, the global credit crisis reached a breaking point. The US government launched the Emergency Economic Stabilization Act, a massive bailout, on October 3, as the contagion of crisis expanded rapidly around the world. The TED spread—a financial expression of how lenders perceive risk—went over four and a half percent on October 10, 2008: an unprecedented picture of the significant financial players stashing their money somewhere safe from the ruinous market.[1] Smaller and developing currencies were hit hard by the rush to hold Treasury bills and seemingly safe currencies like dollars and Swiss francs. Desperate measures were under way to keep trade moving. This was the context of Bitcoin's announcement on Halloween night of 2008. "Bitcoin P2P e-cash paper," posted the pseudonymous Satoshi Nakamoto to a cryptography mailing list, opening the note with, "I've been working on a new electronic cash system that's fully peer-to-peer, with no trusted third party."[2]

The financial chaos not only constituted the backdrop of the announcement but was incorporated into the ledger of the currency itself, once an initial version of the software was working. In the "genesis block" that started the Bitcoin blockchain, Nakamoto included the following text:

> "The Times 03/Jan/2009 Chancellor on brink of second bailout for banks"

which functioned as a kind of time stamp—the equivalent of the *Times* front page (for which that was indeed the headline) photographed next to the stack of cash or the hostage—and a commentary on the perilous moment. To stretch a metaphor, but not too far, it was the opening line of the history that the rest of the blockchain ledger promised to chronicle, transaction by transaction, note by note: the unwinding of a massively overleveraged world, documenting an abject failure of policy, embedded within a new currency. On January 9, the third block of the Bitcoin blockchain incorporated an ASCII art portrait of Ben Bernanke, then chairman of the Federal Reserve. The next day, Hal Finney would post on Twitter (@halfin): "Running bitcoin."

Finney was by then a correspondent of Nakamoto's, the recipient of the second Bitcoin transaction, and actively engaged in explaining, debating, and refining the initial release of the project on the mailing list, where it had been received with cautious interest and considerable tire-kicking skepticism. Some of the people on the list had seen decades of digital cash and anonymous peer-to-peer network projects come and go. Many of the projects faced the same challenges Bitcoin did: problems of scale, security, and value.[3] Finney had seen them all, too; indeed, he had created several of those projects. He saw something new in the Bitcoin paper, and his first take was more hopeful—"Bitcoin seems to be a very promising idea"—but of course he had been looking for something like this for a long time.[4]

Finney's was not the only name in the development of early Bitcoin that readers will recognize. Nakamoto corresponded with Adam Back, who suggested looking at Wei Dai's b-money project, and Nakamoto cited Back, Dai, and Merkle in the original Bitcoin paper. Finney mentioned Nick Szabo's bit gold project as a subject of further comparison and discussion; the mailing list that hosted the announcement was run by Perry Metzger, the cypherpunk who set up and hosted the first Extropian email forum; even Ted Nelson of Xanadu would turn up later, with a suggestion for the real identity behind the pseudonymous Nakamoto.[5]

All the technical components and concepts used in Bitcoin already existed by 2008. Many of them have been introduced in previous chapters, including proof-of-work systems, public key cryptography, and Dai's conceptual outline of b-money's broadcast and competition protocol. The earlier drafts of the project—discussed in correspondence between Nakamoto and Dai—still referred to it as "electronic cash." Debates, proposals, programs, and primitives going back decades were the milieu out of which the first version of Bitcoin was created: a conceptual thread that runs through Extropians, cypherpunks, and experimental infrastructure projects, like AMIX and Xanadu, to the earliest sketches of what digital cash might look like.

What came together over the months before and after Halloween in 2008—in the conversations, suggestions, and refinements around Nakamoto's proposal and its initially rather crude and eccentric implementation as code—was an *incremental* technological advance, with one striking theoretical breakthrough.

Given all the puffery, hype, and change-the-world hand waving that would subsequently surround Bitcoin with a rhetorical fog, Nakamoto's own correspondence and the documentation and materials is refreshing in its lack of pretense and its careful interest in prior work; part of Nakamoto's conversation with Dai concerned how to accurately cite his b-money proposal. (After the first release, Nakamoto wrote to Dai of the Bitcoin project: "I think it achieves nearly all the goals you set out to solve in your b-money paper."[6]) This was not a technology that fell out of the cargo bay of a UFO; it incorporated decades of published research into cryptography and computation, from peer-to-peer networking technologies to digital time stamping to the conceptual outlines of digital cash schemes—the oldest citation in the original paper is a probability theory problem called "Gambler's Ruin" from 1957.

Bitcoin was a hybrid technological move, a patchwork of previous developments in a new arrangement, with missing pieces, kludges, and plenty of areas in need of further improvement. Reading through the Bitcoin paper a week after it was first circulated, Finney wrote a lengthy response that combined encouragement with a string of precise technical questions seeking to figure out how many parts of the actual system would function. Knowing that Nakamoto was working on the software, he gently recommended: "I think a more formal, text description . . . would be a helpful next step."[7]

THE CURRENCY OF COMPUTATIONAL WORK

As we look at how the first version of Bitcoin worked, we can see precedent technologies and tools described in previous chapters snapping into place. This does not mean that they were direct antecedents or inspirations—Nakamoto apparently learned about Dai only after corresponding with Back, for instance—but it does reveal a shared set of problems and approaches to solving them. The most prominent problem was implied by Finney's note on b-money for the Extropian community in 2002: "Money is not about atoms, it is about bits. Extropians should shun old-fashioned views of money as based on material goods." B-money, bit gold, the RPOW system, and now Bitcoin seemed on their face to meet this demand—to create completely *computational currency*, without any material substrate that backed, substantiated, or guaranteed: cash as information, information as money.

By this Finney did not mean only what Dee Hock meant, the Visa CEO envisioning exchanges of electronic value in the form of "guaranteed alphanumeric data" in the 1970s. What interested Hock was how money could be stored as digital-electronic information—as arranged energy—and how the transmission, receipt, and verification of money would be done over telephone cables, radio waves, and as yet unknown communications media. Finney sought the step beyond this: money that was computational all the way down the stack, rather than a change of format. (Even Chaum's DigiCash, brilliant as it was, was a way to create temporary digital versions of existing money.) Instead of putting a smartphone in the middle of a transaction that could also have been conducted with a checkbook—instead of rendering an existing transactional relationship digital and electronic—Finney sought money that was itself the product of a series of computational processes.

Hence the *crypto-* in cryptocurrency. The prefix is often taken to mean "encrypted," in the sense of "secret," and conflated with the initial Bitcoin promise that "participants can be anonymous"; but this understanding, while not wrong, is misleading. The core of the Bitcoin system as it was first presented—and similar to the components of bit gold, b-money, and RPOW tokens—was a set of cryptographic (or cryptoadjacent) processes, like those partial hash collision problems used in proof-of-work systems. These cannot be separated from computation itself: the processes emerged from and work practically only in the intersection of cryptographic mathematics, computer science, and what Diffie and Hellman called "cheap . . . general purpose digital hardware."[8]

When Finney downloaded the draft of Nakamoto's "Bitcoin v0.1" software, what did he get? "The main properties," Nakamoto promised in the paper, were the following:

> Double-spending is prevented with a peer-to-peer
>   network.
> No mint or other trusted parties.
> Participants can be anonymous.
> New coins are made from Hashcash style proof-of-work.
> The proof-of-work for new coin generation also powers
>   the network to prevent double-spending.[9]

The problem of "double-spending" has appeared in various forms throughout this book: digital information is, by design, perfectly reproducible. How do you prevent a digital money token from being spent twice, or many times over, by the same person? What's to stop cutting-and-pasting money? To take the same problem from the other side, what is to stop the creator of some new Magic Computer Money (MCM) from creating many more MCM tokens than they claim exist?

You could beat double-spending on the part of a currency's users by having transactions reconciled through a central server or ledger, but then you had to trust the server. RPOW made the server visible as it accepted spent RPOW tokens and issued unspent ones; Finney's "transparent server" system would provide access to what the server was at any time doing without making itself vulnerable to manipulation. Bit gold and b-money both maintained shared public ledgers: Szabo's project had its distributed, "unforgeable . . . chain of digital signatures" attesting to who owned what at any time, and Dai's b-money had its system of voting on the cost of new money and the public broadcast of activity. All three shared some kind of proof-of-work challenge for making new money—a way of producing "costly bits."

Nakamoto's Bitcoin fused these ideas together, putting bank, cash, and mint in one: "The proof-of-work for new coin generation also powers the network to prevent double-spending." It had a single, shared, widely distributed, append-only digital ledger—a ledger that tracked every transaction, bundled into "blocks" of activity, with the past and current ownership of every bitcoin. Information could be added to this ledger but never removed or altered. All the "nodes"—participants on the Bitcoin network—had a copy of the ledger, that chain of blocks (Nakamoto never used the term *blockchain* in the original paper): the documentation of each event in which the rights to claim a given bitcoin were signed over from one address to another. The hash value of each new transaction, time-stamped and signed with a cryptographic private key by both parties, was broadcast to all the nodes to check. New transactions not yet added to the ledger accumulate into a new block, and all the nodes start trying to generate a difficult proof-of-work hash of that data. (Technically, for security reasons, they actually have to apply the hashing function twice—still more challenging.) This is called *mining*, for reasons that will become clear soon.

The first node to succeed at the hashing challenge sends the block to all the others, who add the new block in the chain to the record they keep—at least in theory. In practice, the structure of the Bitcoin network means there may be multiple candidates for the new block at the same time—mining computers at different places on the Earth's surface might have microseconds of lag in transmitting their results, for instance. If there are divergent chains of blocks, if nodes are trying to circulate different next entries for the master ledger, then everyone on the network automatically goes with the longer chain of entries: the one that has had more of the total processing power of the network as a whole devoted to it.

This, combined with the escalating difficulty of the proof-of-work challenges, means that—in theory—no node can produce forged transactions or maliciously interfere with the overall operation of the ledger without consistently beating the rest of the network in solving the problems. The bad node would have to control more than half the total computing power of the entire network to pull off such a scheme (which turned out down the line to be a much less reliable protection than it first appeared—but let us stay with the initial version). Through this system, the blockchain arrives at a consensus about the ledger—but a very particular sort of "consensus," grounded not in collective decision making but in the steadily decreasing probability that an alternative version will successfully challenge the canonical record.[10]

If the proof-of-work challenges become steadily more difficult and expensive to solve, why would any of the nodes bother mining? "New coin generation." The node that solves the current proof-of-work challenge first would be assigned the rights to claim fifty new bitcoins (since halved to twenty-five), as well as a transaction fee. Thus "mining"—as if you were digging for resources in a video game and every thirty button presses had a chance of rewarding you with ore (Szabo likewise referred to "bit gold miners" in his description of the computational work of producing hashes of the "challenge strings" in his bit gold proposal). Because the difficulty of the proof-of-work problem can be incrementally increased with every solution or set of solutions, you can design the system so the problem becomes harder as more computers join the network, always taking a set length of time to solve. This keeps the speed of the introduction of new money consistent, and the money itself becomes more expensive to produce as the network of all Bitcoin nodes becomes more powerful.

The total number of coins generated is finite, Nakamoto wrote in the original paper: "Once a predetermined number of coins have entered circulation, the incentive can transition entirely to transaction fees and be completely inflation free." In the matter-of-fact way of one who doesn't know how significant this choice is going to be, Nakamoto added a detail in the announcement for the first version of the software on January 8, 2009: "Total circulation will be 21,000,000 coins. It'll be distributed to network nodes when they make blocks, with the amount cut in half every 4 years."[11]

That's the ledger. The ledger tracks the coins. The work of adding to the ledger creates the coins. What are the coins?

THE CHAIN OF SIGNATURES

Back in the late 1980s, Tim May asked the cypherpunk community, "What is a 'digital coin'?" Here was one answer: it was not a "coin" at all—not some discrete string of bits, some unit of data—but a system for the collective verification of ownership, with no existence outside that system of verification.[12] No coin exists without a Bitcoin account that currently owns it; the "coin" itself is the property of being owned. (The whole apparatus could be summarized by Ted Nelson's description of Xanadu in the 1970s: a "technical structure and an ownership convention."[13])

This is one of the implications of Nakamoto's premise: "We define an electronic coin as a chain of digital signatures." A coin cannot be separated from the history of the signed transactions in which it has been exchanged—in fact, it is *nothing but those transactions.*

You don't own a bitcoin—you don't have possession of the bits because there are no bits that constitute a given bitcoin to be possessed. Rather, you hold the right in the ledger to claim a particular bitcoin and to assign that right to someone else. A transaction does not mean that the bitcoin "changes hands" (never have bodily metaphors been so misleading) but that the right, the claim, is reassigned through a transaction update added to the ledger.

In Szabo's bit gold, the end of the last solved problem acted as the "challenge string" for finding the next rare hash, inextricably linking the entries in the chain of title all the way back to the very first; in NIST's reliable random number generator, every new broadcast includes the hash of the previous broadcast, which in turn incorporates the one before. In Nakamoto's Bitcoin, the hash of the block of recent transactions on the ledger, once verified and accepted, becomes the starting point for the next block, linking them into a continuous chain of transactions that runs all the way back to the "genesis block"—with its announcement of the banking bailout—and the experimental transactions between Nakamoto and Finney. Likewise, the "coins" of Bitcoin themselves are just chains of digital signatures: records of the right to claim. The money is the product of an archival system with meticulous, automated records of provenance and chains of custody, but no actual items—transaction records and ownership logs for objects whose existence is constituted by their transaction records and ownership logs.

One of the promises on Nakamoto's list was that "participants can be anonymous." That conditional "can be" sidesteps the trade-off the ledger-and-signature system actually demanded. It required no photo ID, no email address, no Vingean true name; all you needed to hold and transact bitcoin was an address on the ledger, which was just a newly generated cryptographic public key (or, to be more precise, a hash of that key). What could be more anonymous? But every transaction your address engaged in was permanently visible in the public ledger. Chaum's Digi-Cash was transactionally anonymous, even more than banknotes themselves were: once withdrawn from your (named, identified) account at the bank, the money could not be used to connect a purchase to you. Bitcoin had the opposite arrangement, with an anonymous account using money that was unconditionally visible, traceable, and public. (Subsequent projects have been working on truly anonymous, untraceable cash, whether through building on top of Bitcoin or developing new cryptocurrencies.[14]) Imagine if every banknote could be unrolled like a genealogical scroll, with the whole tale of its circulation for your review.

For the curious, every single prior transaction can be immediately assembled and the network of all interactions put into place. As subsequent events would reveal, accidentally associating a Bitcoin address with something that can be connected with your real identity, like an email address, a forum posting, a postal address, or an attempt to sell bitcoin for other currencies or goods would reveal not just your identity but—through the transaction history in the ledger—a time-stamped log of your activities and the network of your colleagues. People have tried to use numerous addresses to conceal activity, but that strategy proved vulnerable to the network-graph disambiguation, revealing common connections and associations. The humans may try to conceal themselves, but their money has an identity, and it never forgets.

51° 33' 31.6224" N 2° 59' 57.987" W

To understand the peculiar arrangements and paradoxes this system could produce, consider the case of James Howells in Wales.

"He actually took me out in his truck to where the landfill site is," Howells recalled in 2013, all the way to "the current ditch they're working on."[15] Anything thrown in the trash over the past few months in the town would now be somewhere in that field, under three or four feet of garbage and mud, sodden with Welsh rain. Somewhere down there was a discarded hard drive worth, at that time, nearly thirty million dollars. The drive itself wasn't worth much, of course—it was part of a Dell laptop knocked out of commission by a spill and stripped for parts. It sat in a drawer for three years until Howells, finding it while cleaning up, threw it away.

On the drive was a stray relic of 2009: a string of letters and numbers—a set, that is, of decaying sub-microscopic stripes of magnetic variance. These are, or were, the private key for a Bitcoin wallet—an address assigned exclusive rights to trade eight thousand bitcoins. (The tenses are a tricky issue here, as we will see.) The bitcoins were the product of idle "mining" for a few months in 2009 until late April, when the Bitcoin platform was new, the nodes few, and the challenges exceptionally easy. Howells stopped due to the constant fan noise and heat of the laptop at work solving the partial hash collision problems for a "currency" that was then little more than a hobbyist project. Without the private key, there was no way to access or transact those bitcoins. By 2013, their value—what others were willing to pay for them in other currencies—had gone from nothing to more than a thousand dollars each.

Howells looked into excavating the landfill, not a simple task: hiring a team, renting two diggers and protective equipment, to root through several months of wet trash—a different kind of mining—in a lot the size of a soccer field looking for something about the size of a pack of cigarettes. Of course there might be other discarded hard drives in those months of garbage and mud; which was the exact model? And how much would the forensic data recovery work cost, and could they in fact recover anything, and how long would it take to discover if they had the wrong drive? Schemes with documentary crews to film and help finance the dig were proposed. "Why aren't I out there with a shovel now?" he asked himself in interviews.

You can see where the hard drive is, more or less: in the landfill in the town of Newport, Wales, on the bend of the Ebbw River, at about 51° 33′ 31.6224″ N and 2° 59′ 57.987″ W. You can see where the bitcoins are, too: they sit at the address 198aMn6ZY-AczwrE5NvNTUMyJ5qkfy4g3Hi on the Bitcoin blockchain where they will remain, visible and inaccessible, present but lost, for as long as the blockchain itself persists.[16]

THE TRUST BULB

Finney, at the very outset of the Bitcoin system, noticed the paradox that made Howells quit mining: computational currency, money that was entirely about bits rather than atoms, moved a lot of atoms around. Air molecules caromed back and forth, dissipating heat from the microchips as they tried solution after solution to the partial hash collision problem; fans spun; Finney's son uninstalled the software when he noticed how much work it was demanding of his laptop. Though classified and described as "virtual currency," Bitcoin was far more material in practice than, say, a seventeenth-century merchant's bill of exchange. What secures the scarcity of this kind of digital cash is the transformation of electricity into heat by friction; it is a currency whose production and transaction is constrained by expenditure, by waste. Bitcoin wasn't magic but a technology in context, and part of that context was the power grid, the business of microchip fabrication, and the planet's atmosphere.

A wire in use must dissipate power, and that means generating heat. Wires, especially at the microscopic and submicroscopic scale of the labyrinths of wire in microchips, are so small, and the distances so slight, that we can almost think of them as abstract objects, like the frictionless boards and massless pulleys of introductory physics—a "costless and volumeless idealized connection," to quote the engineer and scientist Danny Hillis.[17] But moving current through a conductor takes time (recall Grace Hopper with her nanoseconds) and results in Joule heating, collisions between electrons and atomic ions giving off kinetic energy: an amount of heat proportional to the square of the current. You can feel this on your skin in the warmth of an incandescent lightbulb, whose filament shines with resistance to the current passing through it.

Heat has been a problem for electronic computing from the beginning; the sound of computation was—and is—the roar of the fans.[18] The landmark Cray supercomputers were masterpieces in the circulation and management of heat: massive, furniture-size heat sinks that happened to also compute. All the patents for the original Cray-1 were for innovations in cooling.[19] Seymour Cray, the architect of those machines, also held a patent for the use of an inert liquid—one that doesn't conduct electricity, making it safe for computer components—in which you could immersion-cool circuit boards: "Unfortunately, that theoretically possible high density [of microchips] cannot be achieved in practice unless a very considerable amount of heat generated by such a high density assemblage of circuits can be successfully removed."[20] Just such "high density assemblages" are running now in secure facilities around the world, wherever there's access to cheap or free electricity, with the same liquid (Fluorinert) boiling in tanks filled with racks of boards mounted with grids of microchips. The chips are generating billions of hashes per second, trying to produce a cosmically unlikely collision, one that proves nothing but its own arduous discovery: they're mining Bitcoin.

The SHA-256 algorithm at work in the partial collision challenges is not in itself interesting; you could work it out by hand—producing guesses at the solution to mine for Bitcoin with a pencil and paper—though "the process is extremely slow compared to hardware mining and is entirely impractical."[21] Ken Shirriff, who took on this quixotic task, determined that with pencil and paper he could produce a single hash of a full Bitcoin block—a single guess at the challenge—in about a day and a half, a rate of 0.67 hashes per day ("although I would probably get faster with practice"); by contrast, chips custom-built to solve Bitcoin-type hashing problems are rated in terms of trillions of hashes produced per second. Shirriff also worked out his relative energy consumption, sitting at a table cranking through the steps of SHA-256 at his resting metabolic rate: about one hash produced per ten megajoules of energy, by contrast to the typical (at that time) Bitcoin-hashing hardware rate of about one thousand megahashes per joule of energy—meaning that the human is about ten quadrillion times less efficient than the machine.[22]

Bitcoin was in theory and in practice inseparable from the process of computation run on cheap, powerful hardware: the system could not have existed without markets for digital moving images, especially video games, driving down the price of microchips that could handle the onerous business of guessing. It also had a voracious appetite for electricity, which had to come from somewhere—burning coal or natural gas, spinning turbines, decaying uranium—and which wasn't being used for something arguably more constructive than this discovery of meaningless hashes. The whole apparatus of the early twenty-first century's most complex and refined infrastructures and technologies was turned to the conquest of the useless. It resembled John Maynard Keynes's satirical response to criticisms of his capital injection proposal by proponents of the gold standard: just put banknotes in bottles, he suggested, and bury them in disused coal mines for people to dig up—a useless task to slow the dispersal of the new money and get people to work for it. "It would, indeed, be more sensible to build houses and the like; but if there are political and practical difficulties in the way of this, the above would be better than nothing."[23]

The process of policing transactions and preventing double-spending—and thereby the perception of the trustworthiness, confidence, and value of currency in the eyes of its holders—required turning the physics of computation into a kind of friction brake. It was a process of deliberate inefficiency to generate a by-product, like Joule heating as a source of visible light. Like the incandescent bulb, heat is almost all it produces. Its social function is an infinitesimal side effect: the trust bulb as a replacement for those "trusted third parties." In this way, and in only this way, did Bitcoin share something with silver and gold: you know them partially through their thermal conductivity. They prove themselves in part through heat.

You may have wondered through all this about the other, thoroughly material component of a currency: that it's current and it passes. What makes a currency is that it will be accepted: by the state in payment of taxes, by merchants in settlement of debts, by kinship networks, friends, and communities in the circulation of promises, esteem, prestige, and affection. The most important component is still missing in all the technical complexity of the apparatus of cryptocash explained here: Who wanted it, and why?

The trust produced by Bitcoin's hash collision problems was not, in fact, trust in the *value* of the currency, which could only be produced by the acceptance of others. It was trust in its scarcity: that you could verify, for yourself, precisely how many bitcoins existed, how many were in circulation, and how many were being added. All the electricity, the specialized chips, the boiling Fluorinert, the roar of the fans, served to guarantee that no duplicate "coins" existed and that new coins were being irrefutably produced in a predetermined and fixed amount, staying rare and getting rarer, "analogous to gold miners expending resources to add gold to circulation," as Nakamoto put it.[24] The coins, chains of digital signatures on a network that consumes electricity while generating no other product—coins that cannot be expended outside that same network, coins for which there is no other value and no inherent demand—were at every point compared to gold in incessant social efforts to drum up commitment to their value. (The anthropologists of money Bill Maurer, Taylor Nelms, and Lana Swartz have called this "digital metallism": the grounding of value outside human society, "through algorithmic control of the money supply," in the model of gold, yet relying on "the social dynamics of community and trust" and the production of excitement through prose, videos, stunts, manifestos, even poetry.[25]) When required to provide a birthday for an account, Nakamoto chose April 5, 1975. On April 5, 1933—in the midst of another global financial crisis—Roosevelt signed Executive Order 6102, which forbade the hoarding of monetary gold in the United States, a moment that looms large in libertarian nightmares. (Why 1975? The Roosevelt order's prohibitions were fully relaxed, and Americans could own and trade monetary gold again.)[26]

At the very first appearance of the Bitcoin proposal on the cryptography mailing list in 2008, conversation veered toward the nature of money and the possibility of "objective value" in digital cash, threatening to swamp the technical debate. Perry Metzger, the list's administrator, had to step in: "I'm a rabid libertarian myself, but this isn't the rabid libertarian mailing list. Please stick to discussing either the protocols themselves or their direct practicality, and not the perils of fiat money, taxation, your aunt Mildred's gold coin collection, etc."[27] The first few years of Bitcoin's adoption were shaped by the circumstances of contemporary crisis and the particular fantasies of libertarian escape that provided a framework for its value: scarce cryptomoney to offset "the perils of fiat money," emergency coinage for extraordinary times.

CHAPTER 11

ESCAPE GEOGRAPHIES

We now discover the context of libertarian speculative currency, where Bitcoin found its most devoted initial audience. Tracing these currencies—and understanding the significance of coins and precious metals in particular—takes us into rogue mints, agorist fiction, wildcat banks, digital gold currencies, the coinage of nonexistent high-seas micronations, and finally the aftermath of the Sealand project to create an offshore data haven: imaginative territory suited to Bitcoin's version of digital cash.

THE DROP

Coins carry a weight—literally and figuratively—for libertarians, Austrian School proponents, Objectivists, and the hardcore, hard-money theorists of the (mostly) far right wing: they are minted as a numismatic artifact from future history. Coins symbolize access to and control over tangible forms of value, physical manifestations of new sovereign orders. They are artifacts from and investments in a new arrangement of territorial power in the world: tokens from the geographical outside. Sometimes they are just symbols, issued at a loss to bolster morale; sometimes they are sold at a premium, a fund-raising tool to be redeemed in a time to come. In every case, they conjure a different order of values.

By the time of his arrest in 2009, Bernard von NotHaus was the mintmaster of the Royal Hawaiian Mint Company and

self-described monetary architect of Liberty Dollar coins
through Sunshine Minting in Coeur d'Alene, Idaho, under the
aegis of his National Organization for the Repeal of the Federal
Reserve and the Internal Revenue Code (NORFED). (He was
also high priest of the Free Marijuana Church of Honolulu—
"One Toke to God"—which he founded.) But his story began
in 1974, when he produced a nineteen-page essay with his partner, Telle Presley: "To Know Value—An Economic Research
Paper."[1]

This eccentric document was the result of a "spiritual epiph-
any"; it opens with a dedication to "the Dreams of Aldous
Huxley" and quotes Swami Kriyananda alongside goldbugs,
deflationary theorists, and issues of *TV Guide*. At heart, it is a
statement about ontology and epistemology: about how something is "real" and how it is *known* to be real. The argument is
neither complex nor convincing, filled as it is with circular logic,
crisis-mongering, and Yoda-as-economist statements like: "Why
buy gold? Because of what it is. It is gold." In its directness,
though, it is an exemplary document of the fundamental conviction of precious metal coinage—of specie—as a kind of
superior monetary knowledge. "Gold is only uncertain for
those who do not know," they wrote. "Each individual sees the
commodity, evaluates it, and agrees to accept it": a sequence of
ways of knowing, with mystical implications.[2]

Appropriately, then, the legal struggle over the currencies von
NotHaus would issue ultimately turned on a string of questions
not about value but about knowledge—about the cultural and
legal meaning of a coin. Because it's not a coin, first of all: it's a
"medallion." In the United States, it's illegal to "make or utter or
pass . . . any coins of gold or silver or other metal . . . intended
for use as current money." The Liberty Dollar's "private volun-
tary barter currency" was therefore not issued in coins and notes

but instead in "medallions" and "warehouse receipts" redeemable for metal from a facility in Idaho. The receipts existed in paper and as digital "eLibertyDollars"—a form of "digital gold currency," a curious offshoot of electronic money.

The minters were meticulously explicit in their issue statements and purchase agreements that they were not creating money: "*never* claimed to be, does *not* claim to be, is *not,* and does *not* purport to be, legal tender," they wrote. To purchase a "New Liberty Dollar" silver piece—from a different organization with a shared ideology and audience—you must begin by answering a series of questions: "Do you understand that the New Liberty Dollar is 1 troy ounce .999 fine silver private issue silver piece medallion, and not any government issued coin? . . . Do you understand that silver pieces such as these New Liberty Dollars may also have numismatic, artistic, sentimental, historic, or other value[?]"[3] You should, in theory, encounter these pieces of metal as something you know in person, in an immediate and bodily way, rather than with reference to a bank or a nation—though the coins were, at the same time, meant to call exactly these abstract entities into question for you. Von NotHaus's motion for a retrial in his case turned on this paradox: "The jury's verdict conflates a program created to function as an alternative to the Federal Reserve system with one designed to deceive people into believing it was the very thing Mr. von NotHaus was protesting in the first place."

Like the "sovereign citizen" movement, with which the Liberty Dollars were closely connected, these ideas are based on a sense of *realness*. There is real experience, which is immediate, in the body "on the land," and there is the pernicious fiction of government and society. The coins mean something because you can hold them, weigh them, assay them. The receipts mean something because you could, in theory, go to Coeur d'Alene to redeem an equivalent quantity of silver; indeed, the receipts noted that, after five years, 1 percent of the value of the silver would be kept in fees for storage and insurance.[4] Someone has to drive the forklift and stack the pallets of silver ingots in the strong room of the warehouse in Idaho, inspect the fire sprinklers, and watch the CCTV feed: the realness of storage and maintenance.

The key sales technique to use on people ideologically unconverted to this radical money, as taught through the Liberty Dollar University training program, was "the Drop": "The NORFED member," summarized an undercover FBI agent, "holds out an ALD [Liberty Dollar] coin and drops the coin in the person's hand so that they can feel the weight of the silver. The NORFED member then asks, 'Do you take silver?'"[5] Never, the agent points out, does the member "describe or offer any explanation that the ALD is an alternative currency." The feeling in the palm is the prelude to the idea: money from the real world, and money for the coming disaster.

Implicit throughout was a simple future of decisive crisis, familiar from decades of libertarian prognostication and daily ads on *Fox News*. A crash is coming for the US dollar, with hyperinflation, unsustainable deficits, trade wars, and systemic crises combining to produce financial collapse. Gold, silver, and platinum will come (back) into their own, and decades of keeping coins buried under your floorboards will suddenly prove worthwhile.

This money is an act of allegiance to a state of affairs that does not yet exist, a value meant to pass—to become current—not in the fullness of ordinary time, in Keynes's "indefinitely postponed future" of accumulating wealth, but in an extraordinary period of crisis, contraction, and breakdown.[6] "Tell them," wrote von NotHaus for the (old) Liberty Dollar Association, of those unconverted to his bimetallic standard, "to get ready for the *Nazi-ization of America* and a reign of terror, the like of which this country has never seen. Tell them to get out of government money, seek privacy at all costs and buy silver to stave off the rainy days/years ahead"[7] (emphasis in original). It is an opportunity for commitment to an order at once archaic and futuristic—with "digital warehouse receipts" for silver and gold, email-ready units of money based in fantasies of stateless, objective value older than Croesus. A few pages later comes the contract and an order form for Liberty Dollars: the prospect of disaster is a sales pitch.

FEDERAL BLUES

"With Pecunix, I understand it is a goldbacked [*sic*] digital currency," wrote Ross Ulbricht, as he developed the plan that would become the Silk Road cryptomarket for drugs and other contraband—Bitcoin's first significant transaction platform. "Can I anonymously and securely withdraw funds in the form of fiat currency or gold?"[8]

Pecunix was a digital gold currency (DGC). Other DGCs included OSGold, IntGold, e-bullion, the Aspen Dollar, the Second Amendment Dollar (issued by a gun store in Kentucky), GoldMoney (operating out of the tax haven Jersey in the Channel Islands), and e-gold.[9] They shared various promises around the properties of gold: borderless transactions, transferable into many currencies, with the stability of bullion—the promise of gold as a safe harbor from the coming emergency—and, handled appropriately, the possibility of anonymity.

E-gold exemplified the field: launched by an American libertarian oncologist in 1996, years before the formation of PayPal and more than a decade ahead of Bitcoin, it promised (and trademarked) "Better Money" for payment around the world. It was inspired in part by Vera Smith's *The Rationale of Central Banking and the Free Banking Alternative* (originally published in 1936), which began as her doctoral dissertation under Friedrich Hayek, envisioning a world of "free banks" issuing banknotes as "promises to pay . . . on demand in the generally accepted medium which we will assume to be gold."[10] E-gold accounts were denominated in grams and troy ounces of metal, and the site maintained meticulous lists of every single bar of metal with its brand, weight, serial number, and current location. Again, this was a digital currency available to a particular kind of knowledge: "Weight units have a precise, invariable, internationally recognized definition," noted the e-gold site, and the assets had a chain of provenance, quantification, and custody few objects could claim—bar #9272–41 from the US Assay Office, for example, .9950 purity, weighing 380.775 oz t.

In October 2008, as Nakamoto was presenting the idea of Bitcoin on a mailing list, e-gold was suspending their operation and turning over their assets, after pleading guilty to numerous felony charges. (The platform had become a high-volume venue for specialists in credit card fraud, Ponzi schemes, and money laundering.) A year later, Ulbricht was weighing the pros and cons of other DGCs for doing business on a secret marketplace: "I can see how it would work as a closed system, but is there a way to integrate it with the rest of the economy securely?" His interlocutor was Arto Bendiken, a young cypherpunk software developer, whose site featured things like a lecture transcript from the Mises Institute on currency debasement in the monetary policies of the Roman Empire. Both men described themselves as agorists.

"The great thing about agorism," Ulbricht wrote, "is that it is a victory from a thousand battles. Every single transaction that takes place outside the nexus of state control is a victory for those individuals taking part in the transaction. So there are thousands of victories here each week and each one makes a difference, strengthens the agora, and weakens the state."[11] (And every transaction would be conducted in Bitcoin.) Agorist theory was developed by the Canadian libertarian Samuel Edward Konkin III in the 1970s: the proliferation of unregulated covert market-places would draw people away from state arrangements and fiat currencies into alternative zones of countereconomics and counterinstitutions. It was popularized by his friend J. Neil Schulman's 1979 novel *Alongside Night*. For Ulbricht, *Alongside Night* and Konkin's work were "the missing puzzle piece!" in building the Silk Road—a convergent evolution with Tim May's Xth Column: spurring the adoption of new currencies and encrypted platforms by offering access to contraband and illicit goods.

In *Alongside Night*, set in 1999, the United States is sinking into a currency crisis, complete with rapid inflation of the new, infe-rior, federally issued "blues": "blue-colored notes, no engraving on one side, on the other side hasty engraving . . . resembled *Monopoly* money." (A hallmark of libertarian fiction is detailed at-tention to the look and feel of different kinds of money.) There are bank runs, credit freezes, rationing, and jackbooted govern-ment thugs seizing private gold. The main character's father, Nobel Prize–winning economist Martin Vreeland, predicted all this—any resemblance to Nobel Prize–winning Chicago School economist Milton Friedman, responsible for some of the most extreme free market policies ever enacted, is purely coinciden-tal. (Friedman was, with fellow Nobel winner Hayek, another apologist for Pinochet's Chile as an experiment in radical privatization; his disciples were its architects.) Vreeland's son escapes to join the Revolutionary Agorist Cadre, who are con-structing a parallel society with their own contracts, arbitration systems, markets, militant teams, counterintelligence, and, of course, money—"AnarchoBank" coins and gold-backed digital assets issued by wildcat banks.

In one of the Agorist hideouts the protagonist finds a library, which provides the audience of *Alongside Night* with a reading list. The nonfiction shelf has books by Mises and Rothbard. The fiction includes Ayn Rand's *Atlas Shrugged* and Robert Heinlein's *The Moon Is a Harsh Mistress*, canonical novels of American libertarianism that contain the same historical-spatial structure as *Alongside Night* itself. They are set in the future when systems of governance have become dysfunctional and are beginning to break down. Characters move to or inhabit alternative zones, where they can live outside the emergency, exacerbate the existing crisis, and return to the changed world on the other side of the disaster where their utopia becomes possible. " 'The road is cleared,' says Galt," as Rand's characters look over the devastated landscape at the end of *Atlas Shrugged*. " 'We are going back to the world.' " Over Penn Station at the end of *Alongside Night*, "two banners flew at half staff, commemorating the dead of Utopia. . . . Things were looking up for a change." (The two flags in Schulman's book are the black flag of anarchism and the "Don't Tread on Me" Gadsden flag; the current agorist flag is gray and black, the colors of their preferred markets.) Heinlein's lunar revolutionaries prepare to head out to the asteroids: "Some nice places out there, not too crowded."

In these fictions and in agorist and libertarian practice, using the right money (and using money right) is a philosophical way of knowing value, the passport to a new physical territory, the commitment to a particular future of crisis to come, and the entryway to a different model of society, all at once—their cosmogram, a way to align themselves with objective reality, against arbitrary fiat, as a kind of financial pilgrimage. You must find "trustworthy countereconomic contacts," enter "the agora," leave your home to follow "John Galt," and abandon "Authority scrip" in favor of "Hong Kong Bank notes, backed by honest Chinese bankers instead of being fiat of bureaucracy. One hundred Hong Kong dollars was 31.1 grams of gold (old troy ounce) payable on demand at home office."[12] By doing this, you join an alternate history and its inevitable future. "Whenever destroyers appear among men, they start by destroying money," wrote Rand in *Atlas Shrugged,* about two-thirds into one of those Randian monologues for which the other characters obligingly sit still page after page. "Destroyers seize gold and leave to its owners a counterfeit pile of paper. This kills all objective standards and delivers men into an arbitrary power of an arbitrary setter of values. . . . Paper is a check drawn by legal looters upon an account which is not theirs: upon the virtue of the victims. Watch for the day when it bounces, marked: 'Account overdrawn.'"[13] The reckoning—in both the current sense of the word and the archaic, when it referred to settling a bill—is coming, and adopting money with "objective value" makes surviving the reckoning possible: to adopt it is to become part of the next society.

The physical properties of gold exemplify the hard, gleaming, cold, elemental personalities Rand's "utopia of greed" hoped to generate. Gold's properties of being objective, measurable, and quantifiable are necessary for a social philosophy in which the accumulation of money itself is the direct expression of human worth, the social order embedded in its cosmogram. Rand's monetary speculations were epistemological statements. Each coin from Galt's mint would work as an assertion about truth, and grasping that philosophy would put you in exactly the position to become objectively rich. The three-foot-high gold dollar sign erected in Galt's Gulch, the Objectivist fortress in the Rockies, works like the reference kilograms kept by metric institutions: the benchmark by which the world can be accurately assessed and against which the humans who live in Rand's fantasy can be calibrated.

Knowledge *is* money, and money knowledge. When the libertarian pirate Ragnar Danneskjöld shows up in *Atlas Shrugged* to pay back Hank Rearden for "the money that was taken from you by force" (taxes and so on), he gives him, of course, a bar of gold: "an objective value."[14] Rearden's encounter with the ingot is love and truth at once: "Rearden saw the starlight run like fire along a mirror-smooth surface. He knew, by its weight and texture, that what he held was a bar of solid gold." This was not the only fantasy of men from the sea bearing speculatively real (and really speculative) utopian money—objects from a dream of a different way of knowing value that lay on the far side of longed-for catastrophe, a dream into which early Bitcoin was easily folded.

COIN AND COUNTRY

"In this philosophic struggle, no one person in recent years has done more in behalf of the cause of freedom than Ayn Rand": so wrote Werner Stiefel, under the pen name Warren Stevens, in a 1968 booklet supporting his utopian project Atlantis.[15] Stiefel, a skin care magnate, had bought a motel in Saugerties, New York, which he dubbed "Atlantis I." It was an inexpensive base for housing his growing team of libertarians (with whom Rand would have had many doctrinal disagreements, but let that pass) in search of some new territory offshore of every existing government: a "seastead" before the term was coined—a sovereign platform in international waters where new social systems and their new money could be based. The motel rooms would function as stand-ins for the staterooms of the eventual ship— the *Atlantis II*—that would operate on the high seas, bringing in supplies and income for Atlantis III, an island, purchased or made, to act as the free port, redoubt, and bank of his future market-driven society. It would be an outpost in what historian Raymond Craib calls the "escape geography" of libertarian fantasy—the space that would later adopt Bitcoin.[16]

In his hotel, the alpha-version testbed for Atlantis, Stiefel planned the coins and had them struck before that society came through.[17] He struck them before the string of disasters that accompanied Operation Atlantis—the derelict oil rig destroyed by a hurricane, the citizens being mistaken for pirates and driven off by a Haitian vessel at gunpoint, the reinforced concrete barge *Atlantis II* (built under a geodesic dome licensed from Buckminster Fuller) foundering on the Hudson, breaking an axle, and ultimately sinking near the Bahamas. The Atlantean "decas" were ten grams of sterling silver, carrying a ship's wheel on the face and a setting sun at sea on the reverse, with the inscriptions REASON, FREEDOM, and TEN GRAMS SILVER 97.5 FINE on the facing sides. The two sides were guarantors of each other: reason and silver. You could hold a deca and fantasize about holding "money of intrinsic value" from a hurricane-lashed rational society built on a sandbar.

Or, rather, you could fantasize about the fantasy of holding such a coin. The run of decas was actually very small, as were those of all libertarian enclave coin issues. (The decas were stamped out using a hydraulic soap press.) Photographs of the coins were run alongside pictures of islands, reefs, and cays in Operation Atlantis publications: coins and islands were symbols of territory in which you could imagine a utopian project. In the absence of actual country, the coins stood in—pieces of terrain you could hold in your hand and carry in your pocket.

"A more serious effort was done in the early 70s by the Minerva folks," wrote a contributor to the cypherpunk mailing list,

"who built up an island out of coral reefs in the South Pacific"—
prior to, as a contributor to *Extropy* put it, "the unfortunate ending of the lamented Minervan Republic." Minerva was a particularly audacious attempt to claim a new country and a new
currency, one cypherpunks and Extropians alike hoped would
prefigure new geographic zones for prototyping various fantasies of the future. The bizarre story of Minerva and the related
Phoenix Foundation has been told elsewhere: It entangled tax-
dodging investment advisers and entrepreneurs inspired by the
work of Mises and other Austrian economists with aristocrats,
offshore bankers and land speculators, gold dealers, and the as-
sassin, mercenary, and weapons magnate Mitchell Livingston
WerBell III. (WerBell's side projects included designing the
world's best firearm suppressor and acting as the go-between for
Bobby Vesco, that colossus of financial crime, and President
Nixon). Minerva was an attempt to produce a libertarian political and financial geography through the production of new territory (a sandbar) and a convoluted land deal—which was also
an armed insurrection and a religious movement and a bizarre
neocolonial power grab—in the New Hebrides (now Vanuatu)
in 1977.[18]

Of course the Minervans too issued coins, during their attempt to flee "aspects" of the state (as Craib puts it). Minted in
Lanchester, California, the coins carried the head of Vanuatan
independence movement leader Jimmy Stevens over the motto
"Individual Rights for All," again serving as tokens of place and
promise. "The sudden appearance of gold and silver coins bearing Jimmy Stevens' likeness must have been a convincing argument for Phoenix's power" among the country's notional
future citizens, wrote anthropologist Monty Lindstrom in his
study of the hybrid libertarian-messianic project.[19] For the other

Minervan attempt at creating an offshore libertarian paradise—the artificial sandbar—their coins featured the goddess Minerva herself with the latitude and longitude coordinates of their country-to-be: another metallic proof of a thing that did not yet exist (and indeed never would). The coins were minted to be circulated among believers, part of the existence proof for a libertarian enclave in the emergency to come.

The various flavors of libertarianism that converged on digital cash were built on the two outsides that met in the icon of the coin: a territorial outside—from the networked agora to the high seas—from which the coin is issued and where it can be transacted, and a temporal outside, a future of crisis and collapse in which libertarian beliefs would be validated and the money that embodies them would be redeemed. The "escape geography" of libertarian fantasy was intertwined with the "escape temporality" of libertarian currency; the future in which their money could pass would be situated in some contemporary territory.

SOVEREIGNTY ALONE

In 1997, Ryan Lackey was at MIT, in the running for an entrepreneurship prize for "a distributed data store, using strong cryptographic protocols to provide privacy, authentication, and protection from censorship, in a market-based scheme."[20] On the cypherpunks list, he asked, "What would it take to start an anonymous, private, secure, etc. etc. bank issuing e-cash, located in a country without taxes/etc.?"[21] He discussed guns at length with May, prompting Wei Dai's puzzled question (previously mentioned in the context of his b-money proposal): "If we can defend ourselves with guns, why would we need crypto?" Lackey's signature block on his posts was a quote from *Atlas Shrugged,* when Dagny Taggart "calmly and impersonally" shoots a guard "who had wanted to exist without the responsibility of consciousness."

Two years later, he'd dropped out of MIT, worked on an e-payments start-up in Anguilla, and found his way to Sealand as a member of HavenCo's board of directors, offering data storage and management not just offshore but "off-government," in the words of a hyperbolic and credulous *Wired* cover story in 2000.[22] HavenCo's chair was Sameer Parekh, who previously appeared in this book transcribing Thoreau's *Civil Disobedience* to share online and hanging out with the cypherpunks. The CEO of HavenCo was Sean Hastings—also of that Anguillan start-up—who had been a lively contributor to philosophical debates on the Extropian mailing list, especially around artificial intelligence, and developed the "Value and Obligation eXchange Protocol," a contract-barter transaction platform. (Hastings would go on to work on seasteading projects with Patri Friedman, the grandson of Milton Friedman.)

Sealand's legal status was a vexed issue.[23] It was an anti-aircraft artillery platform built off the coast of Essex in the North Sea, abandoned by the government after the war and claimed as sovereign territory by the family that hoisted themselves aboard in 1967. They were part of a larger history of ships, forts, and offshore platforms around the UK repurposed for renegade radio, as recounted in Adrian Johns's *Death of a Pirate*—a strange mix of DJs, gangsters, bohemians, and proto-Thatcherite disciples of free market discipline.[24] Sealand pushed their assertion of sovereignty farther than most, albeit with tongue mostly in cheek. (Their case was not helped by the many forged Sealand passports in circulation—one was found in possession of serial killer Andrew Cunanan after he shot Gianni Versace—including thousands allegedly sold by a Spanish document-forging ring to

Hong Kong citizens in advance of the country's handoff.) This playful-serious sovereignty suggested, in *Wired*'s phrase, "a tantalizing gray zone" where a truly offshore jurisdiction could effectively become a six-thousand-square-foot physical instantiation of the fantasy of cyberspace—a concrete utopia and the perfect place for "untraceable bank accounts." As Lackey later recalled, "The biggest inspiration was Vernor Vinge, 'True Names.'"[25] The Other Plane would finally have a footprint; digital cash would have an appropriate zone, nowhere@cyberspace.nil, a node on the network now with latitude and longitude coordinates.

In theory, this would be a proper fortress for anonymous payments, digital banking, and many other offshore services, provisioned with high-bandwidth connectivity, generators, batteries, and telecommunications gear. In a perfect techno-thriller detail, the machine rooms would have atmospheres of pure nitrogen, to protect from rust and fire—a technique called *inerting* used on oil rigs—which would also suffocate anyone without a breathing apparatus.

In practice, Lackey lived on canned food in the dark—keeping San Francisco hours on Greenwich time, for business reasons and to avoid constant proximity to other people on the platform—pushing bits over a slow Internet connection that got slower when their telecom provider went bankrupt and they fell back on a satellite link, frustrating their ten or twelve customers (mostly casinos). Little was installed, the racks stayed largely empty, and "critical components of technical infrastructure," he said in his bridge-burning presentation at the hacker conference DEF CON after leaving Sealand, "were not deployed due to lack of funding."[26] Ironically, payment itself was a constant problem. HavenCo had reincorporated in Cyprus from Anguilla, and paying them as a service provider was a difficult process, with investor funds coming in through Western Union and credit cards; the security team was paid in cash. As Lackey ruefully put it afterward, "Sovereignty alone has little value without commercial support from banks."

Lackey had planned to launch his own gold-backed currency, using anonymous digital cash protocols, from this extranational haven—like von NotHaus's "warehouse receipts," combined with Chaum's transactional secrecy, based not in Idaho but in a sandbox monarchy the size of an office park. In the end, he left $40,000 in debt and was owed much more. As the legal scholar James Grimmelmann pointed out, by putting themselves outside other legal systems the HavenCo team was, in fact, a subject of Sealand and its prince and prince regent. If Lackey sued them in court and won, he would undercut the pretense of Sealand's sovereignty that he was trying to defend.

In November 2008, a participant in a cryptography mailing list interrupted the discussion about a new proposal for an electronic cash called "Bitcoin" with an announcement: "HavenCo, which ran a datacenter on the 'nation' of Sealand, is no longer operating there." In fact, they had been long gone; shutting down their website in 2008 came years after Sealand's hosting had moved to a data center in London. The facts were wrong, but the timing could not have been more perfect. The fantasy was migrating back from a literal platform in the ocean to a metaphorical one on the network.

CHAPTER 12

DESOLATE EARTH

We come to the last chapter and look at how early Bitcoin itself was understood as a utopian, speculative currency in the context of libertarian dreams: digital cash built for verifiably inflation-proof production, in anticipation of a redemptive economic emergency. Every digital cash project has been organized around a bigger agenda, from protecting privacy to ensuring posthumanity; early Bitcoin's agenda was creating and securing scarcity in the context of crisis.

ERUDITE METAL

All money is an archive, but coins provide exceptionally vivid examples. Coins tell stories, right on the face: dates, images of divine beings and profiles of temporal powers, and languages and symbols documenting communities, trade networks, regions, and the persistence of common practice.[1] The Gotland coin hoard, buried on an island off the coast of what is now Sweden, includes thousands of dirhams from mints across the Islamic caliphate—the mechanisms of trade, pricing, and negotiation along the Silk Road, as far away as Yemen and the Maghreb, a snapshot of human arrangements and connections across half the world.[2] Even in their damage, coins carry histories of sovereignty, territory, and value. Surfaces were worn away through long handling, new values were set with figures hammered into old coins or deliberately scarred and effaced, mutilating the profile of a hated monarch or adding a message. English suffragettes stamped "VOTES FOR WOMEN" into the head of Edward VII on pennies.[3] Coins were "clipped" to trim off a shaving of silver without changing the face value, or debased for political or military projects; they were cut up into small change, or made into "broken money" and valued by weight.[4] Sometimes they persisted as anachronisms, living fossils: long after the monarchs died and borders shifted, coiners still minted Alexandrian tetradrachmas and Venetian sequins, bezants and Maria Theresa thalers. Thalers—the product of an outstanding silver mine in Bohemia—became standard trade coins in such demand that they continued to be issued with the year of Theresa's death, 1780, for centuries.[5] Thalers passed everywhere: from the territories, colonies, and frontiers of the American continent—*thaler* begat *daalder* begat *daler* begat *dollar*—to the trade networks of the Indian Ocean, where they circulated alongside East African shillings, promissory notes, salt bars, British pounds, measures of grain, and Indian rupees.

With these histories, coins document philosophies and structures of value. They speak of the legacies of ideology, religion, and imagined community—sometimes stories that are elsewhere neglected or never written down. (The writer and critic Joseph Addison said of his obsession with coin collecting that of each coin he cherished not "its metal but its erudition," a "poetical cash" that itself remembers the history that people and cultures forget; he once wrote an autobiography from the perspective of a shilling.[6]) "Individuals might speak of a particular currency's value," Rebecca Spang wrote, "but what they are really doing is relying on their own, barely conscious, expectations of how other human beings will react when presented with bills, coins, and credit cards."[7] Coins document what will pass, who will accept it, and why—which constitutes a shared vocabulary of value. To rebase the currency works—at least in part—to rebase the society. It is to make an ontological statement about *value itself*, about what is most real and how we should therefore act. It lays down bedrock for a cosmogram and with it the arrangement of values within the society. This is therefore an epistemological act as well: an assertion about how the significant values can be known.

Lycurgus, the semimythical lawgiver of ancient Sparta, was reported by Plutarch to have based the currency on iron: heavy, symbolic, reasonably difficult to get without being appealingly precious to others, and wildly inconvenient. "When this money obtained currency," Plutarch wrote, "many sorts of iniquity went into exile from Lacedaemon. For who would steal, or receive as a bribe, or rob, or plunder that which could neither be concealed, nor possessed with satisfaction, nay, nor even cut to pieces with any profit?" That Lycurgus did not, in fact, do exactly that does not detract from the point of Plutarch's account. Plutarch's Lycurgus used iron currency as a forcible leveler of social distinctions, a means to kill off "the unnecessary and superfluous arts," and the motor of radical, autarkic self-reliance that effectively eliminated trade. The iron was a pedagogical tool as well as a social system, a kind of discourse both metaphorical (an expression of values and particular character) and literal—an object that pulled the society out of most markets entirely. Alexander Hamilton, reading Plutarch during the winter of 1777 at Valley Forge, in the midst of founding the new state for which he would serve as Secretary of the Treasury, made a note of this decision: a social model built into the ordinance of money.[8]

Hamilton's colleague, Benjamin Franklin, successfully proposed land banks—"coined land"—for the paper money of the American colonies.[9] The supply of gold and silver, he pointed out, had fluctuated wildly with new discoveries, and precious metals could be exported in trade, ending up in England and bringing business within the colonies to a standstill. Land, instead, would be pledged as collateral for paper money. When money grew scarce and the difficulty of barter grew, people would borrow more against their land to take advantage of the valuable money; when the system was flush with money and its value fell, people would trade to accumulate the cheaper notes with which to pay off their pledges. It would root the trade of the colonies within the colonies themselves, building their economic independence from the Empire and encouraging a form of import substitution (a subject of particular interest to Hamilton as well), and link the holders of currency to their terrain. The notes themselves were authenticated with the leaves of American trees—leaf casts, struck with a copper plate press, being relatively easy to produce and compare but very difficult to counterfeit freehand.[10] (They became an accidental botanical archive as well: a circulating paper library of the forests of New England.) A social framework, a political mission, and a physical place were brought together into the banknotes.[11]

What kind of stories do bitcoins tell? What arguments do they make? What human beings do they assume? What is their cosmogram?

MAGNIFICENT STUPID HONESTY

At the PorcFest gathering in the White Mountains of New Hampshire, silver, Bitcoin, and other cryptocurrencies traded alongside "FRNs," the dismissive term for dollars as "Federal Reserve notes." It was the summer of 2014, seventy years nearly to the day from the Bretton Woods Conference—the founding event of the postwar global monetary order—which took place about a half hour south, at the Mount Washington Hotel.

PorcFest was named for porcupines, spiny creatures that want to be left alone; it was a gathering of libertarians and a recruitment venue for the Free State Project, an initiative to take over towns and counties by moving libertarians in to vote local government more or less out of existence. Vehicles parked around the campground had bumper stickers in support of Bitcoin, agorism, Ayn Rand, cryonics ("Dead? We Can Help!")—even a Ludwig von Mises vanity plate. The silver pieces carried in velvet bags and pouches, the shirtlessness, braided beards, utilikilts, flags and banners, and plant tinctures and cooking smoke created an atmosphere akin to a heavily armed Renaissance fair. This was one of the first communities in the world trying to use cryptocurrencies for everyday, interpersonal transactions.

The merchants under the boughs of the maples and blue spruce had small scales and calculators and handwritten conversion charts for working out the effective payment value of different precious metals—and smartphones, too, for checking the bid-ask spread and doing transactions in Bitcoin. You could buy gumbo, dry socks, coffee, Wi-Fi access (over an antenna mounted on a trailer, connected to a mysterious 4G network on a VPN with an exit node somewhere in Indonesia), paleo cereal (almonds, pumpkin seeds, coconut flakes), and a book of essays by the American individualist anarchist Lysander Spooner. You could make donations and model an imagined condition that would follow the collapse of the state, the economy, and the world, showing your commitment to their particular future. I found the combination of utopian monies baffling: How could the same people so deeply committed to "hard money," "honest money," to barter and bullion and "intrinsic value," decide to adopt cryptocurrencies—a system made of nothing but buggy software, theoretical abstractions, and complex, brittle shared infrastructure?

I kept asking the wrong question. I assumed the answer to this puzzle had to do with what *backed* the currency—since much of the contempt for FRNs and other state monies began with the idea that nothing backed them but promises. The notes were "nothing but paper," warned men wearing END THE FED T-shirts, and the coinage had been debased. (Some transactions in that field were priced in "1964 or before" quarters or dimes—90/10 coins, 90 percent silver and 10 percent copper, as produced by the US Mint from 1932 to 1964, whose metallic value now significantly exceeds their face value.) Gold and silver were useful, even if only as ornament; people discussed other useful assets suited to payments and transactions, like ammunition, with which you could procure venison or maintain the balance of terror with your neighbors—magazines of bullets had the important commodity-money property, as did cigarettes, of being easily subdivided for small transactions, from cartons to packs, packs to loosies.

Cryptocurrencies here seemed like a paradox. I was expecting to find an ontological debate, an argument about what made money real, a penny-ante version of the argument between John Maynard Keynes and Harry Dexter White at Bretton Woods seventy years before. (Keynes presented a kind of global settlement money—the "bancor" or "unitas"—built on agreements and the utility of trade: "There should be a supply of the money proportioned to the scale of the international trade which it has to carry." White argued for a "gold exchange standard," with the US dollar as the world's reserve currency. White won, until 1971.)[12] What I actually found was an epistemological stance: the similar way these disparate forms of money could be known and verified.

What Bitcoin and silver shared was evaluative: you could, in the words of one minter, "trust in yourself" to verify what you held. Cryptocurrencies in circulation are nothing more or less than records of creation, ownership, and transaction in the block-chain ledger: their existence is constituted by the user-visible records of their existence. Silver is bodily: about palm-feel, bit-ing, body heat, weight both on the scale and in the hand, about the look under different lights. Moneyers I spoke to were not even necessarily opposed to paper currency—no more than von NotHaus had been, with his paper warehouse receipts—as long as they felt they could evaluate precisely how much money was in circulation and have a say in its production (recall e-gold, with its ledger of numbered bars; recall b-money, with its protocol for voting on how expensive to make the production of new money; recall Finney's "transparent server"). People argued *against* the use of security features on paper currency, because they serve as a "distraction": they turn the verification of money into some-thing someone else is in charge of, one more step toward an abstract-institutional world of bancors and international order.

During the Japanese occupation of Indonesia in the Second World War, the thaler—that beloved, persistent silver trade coin—was so widely employed that the Office of Strategic Ser-vices (OSS) minted their own for the underground resistance. (The OSS was the ancestor of the American Central Intelligence Agency, cousin of the Special Operations Executive.) Resident OSS mad scientist Stanley Lovell recalled that his crew of mas-ter forgers disliked making real money, but he insisted that the OSS's counterfeit thalers be made with pure silver: "Indonesians would bite the coins and listen to their ring on a hard stone, so I insisted on absolute integrity."[13] Or, as a libertarian mintmas-ter put it to me in the summer of 2014, "Silver is silver, and the weight is the weight."

Many of Bitcoin's seemingly discouraging design choices make a different kind of sense in this light. The whole apparatus of Bitcoin enables *verification* of the currency, both in particular and in general: you can't exchange "bitcoins" outside the network, or have them circulate freely—and therefore be obliged to test whether a given bitcoin is the real thing—since there are no bitcoins, only the rights to trade within the closed ledger. They cannot be destroyed (though they might belong to an address for which the private key has been lost, as James Howells's was, so they can no longer be spent), and they are created at a fixed and finite rate. This verifiability demands an entirely public system—the books are open—and a form of "money" that exists as a record of itself: every notional bitcoin carries its every transaction, from its addition to the ledger onward. You can know what it is, where it's been, and who owns what parts of it with a precision shared only by certain bars of gold with their assay stamps, four-decimal-place purity, serial numbers, and chain-of-custody documents that account for every shelf in every vault they've occupied. Most important, you can do this verification yourself—the responsibility lies with the individual to confirm that their money is real, and to commit to the money's plan and ideas, and to pay the price if they decide poorly.

Bitcoin as it was built and adopted in the early years had what H. G. Wells said of the gold standard: a "magnificent stupid honesty."[14] The Rube Goldberg complexity of its operation concealed the simplicity of its act: to say, with unerring precision, exactly how much money there is, where it is, and how much more there will be. It is a built version of the fantasy of Mises's "praxeological" doctrine: to put "at the disposal of acting man all the information he needs in order to make his choices in full awareness of their consequences."[15] Within Bitcoin's closed universe, perfect verification was possible (at least in theory): hard-money Austrianism reinvented as a video game—SimGold, perhaps—with every rule explicit and specified.

One piece of information was missing, of course: how much a given bitcoin was actually worth. Money is only valuable because people and their institutions take it in payment or exchange, and they do so—if they do so—in the balance of experience and expectation, habit and hope. They believe it can be passed on in turn, redeemed, or settled, whether now or later; that process of thinking takes place in models of history and futurity. Bitcoin's particular architecture had a story to tell about the future, too—one likewise initially suited to working as libertarian money.

REMNANT

Part of early Bitcoin's promise of verifiability was set in the future. With the ledger, you know how many bitcoins exist and the addresses of their current owners; you also know how many bitcoins will ultimately exist (twenty-one million), the rate at which they will be introduced (originally fifty, currently twenty-five at a time), and the work it takes to produce them (growing ever more difficult). (As with many aspects of later Bitcoin, this became more complex with time and use: the code is maintained by a group of contributors who could make—and have made—significant changes, provoking much drama; but let us stay with the initial version and its ideas for now.) This produces a monetary system that enormously rewards its earliest users—who got in when the mining was easy, as James Howells did, idly accumulating thousands running the software on his laptop in 2009—and encourages the use of the money as reserve and collateral, or, seen differently, for hoarding and speculation.

Depending on that perspective, Bitcoin may, then, look like either a realistic alternative asset to state-issued monies, which tend toward mild inflation to boost economic growth (with occasional extreme and disastrous exceptions, like Venezuela), or a curious variant of a deflationary currency experiment, or a bubble-generating pyramid scheme whose value is driven by waves of late-adopting suckers trying to buy their way in. Either way, it poses a question for anyone making a payment with bitcoins: Why would you spend or invest a currency that might increase in value beyond anything you might invest it in or purchase with it? Better to squirrel it away, like gold—except that even gold has its uncertainties, from strikes and rushes (California, Australia, South Africa, Tierra del Fuego) to new markets for it as a commodity. Bitcoin's future is known: decided in advance.

This is a particularly seductive notion for people already prepared for the collapse of the current monetary order. As things go to pieces due to—well, choose your libertarian poison—an idle population addicted to unearned entitlements, the expenditure of blood and treasure on useless wars, the aggrandizement of the state, the death throes of overly regulated capitalism, Bitcoin's schedule will not vary. (Of course, this assumes a lot of messy real-world contingencies, like continued access to effectively unlimited dirt-cheap electricity, microchip fabrication, and reliable global Internet access.) You can't lose your bitcoins in a bank run or have them seized from your safe-deposit box. The right to trade them remains assigned on the ledger. All you have to do is wait.

To hold speculative libertarian money is to anticipate a threshold in time, but not the threshold of the Extropian breakthrough on the far side of which lay runaway prosperity, abundance, and hedonistic space cities. The threshold is the imminent emergency, a crisis eagerly anticipated for decades by the political models of this loose community. The speculative money is not helping to bring that future about, as the Extropian projects were. It is not an investment in transformation. Rather, the coins and cryptocurrency units are *retrospective artifacts*. In the present, the accumulation and storage of apocalyptic goods and currencies in extraterritorial and alternative zones—the caches of fish antibiotics, the repainted and greased AK-47 magazines, the batteries and gas masks—make it possible to imagine the future disaster when this new society would be validated and come into its own. Early Bitcoin businesses sprang up to exploit this shared set of beliefs, offering seeds, survival kits, movement literature, and fund-raising for a 3-D-printed component of an assault rifle, all priced in bitcoins. A T-shirt company that accepted the currency stocked shirts extolling home schooling, raw milk, the threat of gun control, and the prospect of the next financial crisis—with a promise: "Bitcoin Users Not Affected."[16]

The most telling of these marketing strategies was the "Passports for Bitcoin" business. It was an extension of an existing scheme to sell fast-track citizenships through the islands of St. Kitts and Nevis (the smallest sovereign country in the Western Hemisphere), involving the citizenship retailer and Bitcoin investor Roger Ver.[17] Their advertising copy: "Today's news headlines are filled with stories from around the globe about upheaval, increased taxes, and governments exerting more and more control over citizens' freedoms and privacy. The world is rapidly changing and destabilizing, creating more and more risk for people everywhere."[18] This was accompanied by a collage of headlines: "NSA Surveillance," "Terrorism," and so on. (After they went bust under murky circumstances, Ver went on to act as a funder and ongoing patron of the Free Republic of Liberland, a project to claim and inhabit a disputed island in the

Danube, between Croatia and Serbia, in partnership with blockchain governance projects, using Bitcoin as its national currency.) Bitcoin was an offshore account for a new offshore life—"Swiss bank accounts for the millions," as StJude put it in 1992—in a currency whose central bankers and economists had been replaced with a scheduled and unvarying payout, shelter from the awaited storm.[19]

It plugged neatly into the long-standing desire chronicled in the previous chapter for a place outside the existing state apparatus, from which you could cozily observe the inevitable collapse—Galt's Gulch realized—and emerge to buy up the world at fire-sale prices with your stable money. The libertarian venture capitalist and investor Peter Thiel cofounded PayPal as a platform for, in his words, "the creation of a new world currency, free from all government control and dilution—the end of monetary sovereignty, as it were," enabling the rapid movement of your money when things went bad. He went on to be a significant funder of a seasteading venture with Patri Friedman, previously seen in this book with the ex-Sealand crew.[20] (Thiel later resigned from the board of the Seasteading Institute: "They're not quite feasible from an engineering perspective."[21] Friedman stepped down to pursue creating a self-governing "charter city" in Honduras.)

Others, discounting the option of a physical exit, envisioned the libertarian outside embedded in ordinary life. In 1936, the libertarian theorist Albert Jay Nock—deeply antidemocratic, like both Thiel and Friedman, as well as an anti-Semite—proposed a movement called "the Remnant." This secretive community, "building a substratum like coral insects," would operate in historical and social ignorance of the redemptive disaster; they would hold to the ideals, practice the rituals, keep the money, and wait. "The prophet of the present," Nock wrote, "knows precisely as much and as little as the historian of the future." All they can do is prepare for the breakdown, speculating (in both senses) on the ruin and its aftermath.[22] The libertarian coin persists, as the Remnant does, as a reservoir of "objective value" in a deluded world, to become current—to be redeemed—once the existing society has been destroyed. In the last sentence of *Atlas Shrugged*, John Galt makes "the sign of the dollar" over "the desolate earth," inaugurating the new age.

SCARCITY MACHINE

As emergency money, released in the middle of a banking crisis, Bitcoin was suited to such fantasies, and some of them played a role in its adoption. This was a by-product of the technology's design choices and the Austrian and libertarian commitments they reflected. The transparency of the ledger and the verification of ownership, the proof-of-work process, the foreknowledge of the introduction of the remaining quantity of new money—everything, the whole apparatus—was designed to produce a single thing: predictable scarcity.

That is what Bitcoin generates. Abstractly, that is *all* it generates, aside from enormous quantities of heat: verifiable, distributed, trustless scarcity. It provides the certitude that no one else has the right to trade any particular bitcoin, that no copies are being produced, and that the overall number is fixed and will remain so, becoming steadily harder to create. It puts this scarce object into an infrastructure of ownership: the distributed irrefutable ledger of the blockchain—the blockchain that turned out to have so many more interesting and potentially valuable applications, from establishing the ownership of digital artworks to enabling property sharing and access schemes.[23]

This book opened with the challenge of creating digital cash, data that could pass as money, given that digital technology produces, transmits, and verifies perfect copies. The solution in early Bitcoin was a stroke of perverse genius: to build, inside a global technology of informational abundance, a mechanism that makes one particular kind of data provably scarce and impossible to copy. It should not surprise us that a system designed to create a scarce resource would subsequently, in Nigel Dodd's words, "appear not only to replicate but exacerbate the self-same inequities of wealth and power that can be found in the existing financial system"—complete with centralized "mining pools," speculative cartels, and major shares of the total currency held by a small group.[24]

This book holds many visions: Phillip Salin's financial system for his own revivification; Tim May's state-smashing secrets bazaar; Xanadu, a framework for all human knowledge for all time; idea coupons to simultaneously predict and influence the future; a storm-lashed platform notionally offshore of all governments; a dewar transporting its cargo of frozen heads into a hoped-for future. Most of these visions remained sketches, proposals, the occasional prototype, a small company, or a single instance. Not Bitcoin. Bitcoin got built: the infrastructure necessary to produce the permanently scarce digital object really exists, and at a vast scale—the cosmogram in poured concrete, backup generators, QR codes, smartphone apps, and microchip fabrication.

The blockchain is 145 gigabytes at this writing, and being added to by Bitcoin mining facilities that burn, in Nakamoto's words, "CPU time and electricity"—those racks and racks of boards of chips, putting in quantities of computational work that demand the big Greek prefixes that lie beyond giga-: tera-, peta-, exa-. The miners need electricity: how much precisely is difficult to say, but building in places with inexpensive hydropower or Chinese coal-fired plants is very attractive. All of this goes to solving arbitrary challenges that reveal nothing and produce nothing but *difficulty itself* in quantifiable form. This ceaseless expenditure, every second of every hour of every day, secures the shared consensus among the nodes that nothing in the ledger has been altered.

Seen from a sufficient distance, the Bitcoin machine is revealed as the built-out version of one of the most abstract fantasies of value ever conceived. It does not make data valuable—only humans and their institutions, accepting payment, thinking of past and future, can do that—but it does make a certain kind of data verifiably rare, and therefore suitable for hoarding, display, begging, conspicuous waste, and status competition. It may well be the purest and most honest expression of a society that could not figure out what to do with its technological inventiveness—its energy, innovation, and abundance—except to squander it in creating new kinds of artificial scarcity: the monumental folly of our age.

SOMETIME IN THE FUTURE

If this book has succeeded, you now have a history of digital cash, utopian computing projects, and the precursors of contemporary cryptocurrencies in mind: the earliest experiments with "objects made in new ways," blinded e-cash, the CryptoCredits of BlackNet; hashcash and bit gold, RPOW and b-money; Extropian idea coupons and thornes and hayek note sketches; libertarian coinage and certificates and digital gold currencies; and, finally, the initial version of Bitcoin and its chains of digital signatures. You have a sense of the challenge of creating different kinds of digital media objects that can prove, certify, and authenticate themselves—from signatures to postage, ledgers to banknotes—as a chapter in the larger story of how digital objects became authoritative. You also have a sense of the way all currencies, speculative and practiced, carry histories and futures with them: from thalers to energy certificates, air-dollars to buried dirhams, assignats to bitcoins, each with a different and distinct relationship to cosmograms of value, knowledge, power, and time.

I hope this leads to a practical question: To what future, and what arrangements of knowledge and power, does your money belong? Is that the future you hope to realize? If not, what would that money be?

Every kind of money carries a structure of time and history within which it is transacted, hoarded, distributed, and ultimately destroyed or reduced to a collector's item or a museum piece. The ultimate horizon of money's future contains our own deaths—we who transact it—and the end of our societies that made it valuable. It therefore acts as a model of the future—but always the future within a particular time. In their very obscurity and marginality, each of the speculative currency projects in this book offers us an unsullied example of the imagination of their community and their era expressed in monetary proposals and stories. They are theories of the future that also act as testimony of their present.

In this way, Technocratic energy certificates are still futuristic—American Depression-era futuristic, as much an object of their period as dance marathons or the radio broadcast of *The War of the Worlds*. Extropian digital cash and "idea futures" were futuristic in a way that makes them time capsules of the old New Economy, the boom years, Fukuyama's *The End of History* and the transhuman prospect. Early Bitcoin draws on a long-standing libertarian future of inflation-free "hard money" held for an imminent and comprehensive crisis which, in 2008 and 2009, appeared to be actually happening.

Technocracy Inc. became a curious footnote in the cultural history of technology in American life: total submission to a daydream of engineering, with the entire continent tooled into a calibrated motor of scientific management. Howard Scott lived to see himself revealed as the industrialist cosplayer he had always really been, his movement dwindling to a few acolytes puttering around "the Erg Man" in his office.[1]

Crypto anarchy ended up as the partial inspiration and prologue for systems of leaks, document dumps, whistle-blowing, and extortion schemes—an inside-out, hippiefied "desktop NSA," as Bruce Sterling put it—selling exfiltrated data for bitcoins and becoming in turn the pawns and assets of the very governments they were meant to destroy. (It was also the inspiration for numerous online black markets.) Rather than making cash digital and personal activities private, we ended up with a network infrastructure built on advertising and aggressive surveillance that monetizes the *users*, making them into the product to be sold—tagged livestock in feedlots, as Chaum warned, with their attention and payment data just another resource for capture and exploitation.

Like a mirage, Extropianism disappeared into the environment itself, its more eccentric features normalized (relatively speaking) into Singularity bros who pump iron, chew caffeine cubes, and pride themselves on their ultrarationality while fretting about a Gnostic demonology of evil machine intelligence. Extropian money, meant to reverse time's entropic arrow, ended up in a very different future than they had anticipated.

Early Bitcoin and its blockchain was refined and adopted, becoming increasingly unlike the initial version as other institutions, agendas, and systems made use of it. The years after its launch featured a string of crises, adaptations, hacks, bull rallies and busts, schisms and reinventions, with different groups arguing for what it *really* is, could be, or should be.[2] (And, of course, many other cryptocurrencies and related technologies have spun off or been developed independently, from Ethereum to the proliferation of "Initial Coin Offerings"; their stories could be, and will be, other books.) Like Biblical exegetes making the New Testament into the fulfillment and confirmation of Old Testament prophecy, the story of what Bitcoin should be turns on what it is understood to have been. As of this writing, it seems to have found a role that perfectly exemplifies the present moment: a wildly volatile vehicle for baseless speculation, a roller coaster of ups and downs driven by a mix of hype, price-fixing, bursts of frenzied panic, and the dream of getting rich without doing much of anything.

Hal Finney, who quietly became the main character of this book, died in 2014. He was a victim of amyotrophic lateral sclerosis— Lou Gehrig's disease. His body was perfused, cooled below freezing, and placed in long-term storage in the Alcor cryonics facility. Some of his medical expenses were defrayed by selling the Bitcoin he had accumulated in the blockchain's early days; even as he lost control over his hands, he worked on a coding project to better secure Bitcoin wallet software.[3]

In the cold, in the aluminum cask, funded by a complex financial arrangement, Finney is simultaneously in the past, deceased and memorialized in the press and the Bitcoin blockchain; in the present, at −196°C in Arizona; and in the future, where all money is, somewhere over the utopian horizon of hope and expectation. "Hal," wrote Max More, who is now Alcor's CEO, in the announcement of his cryopreservation, "I know I speak for many when I say that I look forward to speaking to you again sometime in the future and to throwing a party in honor of your revival."[4]

ACKNOWLEDGMENTS

My deepest thanks to Mario Biagioli, Raymond Craib, Sara Dean, Charlie DeTar, Quinn DuPont, Paul Edwards, Tung-Hui Hu, Chris Kelty, Bill Maurer, Nicole Marie Miller, Lisa Nakamura, Arvind Narayanan, Helen Nissenbaum, Laine Nooney, Mary Poovey, Kriss Ravetto, Phillip Rogaway, Christian Sandvig, Lana Swartz, John Tresch, and Caitlin Zaloom; to Al Bertrand and the reviewers, editors, and designers at Princeton University Press; to the staff of the Department of Media, Culture, and Communication at New York University; and to those who have asked to remain anonymous. This book would not have been possible without you. All the mistakes are my own.

A NOTE ON THE JACKET ART

The artwork on the dust jacket was created by Joey Colombo, who works primarily with currency. It's a photograph from his Instagram (jdotcolombo), documenting the creation of a live piece at the Outside Lands music festival in 2017: the record of an ephemeral work of art, itself assembled from high-resolution scans, enlargements of pieces from many currencies—cash digitized and transfigured. His work carries out the primal mystery of sacrifice, at the heart of exchange and substitution, this-for-that: the destruction of objects at one scale of value to open the way to another level, the vast outside. In his art, paper money dreams of its redemption; freed from circulating as fungible currency, defaced and unspendable, it can take on new forms. Dense guilloché decorations—originally an anti-counterfeiting measure—reveal themselves as slices of lush nineteenth-century psychedelia, luminous relics of an age of paisley, moiré, hothouse flowers, machine-woven tapestries, and filigreed scrollwork. Eyes and wings proliferate. Archaic fragments of the world's currencies become new mandalas, visionary landscapes, and mediation objects. "When you cut into the present," William Burroughs said of his "cut-up" technique of composition, "the future leaks out," and Colombo's X-Acto precision and technique creates work saturated with weird futurity. The solemn faces of politicians, monarchs, and cultural grandees gaze at us anew from exoskeletal body armor and lapidary helmets, wearing garlands of flowers and leaves, with curling clouds and flaming halos like a Tibetan Buddhist *thangka*: they look like portraits of shamans and seraphim from a place simultaneously ancient and utterly futuristic—envoys from utopia.

NOTES

INTRODUCTION: THE PASSING CURRENT

1. Desan, *Making Money*, 331.

CHAPTER 1: SPECULATING WITH MONEY

1. Akin, *Technocracy*, 29; the book is an invaluable resource for the reader interested in this remarkable moment of American history. See also Segal, *Technological Utopianism*, chap. 6.

2. The cofounders of the party included Marion King Hubbert, a geologist who is better known for the "Hubbert peak" theory of petroleum production, which achieved public notoriety several decades later as "peak oil."

3. As cited in Ahamed, *Lords of Finance*, 435.

4. Ahamed, *Lords of Finance*, chap. 21, includes an extremely entertaining overview of these and other results of the cash crunch in the United States; this paragraph is largely extracted from his account.

5. On this project, see Stites, *Revolutionary Dreams*, chap. 7, and Zielinski, *Deep Time of the Media*, chap. 8.

6. Technocracy Inc., "Total Conscription!"

7. Fezer, "The Energy Certificate."

8. Tresch, *Romantic Machine*, xvii.

9. Ohanian and Royoux, *Cosmograms*, 68.

10. For an excellent brief introduction to these projects—called "demurrage currencies"—in the context of political-utopian projects, see North, *Money and Liberation*, 62–66. The canonical stamp scrip project was the "Wörgl experiment," building on the work of the anarchist economist Silvio Gesell. For an excellent, thorough overview of Gesell's work, see Onken, "The Political Economy of Silvio Gesell." The quote is from Gesell, *The Natural Economic Order*, 121.

11. For a much deeper study of communities and time in the work of making new forms of money, see Maurer, *Mutual Life, Limited*.

12. Ibid., 89.

13. There is rich scholarship in this area, but for purposes of this chapter I point the reader to Graeber, *Debt*, and to Hudson, "How Interest Rates Were Set, 2500 BC–1000 AD."

14. This idea—the promise that other promises will turn out to be worthless—comes from the work of the theorist of finance and globalization Arjun Appadurai:

Banking on Words. For the Yale water bond, see https://news.yale.edu/2015/09/22/living-artifact-dutch-golden-age-yale-s-367-year-old-water-bond-still-pays-interest.

15. For an excellent analysis of the "anxiety, fear, and suspicion at work in the technologies of rational prediction in finance," see Zaloom, "How to Read the Future."

16. The term "reserve technology" is from the historian of technology David Edgerton. See Edgerton, *Shock of the Old*, chap. 1. See also Lisa Servon's work on consumer banking and the danger of monthly fees and overdraft charges—and how the clarity offered by payday loan and check-cashing institutions can be preferable (Servon, *The Unbanking of America*).

17. For a deeper analysis of this, see William Deringer's study of the development of different models of discounting in the seventeenth century: "As it turns out, compound-interest discounting [the model that won] is probably not the method that best reflects how people instinctually feel about the future, even today" (Deringer, "Pricing the Future," 521).

18. Spang, *Stuff and Money in the Time of the French Revolution*, 6.

19. Ibid., 20.

20. Zelizer, *Economic Lives*, 154.

21. This only alludes to a larger question than this study can address: the gendering of different forms of money and payment systems. Along with Zelizer's work, see Waring, *If Women Counted*, Gibson-Graham, *The End of Capitalism*, and Swartz, "Gendered Transactions."

22. Desan, *Making Money*, 6.

23. Ibid.

24. Benjamin, "One-Way Street," 451.

25. Keynes, "The General Theory of Employment," 216.

26. Tresch, "Cosmogram," 74.

27. Dwiggins, *Towards a Reform*, 20.

28. Ibid., 19.

29. Belasco, *Meals to Come*, 181, 182.

30. Wells, *The Shape of Things to Come*, 266.

31. Ibid., 285.

32. Morrisson, *Modern Alchemy*, 176—the book provides the definitive account of this peculiar and fascinating genre.

CHAPTER 2: SECURE PAPER

1. Benjamin, "One-Way Street," 481.

2. Spang, *Stuff and Money*, 46.

3. Ibid., 47.

4. Kafka, *The Demon of Writing*, 77.

5. Spang, *Stuff and Money*, 175.

6. McPhee, *Oranges*, 97.

7. As quoted in Beniger, *Control Revolution*, 163.

8. This argument builds on the research and theories of Beniger, *Control Revolution*, chap. 4.

9. Gitelman, *Paper Knowledge*, ix.

10. For more on the public health history of the death certificate, see Schulz, "Final Forms."

11. Robertson, "The Aesthetics of Authenticity."

12. Poovey, *Genres*, 3.

13. Dwiggins, *Towards a Reform*, 27.

14. Swartz, *Social Transactions*.

15. Gilbert, "Forging a National Currency," 42.

16. Emerich Juettner, better known as Edward Mueller, was a senior citizen in New York City who had given up his job as an apartment superintendent in favor of becoming a junkman after his wife passed away in the 1930s. Scraping along the margins of survival, he turned to counterfeiting in a kind of humble desperation that made him almost impossible to catch: he stuck to one-dollar bills, at which no one looks closely—even when they're as clumsy as his were, printed on stationery store bond paper and awkwardly retouched, even misspelling "Washington." He passed only one or two a day, at most, when his own money ran short. Because he didn't want to harm businesses by paying them with notes they couldn't deposit, he never passed a counterfeit at the same place twice, criss-crossing Manhattan to buy groceries and dog food. Year after year, the Secret Service busted far more sophisticated and dangerous counterfeiting operations, but "Old 880" eluded their intensive search for more than a decade. See McKelway, "Mister Eight-Eighty."

17. See the work of Viviana Zelizer on the issue of earmarking and variably discounting money—especially the landmark article "The Social Meaning of Money." See also research in behavioral economics, particularly the work of Richard Thaler on mental accounting, beginning with "Mental Accounting and Consumer Choice."

18. Gibson, *Zero History*, 345–46.

19. Murdoch, "Software Detection of Currency"; Murdoch and Laurie, "The Convergence of Anti-Counterfeiting"; Kuhn, "The EURion Constellation"; Nieves, Ruiz-Agundez, and Bringas, "Recognizing Banknote Patterns."

CHAPTER 3: RECOGNIZABLE WITHOUT BEING KNOWN

1. This account is drawn from Fitzsimons, *Nancy Wake* (which, though a popular book, was based on interviews with Wake herself and has been verified by secondary scholarship); and Elliott, *The Shooting Star*.

2. Marks, *Between Silk and Cyanide*, 44.

3. Ibid., 590.

4. Wallace and Melton, *Spycraft*, 436.

5. For the curious reader, I'm using the substitution table and the first lines of the one-time pad that Marks himself used in presenting the LOP system to Cmdr. Dudley-Smith. Marks, *Between Silk and Cyanide*, 246.

6. Kahn, *The Codebreakers*, provides a rich overview of decades of different applications of one-time pads, including photographs of concealment tools for the materials. An excellent summary of such a system in diplomatic use is Smith, "Book Ciphers."

7. Shannon, "Communication Theory of Secrecy Systems."

8. Levy, *Crypto*; Singh, *The Code Book*; Plutte, "Whitfield Diffie Interview."

9. Merkle, "Secure Communications over Insecure Channels."

10. Singh, *The Code Book*, 283.

11. Levy, *Crypto*, 270.

12. Diffie and Hellman, "New Directions," 652.

13. Rivest, Shamir, and Adleman, "A Method for Obtaining Digital Signatures"; Blanchette, *Burdens of Proof*.

14. This number is RSA-240, an RSA Factoring Challenge semiprime, created to encourage research into the kinds of numbers used in RSA cryptographic keys. The challenge has been suspended—the field's understanding of the strength of different cryptographic schemes has moved on—but the answer to this challenge number, along with many other RSA factoring challenges, has never been found.

15. Blanchette, *Burdens of Proof*, 81.

16. Diffie and Hellman, "New Directions," 649.

17. Ibid.

18. Blanchette, *Burdens of Proof*, 63.

19. This section is based on Meier and Zabell, "Benjamin Peirce and the Howland Will" and the anonymous "The Howland Will Case."

20. Furthermore, 110 checks of President John Quincy Adams were examined, and some transferred to transparent paper so they could be superimposed on one another—what better reference point than a president?

21. "The Howland Will Case," 577.

22. Twenty years later Charles Peirce's student and friend, the art historian Allan Marquand, built a mechanical device for automatically solving a set of problems in formal logic (housing it in a cedar case made from a post at Princeton's oldest homestead), and Peirce made a recommendation: "I think electricity would be the best thing to rely on." As Marquand diagramed the first electric circuits for logical operations, Peirce published a paper on the prospects for such work. "Precisely how much of the business of thinking a machine could possibly be made to perform, and what part of

it must be left for the living mind, is a question not without conceivable practical importance; the study of it can at any rate not fail to throw needed light on the nature of the reasoning process" (Peirce, "Logical Machines," 165).

23. Peirce, "Of Reasoning in General," 13.

24. Schwartz, *The Culture of the Copy*, 179.

25. For a rewarding philosophical analysis of what "signatures" are in fact doing in cryptography—with particular reference to the blockchain—see DuPont, "Blockchain Identities."

CHAPTER 4: BLINDING FACTOR

1. Greenberger, "The Computers of Tomorrow."

2. McCarthy, "The Home Information Terminal."

3. Stearns, *Electronic Value Exchange*, 44. This book is a splendid history of Visa and Hock, including much fascinating material unavailable elsewhere, and deserves to be much more widely read.

4. Ibid., 195.

5. Armer, "Computer Technology and Surveillance," 10.

6. Ibid., 11.

7. Atwood, *The Handmaid's Tale*, 25.

8. See Eubanks, *Automating Inequality*, particularly chap. 2.

9. Deleuze, "Postscript," 5.

10. Ibid.

11. Ibid., 6.

12. Two vital books for further fleshing out this conversation are Bratton, *The Stack*, and Hu, *A Prehistory of the Cloud*.

13. Gleick, "The End of Cash."

14. Chaum, "Blind Signatures," 199.

15. US Congress, "Federal Government Information Technology."

16. Chaum, as quoted in Greenberg, *This Machine Kills Secrets*, 65. Patents cited include "Electronic lock that can learn to recognize any ordinary key" (6318137) and "Physical and digital secret ballot systems" (20010034640).

17. Biagioli, "From Ciphers to Confidentiality."

18. Chaum, "Prepaid Smart Card Techniques."

19. Chaum, "Security without Identification."

20. Finney, "Protecting Privacy with Electronic Cash," 12.

21. Chaum, "Achieving Electronic Privacy."

22. Gleick, "The End of Cash."

23. See Levy, *Crypto*, 293; Röckelein and Maier, "A Common Currency System"; Gleick, "The End of Cash."

24. Blanchette, *Burdens of Proof*, 60.

25. This opening up of a design space can be read alongside the reinterpretation of computing in the service of liberation described in Turner, *From Counterculture to Cyberculture*.

26. For the general context of the political battle with central banking and its relation to cryptocurrency, see Golumbia, *The Politics of Bitcoin*. One interesting area for further research—unfortunately outside the scope of this book—is the "digital bearer certificate" project developed by Robert Hettinga. Hettinga was a regular cypherpunk correspondent, and his proposals and research suggest an alternative approach that post-Chaum digital money could have taken.

27. Finney, "Why remailers . . . ."

28. Pitta, "Requiem."

29. Narayanan, "What Happened to the Crypto Dream?," 3.

CHAPTER 5: COLLAPSE OF GOVERNMENTS

1. These four paragraphs, including all quotes, are based on her account (Milhon, "Secretions").

2. Jude and Community Memory have been extensively discussed: see Levy, *Hackers*, particularly chap. 8; Felsenstein, "Community Memory"; Doub, "Community Memory"; and Brand, "Spacewar!"

3. Levy, *Hackers*.

4. Liška, "St. Jude's Legacy."

5. All quotes in this paragraph are from Milhon, "Secretions."

6. Meieran, Engel, and May, "Measurement of Alpha Particle Radioactivity," 20–21.

7. For an outstanding journalistic account of the legacies of crypto anarchy and the birth of WikiLeaks—including many of the same people in this book but concerned with whistle-blowing and disclosure rather than money, see Greenberg, *This Machine Kills Secrets*.

8. Hughes, "Nuts & Acorns."

9. May, "Libertaria in Cyberspace."

10. May, "The Cyphernomicon," 17.3.1.

11. May, "The Crypto Anarchist Manifesto."

12. Ibid.

13. May, "The Cyphernomicon," 17.3.1.

14. Ibid.

15. Benkler, *Wealth of Networks*—particularly chap. 3.

16. May, "The Cyphernomicon," 17.3.1.

17. Hughes, "Nuts & Acorns."

18. May, "The Cyphernomicon," 16.3.4.

19. Stadd, "NASA Headquarters Oral History Project."

20. As quoted in Peterson, "Shuttle Pricing," 12.

21. As quoted in Dyson, "Making Markets," 2.

22. Orr, "Join the Information Economy."

23. Ott, "For Your Information."

24. Dyson, "Information, Bid and Asked," 92.

25. Dyson, "Making Markets," 5.

26. For context on Brand and *Spacewar!*, see Turner, *From Counterculture to Cyberculture*, particularly chap. 4.

27. Brand, "Spacewar!"

28. Which, as a practical matter, we almost always do. For an explanation of this and, more profoundly, the challenge of transmission, storage, and replication over noisy channels, see Sterne, *MP3*.

29. For a striking alternative to this argument, see DuPont, "Blockchain Identities."

30. There's a lot to say about this that exceeds the mission of this book, but some good places to start include Kirschenbaum, *Mechanisms*, and his distinction between forensic and formal materiality; Schwartz, *The Culture of the Copy*, particularly chap. 6; and Boon, *In Praise of Copying*, also particularly chap. 6.

31. For more information and considerable insight into Zuse's data storage filmstrips as the intersection of media and computing, see Manovich, *The Language of New Media*, particularly chap. 1.

32. There is an immense literature on this topic; for this book's questions, particularly around duplication and ownership, I would recommend Johns, *Piracy*, as a reference point.

33. Dyson, "Making Markets," 5.

34. Kevin Kelly, a contemporary of Dyson's who edited *Wired* magazine during the stretch when it profiled the cypherpunks and published Wolf's epic account of the Xanadu fiasco—he also wrote at length about digital cash in *Out of Control*—has provided a thoughtful answer to this question, based in the mistakes of past predictions, in several sections of his 2016 book *The Inevitable*.

35. May, "Timed-Release Crypto."

36. As did Rivest, Shamir, and Wagner, along with developing public key cryptography and micropayment systems: see their "Time-Lock Puzzles."

37. The acronymic name is also a computer science in-joke: an XOR—"exclusive or"—is a logical operation that returns a result of 1 only when the inputs differ: 1 XOR 1 gives 0, and 0 XOR 1 gives 1. On such a simple basis you can build very complex things.

38. Xanadu's significance as a concept is hard to overstate, and there is much prior scholarship on the project. For a start, see Barnet, *Memory Machines*; Harpold, *Exfoliations*, chap. 2; and Rayward, "Visions of Xanadu."

39. Nelson, *Literary Machines*, 1/35.

40. Walker, *The Autodesk File*, 500.

41. Ibid., 499.

42. Ibid., 843.

43. Nelson, *Literary Machines*, 0/5.

44. Ibid., 1/25.

45. Ibid., 2/29.

46. Ibid., 2/43.

47. Ibid., 4/29.

48. See under "The Rule of Scarcity" on http://www.caplet.com/adages.html.

49. Miller also claims to have independently invented the hierarchical navigation interface through nested directories that is now commonplace—most familiar from iTunes and the Mac OS X "column view"—as "Miller Columns" in 1980.

50. Nelson, *Computer Lib/Dream Machines*, 41.

51. Miller, Tribble, Pandya, and Stiegler, "The Open Society and Its Media," 18.

52. http://www.overcomingbias.com/2006/11/first_known_bus.html.

53. Walker, *The Autodesk File*, 424.

54. Greenberg, *This Machine Kills Secrets*, 59.

55. May, "Re: Anguilla—A DataHaven?"

CHAPTER 6: PERMANENT FRONTIERS

1. May, "Re: Wired & Batch File."

2. Turner, *From Counterculture to Cyberculture*, 6, 73.

3. These terms from: May, "Re: HACKERS: Crypto Session Being Planned."

4. Vinge, "The Coming Technological Singularity," 12.

5. Vinge, *True Names*, 245.

6. Dai, "Cypherpunks and Guns."

7. Vinge, *True Names*, 285.

8. May, "Re: Blacknet Worries."

9. For the record: the cypherpunk mailing list, the alt.extropian newsgroup, and the newsgroup alt.fan.david-sternlight—an inside joke, Sternlight being famously dubious, touchy, and trollish in his dislike for some applications of cryptography.

10. This phenomenon (including my examples) is described in Rubery, *The Novelty of Newspapers*, chap. 2.

11. For those playing along at home: "Don't let JS see you look at advertisement."

12. May, "Introduction to BlackNet," 242. If you are curious to see May's original, anonymous post and the reaction to it, it was forwarded to the cypherpunk mailing list from one of the recipients (Timothy Newsham) on August 18, 1993, under the subject line "no subject (file transmission)." It can be found in the archive at https://cypher punks.venona.com/raw/cyp-1993.txt.

13. This is quoted from his excellent history of BlackNet's launch and its aftermath, including issues we can't attend to here, like the "assassination market": Rid, *Rise of the Machines*, 278.

14. More, *Utopia*, 249.

15. May, "Introduction to BlackNet," 241.

16. An excellent discussion of the resemblance and connections is Sterling, "The Blast Shack"; see also Rid, *Rise of the Machines*.

17. Brunton, "Keyspace."

18. Hughes, "No Subject"; May, "A Minor Experimental Result."

19. Swartz, "Blockchain Dreams," 85.

20. Turner, "Prototype," 256.

21. Ibid., 259.

22. Lewis, "On Line with William Gibson."

23. Barlow, "Crime and Puzzlement."

24. Turner, "Can We Write a Cultural History of the Internet?," 40.

25. May, "The Cyphernomicon," 8.4.22 and 4.8.2.

26. May, "Introduction to BlackNet," 241.

27. Barlow, "A Cyberspace Independence Declaration."

28. The term "settler frontier" is from Richards, *The Unending Frontier*, 6: frontiers that "required the active political, military, and fiscal engagement and support of an aggrandizing state."

29. May, "The Cyphernomicon," 16.21.5.

30. Barlow, "A Cyberspace Independence Declaration."

31. May, "Untraceable Digital Cash."

32. Stallman, "What Is Free Software?"

33. Martinson, "Another Pax-Type Remailer."

34. Ibid.

CHAPTER 7: NANOSECOND SUITCASE

1. Mitchell, "The Contributions of Grace Murray Hopper," 68.

2. Ibid., 39.

3. For present, practical purposes, that is, setting aside things like quantum entanglement for now.

4. Williams, "Improbable Warriors," 112.

5. Mitchell, "The Contributions of Grace Murray Hopper," 63.

6. A related idea—which Back was not aware of during the development of hashcash—was described in 1992 by Dwork and Naor, "Pricing via Processing." Rivest also proposed antispam applications of the 2004 Peppercoin system he developed with Silvio Micali. See Rivest, "Peppercoin Micropayments."

7. Knott, "Hashing Functions," 275.

8. Morris, "Scatter Storage Techniques."

9. Kirschenbaum, *Mechanisms*, 177.

10. Ibid., 85.

11. Finney, "RPOW Theory."

12. For the sake of accuracy, it bears mentioning that Google engineers and the CWI Amsterdam were in fact able to engineer a collision for SHA-1 in February of 2017: to produce identical hashes for different data, endangering various SHA-1–based systems for certification and signing—but the work described here precedes that demonstration. See https://security.googleblog.com/2017/02/announcing-first-sha1-collision.html.

13. "Post-Office Stamps as Currency."

14. Szabo, "Trusted Third Parties Are Security Holes."

15. Szabo, "Bit Gold." This is quoted from his more formal elaboration of the idea in 2005. In 1999 (Szabo, "Intrapolynomial Cryptography"), he referred to "hashcash, MicroMint, bit gold, etc." in the context of benchmark functions; in 1998 (Szabo, "Secure Property Titles with Owner Authority"), he described an aspect of the bit gold system in depth.

16. May, "The Cyphernomicon," 6.3.3.

17. May, "The Cyphernomicon," 6.8.3.

18. May, "Re: Guns: H&K."

19. Dai, "Cypherpunks and Guns."

20. Dai, "PipeNet 1.1 and B-Money."

21. Finney, "Re: Currency Based on Energy."

22. Ibid.

23. It would not be a simple thing to implement—as Bitcoin subsequently demonstrated—and Dai proposed some alternatives: he discussed ways to rely on a set of centralized servers, since keeping synchrony between all those individual ledgers was a considerable challenge, and ways for participants to bid on the difficulty of minting new money to keep the price, in computational work, theoretically fair.

24. Nakamoto, "Citation of Your B-Money Page."

25. Nakamoto, "Re: Citation of Your B-Money Page."

26. Finney, "Re: Currency Based on Energy."

CHAPTER 8: HAYEK IN BIOSTASIS

1. More, "Editorial."

2. More, "Denationalisation of Money," 19.

3. Ibid., 20.

4. "Introduction," 3.

5. A superb summary of the phenomenon of air-mindedness, analyzed in parallel with computing, is available in Edgerton, *The Shock of the Old*.

6. More, "The Extropian Principles," 17.

7. Arne Naess, who sat with the Circle—and would go on to develop the theory of deep ecology—handed out a questionnaire on the streets of Vienna with only one question: "How do you decide what is true?"

8. Mises, *Human Action*, 32.

9. The summary here draws primarily on Hayek, *The Denationalization of Money* and *The Market and Other Orders*; Mises, *Notes and Recollections* (particularly chaps. 1 and 4, and part 4) and *The Theory of Money and Credit*; O'Driscoll and Rizzo, *Austrian Economics Re-examined*; and Jones, *Masters of the Universe*.

10. When he first used this term, Popper referred to "utopian social engineering"; by the time he wrote *The Open Society*, he summarized it as "utopian engineering" (Popper, *Open Society*, 148).

11. Hayek, *Law, Legislation, and Liberty, Vol. 2*, 108–9.

12. It's beyond the scope of this book, but this project has interesting relationships with the set of ideas and political commitments subsequently dubbed "accelerationism." The Cybernetic Culture Research Unit in the UK, one of the agenda setters of accelerationist ideas, were the pessimistic contemporary cousins of the Extropians; they played out a dystopian end game from the same premises, likewise encouraging bubble economies and the invention of new currencies—though in a rhetorical, techno-Gothic spirit that produced no working prototypes.

13. Appadurai, "The Spirit of Calculation," 9, and the larger argument in the context of his *Banking on Words*. See also Zaloom, *Out of the Pits*.

14. Marx, *Grundrisse*, 410.

15. "Spontaneous Orders," 7.

16. Yow, "Mindsurfing."

17. Cypher, "Magic Money Digicash System."

18. Finney, "Protecting Privacy with Electronic Cash."

19. Chaum, "Security without Identification," 1030.

20. Most notably, the autodidact artificial intelligence philosopher Eliezer Yudkowsky, who seeks a kind of predictive conversation with the superintelligence-to-be, and the neoreactionary, racist, and "neocameralist" (imagine a monarchist Technocracy Inc.) software developer Curtis "Mencius Moldbug" Yarvin . . . but

that's another book. Yarvin is currently leading development on Urbit, a clean-slate redesign of cloud computing: "If Bitcoin is digital money," said Yarvin, "Urbit is digital land."

21. Hanson, "Idea Futures," 9.

22. Potvin, "A Solicitation." The date is based on his posting to the Extropian list (Potvin, "Extropians' Net Worths").

23. SEC v. SG Ltd. (2001). No. CIV. A. 00-11141-JLT.

24. Brekke, "Money for Nothing."

25. May, "Untraceable Digital Cash."

26. Spang, *Stuff and Money*, 272.

27. Bell, "Extropia."

28. Machado, "Five Things."

29. Bishop, "my EXTRO 3 perspective"; Szabo, "Future Forecasts," "Intrapolynomial Cryptography," and "Bit Gold."

CHAPTER 9: FUTURE DESIRES

1. Finney, "Exercise and Longevity."

2. This text is excerpted from several different drafts in "The Cryonics Bracelet Contest."

3. Romain, "Extreme Life Extension," 4.

4. de Wolf, "Deconstructing Future Shock," 5.

5. Platt, "Hamburger Helpers," 14.

6. "Excitations/Advances," 6–7.

7. Simberg, "The Frozen Frontier."

8. Lanouette, *Genius in the Shadows*, chapter 16.

9. Szilard, "Memoirs," 4.

10. Ettinger, "The Penultimate Trump."

11. It is not a story of cold sleep, but Edward Bellamy's *Looking Backward* deserves honorable mention here: Julian West, the main character, is hypnotically preserved to reach a new economic future—including "credit cards," a term Bellamy coined. "This card is issued for a certain number of dollars," the future's inhabitant says of the "piece of pasteboard" he hands West. "We have kept the old word, but not the substance. The term, as we use it, answers to no real thing, but merely serves as an algebraical symbol for comparing the values of products with one another."

12. Szilard, "The Mark Gable Foundation," 2.

13. This section is based closely on Krementsov, *Revolutionary Experiments* and *A Martian Stranded on Earth*.

14. Hayek, *The Constitution of Liberty*, 32.

15. Hayek, *Law, Legislation, and Liberty, Vol. 3*, 176.

16. Hayek, *Law, Legislation, and Liberty, Vol. 1*, 38.

17. Ibid., 42.

18. Robin, "Wealth and the Intellectuals." The future-oriented oligarch Hayek anticipates shares a type with the ideal corporate leader, as described by Schumpeter: with a "critical receptivity to new facts," always awake to the next thing, possessed of "extraordinary physical and nervous energy" (Schumpeter, "The Rise and Fall of Families," 123).

19. Drinan, "Review: *Law, Legislation, and Liberty (Volume 3)*," 621.

20. Hayek, *The Constitution of Liberty*, 40.

21. Where to begin rebutting Hayek's claim here? Virtually none of the history of technology corresponds to this account; the excellent place to start is the analysis of innovation, invention, distribution, and production given by Edgerton, *The Shock of the Old*.

CHAPTER 10: EMERGENCY MONEY

1. Brunnermeier, "Deciphering the Liquidity and Credit Crunch."

2. Nakamoto, "Bitcoin P2P e-Cash Paper."

3. To choose three objections: "We very, very much need such a system," wrote cryptographer and cypherpunk James Donald in reply to Nakamoto (Donald, "Bitcoin P2P e-Cash Paper"). "But the way I understand your proposal, it does not seem to scale to the required size." "I think the real issue with this system is the market for bitcoins," another list regular wrote (Dillinger, "Bitcoin P2P e-Cash Paper"). "Computing proofs-of-work have no intrinsic value." Noting a potential concern in the proof-of-work system itself, John Levine—a longtime figure in the world of Internet and email security and trust—pointed out: "This is the same reason that hashcash can't work on today's Internet—the good guys have vastly less computational firepower than the bad guys. I also have my doubts about other issues, but this one is the killer" (Levine, "Bitcoin P2P e-Cash Paper").

4. This initial reception and discussion has been described in journalistic accounts, most notably Popper, *Digital Gold*, conclusion of chap. 2.

5. The reclusive mathematician Shinichi Mochizuki, whose work on the ABC Conjecture has to do with a puzzle about the frequency of prime factors and the additive and multiplicative properties of numbers. There is no particular reason to assume Mochizuki is Nakamoto.

6. Nakamoto, "Re: Citation of Your B-Money Page."

7. Finney, "Bitcoin P2P e-Cash Paper."

8. Diffie and Hellman, "New Directions in Cryptography," 654.

9. Nakamoto, "Bitcoin P2P e-Cash Paper."

10. Greenfield, *Radical Technologies*, chap. 5, provides a superb and lucid explanation for how Bitcoin works for the layperson, including this description of just how little the "consensus" model may reflect common use of the word: "Dissent may persist for a while, but it will expire gradually, as one candidate sequence crosses the threshold past which the likelihood that it can be challenged dwindles toward zero. All mining nodes eventually converge on this single longest chain, which becomes canonical once all its onetime competitors have fallen by the wayside."

11. Nakamoto, "Bitcoin v0.1 Released."

12. For an analysis of Bitcoin's place in the larger world of ledger-based money, see Maurer, "Money as Token and Money as Record."

13. Nelson, *Literary Machines*, 2/29.

14. A good example of the former is the DarkWallet project (https://www.darkwallet.is); the most technically interesting version of a truly anonymous cryptocurrency, at this writing, is the Zcash project (https://z.cash). Amir Taaki, who was the lead developer on DarkWallet and is now starting the Autonomous Polytechnics Group, is by far the most philosophically and politically interesting person in the Bitcoin world; his work rewards investigation.

15. Hern, "Missing: Hard Drive Containing Bitcoins."

16. This address currently holds 8,000 BTC, all produced in a two-month period in 2009, corresponding to Howells's remembered dates. The address has never had an outgoing transaction and has been completely inactive since April 26, 2009—except for an odd scattering of incoming transactions in extremely small amounts beginning in 2014. I believe these are a side effect of the address being used as a sample address in a few pieces of Bitcoin software at that time and subsequently.

17. Hillis, "The Connection Machine."

18. For the conjoined history of computing and air conditioning, see Brunton, "Heat Exchanges."

19. Kolodzey, "CRAY-1 Computer Technology."

20. Cray, "U.S. Patent No. 4,590,538."

21. Shirriff, "Mining Bitcoin with Pencil and Paper."

22. All of this is just solving hashing problems, not trying to do something like signing a Bitcoin transaction, which involves multiplying a lot of very large integers.

23. Keynes, *The General Theory of Employment, Interest and Money*, 129.

24. Nakamoto, "Bitcoin," 4.

25. Maurer, Nelms, and Swartz, "When Perhaps the Real Problem Is Money Itself!," 2.

26. The site for the P2P Foundation requires a birthdate, which it then reflects in the profile's posted age: http://p2pfoundation.ning.com/profile/Satoshi Nakamoto?xg_source=activity. The cryptomarket analyst gwern (https://www

.gwern.net) looking for the incrementing of the age through the archive of the P2P Foundation found that it fell on April 5, 1975.

27. Metzger, "ADMIN: No Money Politics, Please."

CHAPTER 11: ESCAPE GEOGRAPHIES

1. von NotHaus and Presley, "To Know Value."

2. Ibid., 12, 14, 17.

3. "New Liberty Dollar."

4. This appears in the text on the warehouse receipts and can be seen reproduced on a specimen copy. For instance, see Exhibit C, as reproduced in Shelter Systems, "Motion for Return," 33.

5. As entered into evidence in Shelter Systems, "Motion for Return" (from the affidavit), 11.

6. Keynes, "The General Theory of Employment," 213.

7. von NotHaus, "The Nazi-ization of America," 492.

8. Silk Road trial: Government Exhibit 270, 14 Cr. 68 (KBF).

9. For an outstanding survey of the DGC space, see Mullan, *A History of Digital Currency*. The notes on e-gold are from chap. 2 and the primary sources cited there.

10. Smith, *The Rationale of Central Banking*, 169–70.

11. Greenberg, "Collected Quotations of the Dread Pirate Roberts."

12. Heinlein, *The Moon Is a Harsh Mistress*, 155.

13. Rand, *Atlas Shrugged*, 384.

14. Ibid., 253, 258.

15. Stiefel, *The Story of Operation Atlantis*.

16. Craib, "Escape Geographies and Libertarian Enclosures."

17. The fate and operating details of Operation Atlantis are from the research and recollections of Strauss, *How to Start Your Own Country*, and Halliday, "Operation Atlantis."

18. My brief summary of Minerva and the Phoenix Foundation is drawn from Craib, "Escape Geographies," along with McDougall ("Micronations in the Caribbean"), Lindstrom ("Cult and Culture"), and Strauss (*How to Start Your Own Country*). See Craib's in-progress book for a deeper analysis; the working title is *Libertarian Noir: Exit, Enclosure, and the Age of Right Flight*. An excellent, concise summary of the Minerva situation in the context of taxation and sovereignty is available in chap. 3 of van Fossen, *Tax Havens*.

19. Lindstrom, "Cult and Culture" 117.

20. "1997 MIT $1K Warm-Up Business Idea Competition," available (still!) at http://web.mit.edu/~mkgray/afs/bar/afs/athena/activity/other/50k/old-www/1k97/1k97-summary.htm.

21. Lackey, "Starting an e-Cash Bank."

22. The article was Garfinkel, "Welcome to Sealand." Along with other cited materials from this section, I encourage reading the very entertaining account of Sealand and the cypherpunks in Rid, *Rise of the Machines*, chap. 7.

23. For a superb overview of the legal situation itself and the extensive and profoundly strange related criminal activities, see Grimmelmann, "Sealand, HavenCo, and the Rule of Law."

24. Johns, *Death of a Pirate*, particularly chap. 8.

25. As quoted in Rid, *Rise of the Machines*, 281.

26. Lackey's account of what happened is based on his slide deck for DEF CON following his departure from Sealand (Lackey, "HavenCo: What Really Happened").

CHAPTER 12: DESOLATE EARTH

1. For a detailed argument about the records and histories embedded in money, including coins, see Maurer, "Money as Token."

2. Pettersson, *The Spillings Hoard*. Famously, a single Khazar coin in that particular hoard—the "Moses coin"—provided a material trace of the conversion of the Khazar dynasty to Judaism, a significant and much debated moment in a complex history. For an overview of how coinage—hoarded and minted—can help us understand the Khazar, see Kovalev, "What Does Historical Numismatics Suggest."

3. MacGregor, *A History of the World in 100 Objects*, chap. 95.

4. See Desan, "Coin Reconsidered" (particularly 403–9) for a fascinating account of debasement and "competitive debasement"; two insightful accounts of the practice and meaning of cutting, clipping, or destroying coins are Caffentzis, *Clipped Coins*, and von Glahn, *Fountain of Fortune*, chap. 3.

5. There is a wonderful and thorough account of the history of the thaler in Weatherford, *The History of Money*, chap. 7.

6. Addison, *Dialogues upon the Usefulness of Ancient Medals* and "Autobiography of a Shilling." See also the fascinating explication of Addison and coinage in Spicer, *The Mind is a Collection*, particularly exhibit 13.

7. Spang, *Stuff and Money*, 272.

8. Stadter, "Alexander Hamilton's Notes on Plutarch."

9. Franklin, "A Modest Enquiry."

10. Trettien, "Leaves."

11. Another interesting variant of this idea was the Weimar German *Rentenmark*. For an excellent summary of this project and its context, see Taylor, *The Downfall of Money*, 326–335.

12. For a general overview of this extraordinary conversation, see Steil, *The Battle of Bretton Woods*; for more on Keynes's plan, see Keynes, "International Clearing Union." Later, in a strange turn of events, White would be revealed as a kind of financial spy, working covertly for the Soviet Union to aid their postwar economic success, apparently under the conviction that the stability of the new global order relied on the prosperity of *both* superpowers rather than the triumph of one or the other; among other things, he arranged the Soviet receipt of duplicate plates for printing Allied marks, the legal tender of the postwar German occupation. See Craig, *Treasonable Doubt.*

13. Lovell, *Of Spies and Stratagems*, 29.

14. As quoted in Ahamed, *Lords of Finance*, 20.

15. Mises, *Human Action*, 173.

16. The topic of the assault rifle is covered by del Castillo, "Dark Wallet," and Wilson, *Come and Take It*. The site for the T-shirt company, 7bucktees, has lapsed but can be found in the Internet archive: https://web.archive.org/web/20160412110430/http://www.7bucktees.com/product-category/t-shirts/.

17. Ver is memorably chronicled in Abrahamian, *The Cosmopolites*, particularly chap. 5.

18. The site (passportsforbitcoin.com) has been taken offline but remains available through the Internet archive. It has been the subject of controversy, as you would imagine; for an account of the project's early days, see Clenfield and Alpeyev, " 'Bitcoin Jesus' Calls Rich to Tax-Free Tropical Paradise."

19. Milhon, "Secretions."

20. Thiel, "The Education of a Libertarian."

21. Dowd, "Peter Thiel."

22. See Nock, "Isaiah's Job"; for the effect of these ideas on American conservativism and particularly William F. Buckley, Jr., see Judis, *William F. Buckley, Jr.*, 44–46.

23. For a beautiful evocation of blockchain-based communal property—as well as a few blockchain and cryptocurrency nightmare outcomes—see Greenfield, *Radical Technologies*, chap. 10.

24. Dodd, "The Social Life of Bitcoin," 21.

CONCLUSION: SOMETIME IN THE FUTURE

1. Manley, "The Erg Man."

2. For a detailed overview of these changes, including the wild ride through 2013–2014, see Wolfson, "Bitcoin: The Early Market."

3. Greenberg, "Nakamoto's Neighbor."

4. More, "Hal Finney Being Cryopreserved Now."

BIBLIOGRAPHY

Abrahamian, Atossa. *The Cosmopolites: The Coming of the Global Citizen.* New York: Columbia Global Reports, 2015.

Addison, Joseph. "Autobiography of a Shilling." *Tatler,* no. 249, November 11, 1710.

———. *Dialogues upon the Usefulness of Ancient Medals: Especially in Relation to the Latin and Greek Poets.* Published 1726. https://quod.lib.umich.edu/cgi/t/text/text-idx?c=ecco;idno=004788594.0001.000.

Ahamed, Liaquat. *Lords of Finance: The Bankers Who Broke the World.* New York: Penguin, 2009.

Akin, William. *Technocracy and the American Dream: The Technocrat Movement, 1900–1941.* Berkeley: University of California Press, 1977.

Appadurai, Arjun. "The Spirit of Calculation." *Cambridge Journal of Anthropology* 30, no. 1 (Spring 2012): 3–17.

———. *Banking on Words: The Failure of Language in the Age of Derivative Finance.* Chicago: University of Chicago Press, 2015.

Armer, Paul. "Computer Technology and Surveillance." *Computers and People* 24, no. 9 (September 1975): 8–11.

Atwood, Margaret. *The Handmaid's Tale.* New York: Houghton Mifflin, 1986.

Barlow, John Perry. "Crime and Puzzlement." June 8, 1990. Electronic Frontier Foundation list archive: https://w2.eff.org/Misc/Publications/John_Perry_Barlow/HTML/crime_and_puzzlement_1.html.

———. "A Cyberspace Independence Declaration." February 9, 1996. Electronic Frontier Foundation list archive: http://www.eff.org/Publications/John_Perry_Barlow/barlow_0296.declaration.

Barnet, Belinda. *Memory Machines: The Evolution of Hypertext.* London: Anthem, 2013.

Belasco, Warren. *Meals to Come: A History of the Future of Food.* Berkeley: University of California Press, 2006.

Bell, Tom. "Extropia: A Home for Our Hopes." *Extropy* 8 (Winter 1991/1992): 35–41.

Beniger, James. *The Control Revolution: Technological and Economic Origins of the Information Society.* Cambridge, MA: Harvard University Press, 1986.

Benjamin, Walter. "One-Way Street." In *Selected Writings Volume 1: 1913–1926,* edited by M. Bullock and M. W. Jennings, 444–88. Cambridge, MA: Belknap Harvard, 1996.

Benkler, Yochai. *The Wealth of Networks: How Social Production Transforms Markets and Freedom.* New Haven, CT: Yale University Press, 2006.

Bennett, James, and Phillip Salin. "Privatizing Space Transportation." Issue paper no. 102, Federal Privatization Project. Santa Monica, CA: Reason Foundation, 1987.

Biagioli, Mario. "From Ciphers to Confidentiality: Secrecy, Openness and Priority in Science." *British Society for the History of Science*, 2012. https://ssrn.com/abstract =2427952.

Bishop, Forrest. "my EXTRO 3 perspective." ExI-list archive, August 12, 1995. http:// extropians.weidai.com/extropians.3Q97/1794.html.

Blanchette, Jean-François. *Burdens of Proof: Cryptographic Culture and Evidence Law in the Age of Electronic Documents.* Cambridge, MA: MIT Press, 2012.

Boon, Marcus. *In Praise of Copying.* Cambridge, MA: Harvard University Press, 2010.

Brand, Stewart. "Spacewar! Fanatic Life and Symbolic Death among the Computer Bums." *Rolling Stone*, December 7, 1972. http://wheels.org/spacewar/stone/rolling _stone.html

Bratton, Ben. *The Stack: On Software and Sovereignty.* Cambridge, MA: MIT Press, 2016.

Brekke, Dan. "Money for Nothing." *Wired* 8, no. 9 (September 2000). https://www .wired.com/wired/archive/8.09/stock.html

Brunnermeier, Markus. "Deciphering the Liquidity and Credit Crunch 2007–2008." *Journal of Economic Perspectives* 23, no. 1 (Winter 2009): 77–100.

Brunton, Finn. "Keyspace: WikiLeaks and the Assange Papers." *Radical Philosophy* 166 (March/April 2011): 8–20.

———. "Heat Exchanges." In *The MoneyLab Reader: An Intervention in Digital Economy,* edited by Geert Lovink, Nathaniel Tkacz, and Patricia de Vries. Amsterdam: Institute of Network Cultures, 2015.

Caffentzis, Constantine. *Clipped Coins, Abused Words, Civil Government: John Locke's Philosophy of Money.* New York: Autonomedia, 1989.

Chaum, David. "Blind Signatures for Untraceable Payments." In *Advances in Cryptology: Proceedings of Crypto 82*, edited by David Chaum, Ronald L. Rivest, and Alan T. Sherman, 199–203. New York: Plenum Press, 1983.

———. "Security without Identification: Transaction Systems to Make Big Brother Obsolete." *Comm. ACM* 28, no. 10 (1985): 1030–44.

———. "Achieving Electronic Privacy." *Scientific American,* August 1992, 96–101.

———. "Prepaid Smart Card Techniques: A Brief Introduction and Comparison." DigiCash, 1994. http://ntrg.cs.tcd.ie/mepeirce/Project/Chaum/cardcom.html.

Clenfield, Jason, and Pavel Alpeyev. " 'Bitcoin Jesus' Calls Rich to Tax-Free Tropical Paradise." *Bloomberg Technology*, June 16, 2014. https://www.bloomberg.com/ news/articles/2014-06-15/-bitcoin-jesus-calls-rich-to-tax-free-tropical-paradise.

Craib, Raymond. "Escape Geographies and Libertarian Enclosures." Presentation at Yale's Program in Agrarian Studies, February 2015. https://agrarianstudies.mac millan.yale.edu/sites/default/files/files/CraibAgrarianStudies.pdf.

Craig, R. Bruce. *Treasonable Doubt: The Harry Dexter White Spy Case*. Lawrence: University Press of Kansas, 2004.

Cray, Seymour. "U.S. Patent No. 4,590,538: Immersion Cooled High Density Electronic Assembly." US Patent Office, November 18, 1982.

"The Cryonics Bracelet Contest: Top Contenders." *Cryonics* 7, no. 10 (October 1986): 10–18.

Cypher, Pr0duct. "Magic Money Digicash System." Cypherpunks list archive, February 4, 1994. https://cypherpunks.venona.com/date/1994/02/msg00247.html.

Dai, Wei. "Cypherpunks and guns." Cypherpunks list archive, January 6, 1998. http://cypherpunks.venona.com/date/1998/01/msg00115.html.

———. "PipeNet 1.1 and b-money." Cypherpunks list archive, November 27, 1998. http://cypherpunks.venona.com/date/1998/11/msg00941.html.

del Castillo, Michael. "Dark Wallet: A Radical Way to Bitcoin." *New Yorker*, September 24, 2013. https://www.newyorker.com/business/currency/dark-wallet-a-radical-way-to-bitcoin.

Deleuze, Gilles. "Postscript on the Societies of Control." *October* 59 (Winter 1992): 3–7.

Deringer, William. "Pricing the Future in the Seventeenth Century: Calculating Technologies in Competition." *Technology and Culture* 58, no. 2 (April 2017): 506–28.

Desan, Christine. "Coin Reconsidered: The Political Alchemy of Commodity Money." *Theoretical Inquiries in Law* 11, no. 1, article 13 (January 2010): 361–409.

Desan, Christine. *Making Money: Coin, Currency, and the Coming of Capitalism*. Oxford: Oxford University Press, 2014.

de Wolf, Aschwin. "Deconstructing Future Shock." *Cryonics* 36, no. 2 (February 2015): 5.

Diffie, Whitfield, and Martin Hellman. "New Directions in Cryptography." *IEEE Transactions on Information Theory* IT-22, no. 6 (November 1976): 644–54.

Dillinger, Ray. "Bitcoin P2P e-Cash Paper." Cryptography mailing list, November 6, 2008. http://www.metzdowd.com/pipermail/cryptography/2008-November/014822.html.

Dodd, Nigel. *The Social Life of Money*. Princeton: Princeton University Press, 2014.

———. "The Social Life of Bitcoin." *Theory, Culture & Society* (2017): 1–26.

Donald, James. "Bitcoin P2P e-Cash Paper." Cryptography mailing list, November 2, 2008. http://www.metzdowd.com/pipermail/cryptography/2008-November/014814.html.

Doub, Bo. "Community Memory: Precedents in Social Media and Movements," *Computer History Museum* (blog), February 23, 2016. http://www.computerhistory.org/atchm/community-memory-precedents-in-social-media-and-movements/.

Dowd, Maureen. "Peter Thiel, Trump's Tech Pal, Explains Himself." *New York Times,* January 11, 2017.

Drinan, Robert. "Review: *Law, Legislation, and Liberty (Volume 3)." University of Chicago Law Review* 47, no. 3 (Spring 1980): 621–33.

DuPont, Quinn. "Blockchain Identities: Notational Technologies for Control and Management of Abstracted Entities." *Metaphilosophy* 48, no. 5 (October 2017): 634–53.

Dwiggins, W. A. *Towards a Reform of the Paper Currency, Particularly in Point of Its Design.* New York: Limited Editions Club, 1932. Reprint, New York: First Typophiles; Boston: Godine; Cambridge, MA: Kat Ran Press, 2015.

Dwork, Cynthia, and Moni Naor. "Pricing via Processing or Combatting Junk Mail." *Advances in Cryptology—CRYPTO' 92.* Berlin: Springer, 1993.

Dyson, Esther. "Making Markets." *Release 1.0,* July 14, 1990, 1–15.

———. "Information, Bid and Asked." *Forbes,* August 20, 1990, 92.

Edgerton, David. *The Shock of the Old: Technology and Global History since 1900.* London: Profile, 2008.

Elliott, Geoffrey. *The Shooting Star: Denis Rake, MC: A Clandestine Hero of the Second World War.* London: Methuen, 2009.

Ettinger, R.C.W. "The Penultimate Trump." *Startling Stories,* March 1948, 104–15.

Eubanks, Virginia. *Automating Inequality.* New York: St. Martin's Press, 2017.

"Excitations/Advances." *Extropy* 17, no. 8:2 (2nd Half 1996): 6–7.

Felsenstein, Lee. "Community Memory: The First Public-Access Social Media System." In *Social Media Archeology and Poetics,* edited by Judy Malloy, 89–102. Cambridge, MA: MIT Press, 2016.

Fezer, Harold. "The Energy Certificate." Technocracy Pamphlet Series A, no. 10, July 1938. http://www.technocracyinc.org/energy-certificate-2/.

Finney, Fran. "Exercise and Longevity." *Extropy* 9, no. 4:1 (Summer 1992): 30–33.

Finney, Hal. "Why remailers . . ." Cypherpunk mailing list, November 15, 1992. http://cypherpunks.venona.com/date/1992/11/msg00108.html.

———. "Protecting Privacy with Electronic Cash." *Extropy* 10, 1993, 8–14.

———. "RPOW Theory." RPOW.net. https://web.archive.org/web/20070528042614/http://rpow.net:80/theory.html.

———. "Re: Currency based on Energy." ExI-list archive, February 22, 2002. http://extropians.weidai.com/extropians.1Q02/3361.html.

———. "Bitcoin P2P e-Cash Paper." Cryptography mailing list, November 7, 2008. http://www.metzdowd.com/pipermail/cryptography/2008-November/014827.html.

Fitzsimons, Peter. *Nancy Wake: The Inspiring Story of One of the War's Greatest Heroines.* London: HarperCollins, 2002.

Franklin, Benjamin. "A Modest Enquiry into the Nature and Necessity of a Paper Currency." Philadelphia: Printed and sold at the New Printing-Office, near the Market, 1729. https://founders.archives.gov/documents/Franklin/01-01 -02-0041.

Frye, Curtis D. "Re: Forged messages part of "Operation"?" Cypherpunks list archive, January 10, 1994. http://cypherpunks.venona.com/date/1994/01/msg00117 .html.

Garfinkel, Simson. "Welcome to Sealand. Now Bugger Off." *Wired* 8 (July 2000). https://www.wired.com/2000/07/haven-2/.

Gesell, Silvio. *The Natural Economic Order.* London: Peter Owen, 1958.

Gibson, William. *Zero History.* New York: Putnam, 2010.

———. "The Art of Fiction No. 211" (interviewed by David Wallace-Wells). *Paris Review* 197 (Summer 2011).

Gibson-Graham, J. K. *The End of Capitalism (as We Knew It): A Feminist Critique of Political Economy.* Cambridge, MA: Blackwell, 1996.

Gilbert, Emily. "Forging a National Currency: Money, State-Building and Nation-Making in Canada." In *Nation-States and Money: The Past, Present and Future of National Currencies,* edited by Emily Gilbert and Eric Helleiner. New York: Routledge, 1999.

Gitelman, Lisa. *Paper Knowledge: Toward a Media History of Documents.* Durham, NC: Duke University Press, 2014.

Gleick, James. "The End of Cash." *New York Times Magazine,* June 16, 1996. https://www .nytimes.com/1996/06/16/magazine/dead-as-a-dollar.html.

Golumbia, David. *The Politics of Bitcoin: Software as Right-Wing Extremism.* Minneapolis: University of Minnesota Press, 2016.

Graeber, David. *Debt: The First 5,000 Years.* New York: Melville House Publishing, 2011.

Greenberg, Andy. *This Machine Kills Secrets: How WikiLeakers, Cypherpunks, and Hacktivists Aim to Free the World's Information.* New York: Dutton, 2012.

———. "Collected Quotations of the Dread Pirate Roberts, Founder of Underground Drug Site Silk Road and Radical Libertarian." *Forbes,* April 29, 2013. https:// www.forbes.com/sites/andygreenberg/2013/04/29/collected-quotations-of-the-dread-pirate-roberts-founder-of-the-drug-site-silk-road-and-radical-libertarian/.

———. "Nakamoto's Neighbor: My Hunt for Bitcoin's Creator Led to a Paralyzed Crypto Genius." *Forbes,* March 25, 2014. https://www.forbes.com/sites/an dygreenberg/2014/03/25/satoshi-nakamotos-neighbor-the-bitcoin-ghost writer-who-wasnt.

Greenberger, Martin. "The Computers of Tomorrow." *Atlantic* 213, no. 5 (May 1964): 63–67.

Greenfield, Adam. *Radical Technologies: The Design of Everyday Life.* New York: Verso, 2017.

Grimmelmann, James. "Sealand, HavenCo, and the Rule of Law." *University of Illinois Law Review* 405 (2012): 405–84.

Halliday, Roy. "Operation Atlantis and the Radical Libertarian Alliance: Observations of a Fly on the Wall." Royhalliday.com (website), February 13, 2002. http://roy halliday.home.mindspring.com/rla.htm.

Hanson, Robin. "Idea Futures: Encouraging an Honest Consensus." *Extropy* 8 (Winter 1991): 7–17.

Harpold, Terry. *Ex-foliations: Reading Machines and the Upgrade Path.* Minneapolis: University of Minnesota Press, 2009.

Hayek, Friedrich. *Law, Legislation, and Liberty, Vol. 1: Rules and Order.* Chicago: University of Chicago Press, 1973.

———. *Law, Legislation, and Liberty, Vol. 2: The Mirage of Social Justice.* Chicago: University of Chicago Press, 1977.

———. *Law, Legislation, and Liberty, Vol. 3: The Political Order of a Free People.* Chicago: University of Chicago Press, 1979.

———. *The Constitution of Liberty.* Chicago: University of Chicago Press, 1978.

———. *The Denationalization of Money—the Argument Refined: An Analysis of the Theory and Practice of Concurrent Currencies.* 3rd ed. London: Institute of Economic Affairs, 1990.

———. *The Market and Other Orders.* Chicago: University of Chicago Press, 1990.

Heinlein, Robert. *The Moon Is a Harsh Mistress.* New York: Orb, 1997.

Hern, Alex. "Missing: Hard Drive Containing Bitcoins Worth £4m in Newport Landfill Site." *Guardian,* November 27, 2013.

Hillis, William Daniel. "The Connection Machine." PhD dissertation, Prof. Gerald Sussman. Cambridge, MA: Massachusetts Institute of Technology, 1985.

"The Howland Will Case." *American Law Register (1852–1891)* 38, no. 9 (September 1890): 562–81.

Hu, Tung-Hui. *A Prehistory of the Cloud.* Cambridge, MA: MIT Press, 2015.

Hudson, Michael. "How Interest Rates Were Set, 2500 BC–1000 AD: *Máš, tokos* and *foenus* as Metaphors for Interest Accruals." *Journal of the Economic and Social History of the Orient* 43 (Spring 2000): 132–61.

Hughes, Eric. "No Subject." Cypherpunks list archive, September 21, 1992. http://cypherpunks.venona.com/date/1992/09/msg00001.html.

———. "Nuts & Acorns." Cypherpunks list archive, October 6, 1992. http://cypher punks.venona.com/date/1992/10/msg00020.html.

"Introduction." *Extropy* 1 (Fall 1988): 1–13.

Johns, Adrian. *Piracy: The Intellectual Property Wars from Gutenberg to Gates.* Chicago: University of Chicago Press, 2009.

———. *Death of a Pirate: British Radio and the Making of the Information Age.* New York: W. W. Norton, 2011.

Jones, Daniel Steadman. *Masters of the Universe: Hayek, Friedman, and the Birth of Neoliberal Politics.* Princeton, NJ: Princeton University Press, 2012.

Judis, John B. *William F. Buckley, Jr.: Patron Saint of the Conservatives.* New York: Simon & Schuster, 2001.

Kafka, Ben. *The Demon of Writing: Powers and Failures of Paperwork.* New York: Zone Books, 2012.

Kahn, David. *The Codebreakers: The Comprehensive History of Secret Communication from Ancient Times to the Internet.* New York: Simon & Schuster, 1996.

Kelly, Kevin. *Out of Control: The New Biology of Machines, Social Systems, and the Economic World.* New York: Basic Books, 1995.

———. *The Inevitable: Understanding the 12 Technological Forces That Will Shape Our Future.* New York: Viking, 2016.

Keynes, John Maynard. *The General Theory of Employment, Interest and Money.* London: Macmillan, 1936 (reprinted 2007).

———. "The General Theory of Employment." *Quarterly Journal of Economics* 51, no. 2 (February 1937): 209–23.

———. "The International Clearing Union." In *The New Economics: Keynes' Influence on Theory and Public Policy,* edited by Seymour Harris. New York: Knopf, 1947.

Kirschenbaum, Matthew. *Mechanisms: New Media and the Forensic Imagination.* Cambridge, MA: MIT Press, 2007.

Knott, G. D. "Hashing Functions." *Computer Journal* 18, no. 3 (January 1975): 265–78.

Kolodzey, James. "CRAY-1 Computer Technology." *IEEE Transactions on Components, Hybrids, and Manufacturing Technology* 4, no. 2 (June 1981): 181–86.

Koselleck, Reinhart. *The Practice of Conceptual History: Timing History, Spacing Concepts.* Stanford, CA: Stanford University Press, 2002.

———. *Futures Past: On the Semantics of Historical Time.* New York: Columbia, 2004.

Kovalev, Roman. "What Does Historical Numismatics Suggest about the Monetary History of Khazaria in the Ninth Century?—Question Revisited," *Archivum Eurasiae Medii Aevi* 13 (2004): 97–129.

Krementsov, Nikolai. *A Martian Stranded on Earth: Alexander Bogdanov, Blood Transfusions, and Proletarian Science.* Chicago: University of Chicago Press, 2011.

———. *Revolutionary Experiments: The Quest for Immortality in Bolshevik Science and Fiction.* Oxford: Oxford University Press, 2013.

Kuhn, Markus G. "The EURion Constellation." Security Group presentation, Computer Laboratory, University of Cambridge, February 8, 2002. http://www.cl.cam .ac.uk/~mgk25/eurion.pdf.

Lackey, Ryan. "Starting an e-Cash Bank." Cypherpunks list archive, December 30, 1995. http://cypherpunks.venona.com/date/1995/12/msg00969.html.

———. "HavenCo: What Really Happened." Presentation at DEF CON 11, August 3, 2003. http://www.metacolo.com/papers/dc11-havenco/dc11-havenco.pdf.

Lanouette, William. *Genius in the Shadows: A Biography of Leo Szilard, the Man behind the Bomb.* Chicago: University of Chicago Press, 1994.

Levine, John. "Bitcoin P2P e-Cash Paper." Cryptography mailing list, November 3, 2008. http://www.metzdowd.com/pipermail/cryptography/2008-November/014817.html.

Levy, Steven. "The Cypherpunks vs. Uncle Sam." In *Building in Big Brother: The Cryptographic Policy Debate,* edited by Lance J. Hoffman. Berlin: Springer, 1995.

———. *Crypto: How the Code Rebels Beat the Government—Saving Privacy in the Digital Age.* New York: Penguin, 2001.

———. *Hackers: Heroes of the Computer Revolution* (25th anniversary edition). Sebastopol, CA: O'Reilly, 2010.

Lewis, Peter. "On Line with William Gibson: Present at the Creation, Startled at the Reality." *New York Times,* May 22, 1995.

Licklider, J.C.R. "Memorandum for Members and Affiliates of the Intergalactic Computer Network." Advanced Research Projects Agency, April 23, 1963.

———. "Some Reflections on Early History." In *A History of Personal Workstations,* edited by Adele Goldberg. New York: Addison-Wesley, 1988.

Lindstrom, Monty. "Cult and Culture: American Dreams in Vanuatu." *Pacific Studies* 4, no. 2 (Spring 1981): 101–23.

Liška. "St. Jude's Legacy." July 18, 2015. http://unwittingraconteur.com/index.php/2015/07/18/st-judes-legacy/.

Lovell, Stanley. *Of Spies and Stratagems.* Englewood Cliffs, NJ: Prentice-Hall, 1962.

MacGregor, Neil. *A History of the World in 100 Objects.* New York: Penguin, 2013.

Machado, Romana. "Five Things You Can Do to Fight Entropy Now." September 12, 1994. http://www.euvolution.com/prometheism-transhumanism-posthumanism/transtopa-transhumanism-evolved/5things.html.

Manley, Jared. "The Erg Man." *New Yorker* 12, no. 37 (October 31, 1936): 19–21.

Manovich, Lev. *The Language of New Media.* Cambridge, MA: MIT Press, 2002.

Marks, Leo. *Between Silk and Cyanide: A Codemaker's Story, 1941–1945.* London: Harper Collins, 1998.

Martinson, Yanek. "Another pax-type remailer." Cypherpunks list archive, December 22, 1992. http://cypherpunks.venona.com/date/1992/12/msg00232.html.

Marx, Karl. *Grundrisse: Foundations of the Critique of Political Economy.* London: Penguin, 1973.

Maurer, Bill. *Mutual Life, Limited: Islamic Banking, Alternative Currencies, Lateral Reason.* Princeton, NJ: Princeton University Press, 2005.

————. "Money as Token and Money as Record in Distributed Accounts." In *Distributed Agency,* edited by N. J. Enfield and Paul Kockelman. Oxford: Oxford University Press, 2017.

Maurer, Bill, Taylor Nelms, and Lana Swartz. "'When Perhaps the Real Problem Is Money Itself!': The Practical Materiality of Bitcoin." *Social Semiotics* (2013). DOI:10.1080/10350330.2013.777594.

May, Timothy. "The Crypto Anarchist Manifesto." Cypherpunks list archive, November 22, 1992. http://cypherpunks.venona.com/date/1992/11/msg00204.html.

————. "A Minor Experimental Result." Cypherpunks list archive, December 13, 1992. http://cypherpunks.venona.com/date/1992/12/msg00124.html.

————. "Timed Release Crypto." Cypherpunks list archive, February 10, 1993. http://cypherpunks.venona.com/date/1993/02/msg00129.html.

————. "Re: Wired & Batch File." Cypherpunks list archive, February 11, 1993. http://cypherpunks.venona.com/date/1993/02/msg00159.html.

————. "Libertaria in Cyberspace." Cypherpunks list archive, August 9, 1993. http://cypherpunks.venona.com/date/1993/08/msg00168.html.

————. "Re: HACKERS: Crypto Session Being Planned." Cypherpunks list archive, October 7, 1993. http://cypherpunks.venona.com/date/1993/10/msg00307.html.

————. "Re: Blacknet Worries." Cypherpunks list archive, February 20, 1994. http://cypherpunks.venona.com/date/1994/02/msg01131.html.

————. "The Cyphernomicon: Cypherpunks FAQ and More." September 1994. https://web.archive.org/web/20170805063522/http://www.cypherpunks.to:80/faq/cyphernomicron/cyphernomicon.txt.

————. "Re: Anguilla—A DataHaven?" Cypherpunks list archive, August 14, 1996. http://cypherpunks.venona.com/date/1996/08/msg01155.html.

————. "Introduction to BlackNet." In *High Noon on the Electronic Frontier: Conceptual Issues in Cyberspace,* edited by Peter Ludlow. Cambridge, MA: MIT Press, 1996.

————. "Untraceable Digital Cash, Information Markets, and BlackNet." Talk at Computers, Freedom, and Privacy 1997. http://osaka.law.miami.edu/~froomkin/articles/tcmay.htm.

————. "Re: Guns: H&K, G3, 7.62 v 5.56 [Guns]" Cypherpunks list archive, January 2, 1998. http://cypherpunks.venona.com/date/1998/01/msg00006.html.

McCarthy, John. "The Home Information Terminal—A 1970 View." *Man and Computer: Proceedings of International Conference,* Bordeaux, 1970, 48–57. Basel: Karger, 1972.

McDougall, Russell. "Micronations of the Caribbean." In *Surveying the American Tropics: A Literary Geography from New York to Rio,* edited by Maria Cristina

Fumagalli, Peter Hulme, Owen Robinson, and Lesley Wylie. Liverpool: Liverpool University Press, 2013.

McKelway, St. Clair. "Mister Eight-Eighty." In *Reporting at Wit's End: Tales from the New Yorker*. New York: Bloomsbury, 2010.

McPhee, John. *Oranges*. New York: Farrar, Straus, and Giroux, 1966.

Meier, Paul, and Sandy Zabell. "Benjamin Peirce and the Howland Will." *Journal of the American Statistical Association* 75, no. 371 (September 1980): 497–506.

Meieran, E. S., P. R. Engel, and T. C. May. "Measurement of Alpha Particle Radioactivity in IC Device Packages." *17th Annual Reliability Physics Symposium*, 1979, 13–22.

Merkle, Ralph C. "Secure Communications over Insecure Channels." *Communications of the ACM* 21, no. 4 (1978): 294–99.

Metzger, Perry. "ADMIN: No Money Politics, Please." Cryptography mailing list, November 7, 2008. http://www.metzdowd.com/pipermail/cryptography/2008 -November/014824.html.

Michell, Humfrey. "The Iron Money of Sparta." *Phoenix*, supplement to vol. 1 (Spring 1947): 42–44.

Milhon, Judith. "Secretions." Cypherpunks list archive, September 25, 1992. http:// cypherpunks.venona.com/date/1992/09/msg00013.html.

———. "Public vs. Private." Cypherpunks list archive, October 3, 1992. http:// cypherpunks.venona.com/date/1992/10/msg00005.html.

Miller, Mark, E. Dean Tribble, Ravi Pandya, and Marc Stiegler. "The Open Society and Its Media." *Extropy* 12, no. 6:1 (1st Quarter 1994): 18–23.

Mises, Ludwig von. *The Theory of Money and Credit*. Rev. ed. New Haven, CT: Yale University Press, 1953.

———. *Human Action: A Treatise on Economics—the Scholar's Edition*. Auburn, AL: Ludwig von Mises Institute, 1998.

———. *Notes and Recollections, with the Historical Setting of the Austrian School of Economics*. Indianapolis: Liberty Fund, 2014.

Mitchell, Carmen L. "The Contributions of Grace Murray Hopper to Computer Science and Computer Education." PhD dissertation. Denton: University of North Texas, 1994.

More, Max. "The Extropian Principles." *Extropy* 6 (Summer 1990): 17–18.

———. "Denationalisation of Money: Friedrich Hayek's Seminal Work on Competing Private Currencies." *Extropy* 15, no. 7:2 (2nd/3rd Quarter 1995): 19–20.

———. "Editorial." *Extropy* 15, no. 7:2 (2nd/3rd Quarter 1995): 8.

———. "Hal Finney Being Cryopreserved Now." ExI-list archive, August 28, 2014. https://web.archive.org/web/20180611154221/http://lists.extropy.org/piper mail/extropy-chat/2014-August/082585.html.

More, Thomas. *Utopia*. Oxford: Clarendon Press, 1904.

Morris, Robert. "Scatter Storage Techniques." *Communications of the ACM* 11, no. 1 (January 1968): 38–44.

Morrisson, Mark S. *Modern Alchemy: Occultism and the Emergence of Atomic Theory*. Oxford: Oxford University Press, 2007.

Mullan, P. Carl. *A History of Digital Currency in the United States: New Technology in an Unregulated Market*. New York: Palgrave, 2016.

Murdoch, Steven J. "Software Detection of Currency." 2012. www.cl.cam.ac .uk/~sjm217/projects/currency/.

Murdoch, Steven J., and Ben Laurie. "The Convergence of Anti-counterfeiting and Computer Security." 21st Chaos Communication Congress, December 27–29, 2004. http://sec.cs.ucl.ac.uk/users/smurdoch/talks/ccc04_counterfeiting. pdf.

Nakamoto, Satoshi. "Bitcoin: A Peer-to-Peer Electronic Cash System." 2008. https://bitcoin.org/bitcoin.pdf.

———. "Citation of Your B-Money Page." Email to Wei Dai, August 22, 2008. http://www.gwern.net/docs/2008-nakamoto.

———. "Bitcoin P2P e-Cash Paper." Cryptography mailing list, October 31, 2008. http://www.metzdowd.com/pipermail/cryptography/2008-October/014810. html.

———. "Bitcoin v0.1 Released." Cryptography mailing list, January 8, 2009. http://www.metzdowd.com/pipermail/cryptography/2009-January/014994. html.

———. "Re: Citation of Your B-Money Page." Email to Wei Dai, July 10, 2009. http://www.gwern.net/docs/2008-nakamoto.

Narayanan, Arvind. "What Happened to the Crypto Dream? Part 1." *IEEE Security & Privacy* 11, no. 2 (March/April 2013): 2–3.

Nelson, Theodore. *Computer Lib/Dream Machines*. Redmond, WA: Microsoft Press, 1987.

———. *Literary Machines 93.1*. Sausalito: Mindful Press, 1993.

"New Liberty Dollar." 2013. http://newlibertydollar.com.

Nieves, Javier, Igor Ruiz-Agundez, and Pablo G. Bringas. "Recognizing Banknote Patterns for Protecting Economic Transactions." *2010 Workshop on Database and Expert Systems Applications*, 2010, 247–249.

Nock, Albert Jay. "Isaiah's Job." *Atlantic Monthly*, June 1936, 641–49.

North, Peter. *Money and Liberation: The Micropolitics of Alternative Currency Movements*. Minneapolis: University of Minnesota Press, 2007.

O'Driscoll, Gerald, and Mario Rizzo. *Austrian Economics Re-examined: The Economics of Time and Ignorance*. New York: Routledge, 2015.

Ohanian, Melik, and Jean-Christophe Royoux. *Cosmograms*. Berlin: Sternberg Press, 2005.

Onken, Werner. "The Political Economy of Silvio Gesell: A Century of Activism." *American Journal of Economics and Sociology* 59, no. 4 (October 2000): 609–22.

Orr, Joel. "Join the Information Economy." *Computer Aided Engineering*, April 1992, 84.

Ott, Christopher. "For Your Information." *Salon*, August 3, 1999. http://www.salon.com/1999/08/03/info_markets/.

Peirce, Charles Sanders. "Logical Machines." *American Journal of Psychology* 1 (1887): 165–70.

———. "Of Reasoning in General." In *The Essential Peirce: Selected Philosophical Writings (1893–1913)*. Bloomington: Indiana University Press, 1998.

Peterson, Chris. "Shuttle Pricing and Space Development." *L5 News*, January/February 1985, 8–16.

Pettersson, Ann-Maria. *The Spillings Hoard: Gotland's Role in Viking Age World Trade*. Visby, Sweden: Gotlands Museum, 2009.

Pitta, Julie. "Requiem for a Bright Idea." *Forbes*, November 1, 1999. https://www.forbes.com/forbes/1999/1101/6411390a.html.

Platt, Charles. "Hamburger Helpers." *Cryonics* 179, no. 19:4 (4th Quarter 1998): 13–16.

Plutte, Jon. "Whitfield Diffie Interview." March 28, 2011. Computer History Museum, CHM reference number X6075.2011.

Poovey, Mary. *Genres of the Credit Economy: Mediating Value in Eighteenth- and Nineteenth-Century Britain*. Chicago: University of Chicago Press, 2008.

Popper, Karl. *The Open Society and Its Enemies*. Single-volume ed. Princeton, NJ: Princeton University Press, 2013.

Popper, Nathaniel. *Digital Gold: Bitcoin and the Inside Story of the Misfits and Millionaires Trying to Reinvent Money*. New York: Harper, 2016.

"Post-Office Stamps as Currency." *New York Times*, October 2, 1862.

Potvin, Richard. "A Solicitation to Extropians to Buy Virtual Shares." January 9, 2000. http://www.webspawner.com/users/extrosgpotvin/.

———. "Extropians' net worths." ExI-list archive, January 9, 2000. http://extropians.weidai.com/extropians.1Qoo/0488.html.

Rand, Ayn. *Atlas Shrugged*. New York: Signet, 1996.

Rayward, W. Boyd. "Visions of Xanadu: Paul Otlet (1868–1944) and Hypertext." *Journal of the American Society of Information Science* 45 (1994): 235–50.

Richards, John. *The Unending Frontier: An Environmental History of the Early Modern World*. Berkeley: University of California Press, 2006.

Rid, Thomas. *Rise of the Machines: A Cybernetic History*. New York: W. W. Norton, 2016.

Rivest, Ronald. "Peppercoin Micropayments." *Proceedings Financial Cryptography 2004*. Berlin: Springer, 2004.

Rivest, Ronald, Adi Shamir, and Leonard Max Adleman. "A Method for Obtaining Digital Signatures and Public-Key Cryptosystems." *Communications of the ACM* 21, no. 2 (1978): 120–26.

Rivest, Ronald, Adi Shamir, and David Wagner. "Time-Lock Puzzles and Timed-Release Crypto." Laboratory for Computer Science technical memo MIT/LCS/TR-684 (February 1996).

Robertson, Frances. "The Aesthetics of Authenticity: Printed Banknotes as Industrial Currency." *Technology and Culture* 46, no. 1 (January 2005): 31–50.

Robin, Corey. "Wealth and the Intellectuals." In *Hayek: A Collaborative Biography: Part V, Hayek's Great Society of Free Men*, edited by Robert Leeson. London: Palgrave Macmillan UK, 2015.

Röckelein, Wolfgang, and Ronald Maier. "A Common Currency System for Spontaneous Transactions on Public Networks: Is it Feasible?" *Proceedings of the Ninth International Conference on EDI-IOS Electronic Commerce for Trade Efficiency and Effectiveness*, June 1996.

Romain, Tiffany. "Extreme Life Extension: Investing in Cryonics for the Long, Long Term." *Medical Anthropology: Cross-Cultural Studies in Health and Illness* 29, no. 2 (May 2010): 194–215.

Rubery, Matthew. *The Novelty of Newspapers: Victorian Fiction after the Invention of the News*. Oxford: Oxford University Press, 2009.

Schulz, Kathryn. "Final Forms," *New Yorker*, April 7, 2014, 32–37.

Schumpeter, Joseph. "The Rise and Fall of Families within a Class." In *Imperialism and Social Classes: Two Essays*. New York: Meridian Books, 1966.

Schwartz, Hillel. *The Culture of the Copy: Striking Likenesses, Unreasonable Facsimiles*. New York: Zone Books, 1996.

Scott, Howard. "Technology Smashes the Price System: An Inquiry into the Nature of Our Present Crisis." *Harper's Magazine* 166 (January 1933): 129–42.

Segal, Howard. *Technological Utopianism in American Culture: Twentieth Anniversary Edition*. Syracuse, NY: Syracuse University Press, 2005.

Servon, Lisa. *The Unbanking of America: How the New Middle Class Survives*. New York: Houghton Mifflin, 2017.

Shannon, Claude. "Communication Theory of Secrecy Systems." *Bell System Technical Journal* 28, no. 4 (1949): 656–715.

Shelter Systems, LLC. "Motion for Return of Property." Case No. MS-07-6337-MHW, June 17, 2008.

Shirriff, Ken. "Mining Bitcoin with Pencil and Paper: 0.67 Hashes per Day." *Righto.com* (blog), September 2014. http://www.righto.com/2014/09/mining-bitcoin-with-pencil-and-paper.html.

Simberg, Rand. "The Frozen Frontier, or: How Alcor Will Open Up Space." *Cryonics* 115, no. 11:2 (February 1990): 51–55.

Singh, Simon. *The Code Book: The Science of Secrecy from Ancient Egypt to Quantum Cryptography*. New York: Anchor, 1999.

Smith, David. "Book Cyphers in External Affairs Canada (1930s–1980s)." January 2005. http://www.jproc.ca/crypto/otfp_otlp.html.

Smith, Vera. *The Rationale of Central Banking and the Free Banking Alternative*. Indianapolis: Liberty Fund, 1990.

Spang, Rebecca. *Stuff and Money in the Time of the French Revolution*. Cambridge, MA: Harvard University Press, 2015.

Spicer, Sean. *The Mind Is a Collection: Case Studies in Eighteenth-Century Thought*. Philadelphia: University of Pennsylvania Press, 2015.

"Spontaneous Orders." *Extropy* 1 (Fall 1988): 7.

Stadd, Courtney. "NASA Headquarters Oral History Project." Interviewed by Rebecca Wright, Washington, DC, January 7, 2003. https://www.jsc.nasa.gov/history/oral_histories/NASA_HQ/Administrators/StaddCA/StaddCA_1-7-03.htm.

Stadter, Philip. "Alexander Hamilton's Notes on Plutarch in His Pay Book." *Review of Politics* 73, no. 2 (Spring 2011): 199–217.

Stallman, Richard. "What Is Free Software?" Free Software Foundation. https://www.gnu.org/philosophy/free-sw.en.html.

Stearns, David. *Electronic Value Exchange: Origins of the VISA Electronic Payment System*. London: Springer-Verlag, 2011.

Steil, Benn. *The Battle of Bretton Woods: John Maynard Keynes, Harry Dexter White, and the Making of a New World Order*. Princeton, NJ: Princeton University Press, 2013.

Sterling, Bruce. "The Blast Shack." *Webstock* (blog), December 22, 2010. https://medium.com/@bruces/the-blast-shack-f745f5fbeb1c.

Sterne, Jonathan. *MP3: The Meaning of a Format*. Durham, NC: Duke University Press, 2012.

Stiefel, Werner ("Warren K. Stevens"). *The Story of Operation Atlantis*. Saugerties, NY: Atlantis Publishing Company, 1968.

Stites, Richard. *Revolutionary Dreams: Utopian Vision and Experimental Life in the Russian Revolution*. Oxford: Oxford University Press, 1991.

Strauss, Erwin. *How to Start Your Own Country*. Boulder, CO: Paladin Press, 1999.

Strugatsky, Arkady and Boris. *Roadside Picnic*. New York: Macmillian, 1977.

Swartz, Lana. "Gendered Transactions: Identity and Payment at Midcentury." *Women's Studies Quarterly* 42, no. 1/2, "Debt" (Spring/Summer 2014): 137–53.

———. "Blockchain Dreams: Imagining Techno-Economic Alternatives after Bitcoin." In *Another Economy Is Possible*, edited by Manuel Castells. London: Polity Press, 2017.

———. *Social Transactions: The Cultural Politics of Money Technology.* New Haven, CT: Yale University Press, forthcoming.

Szabo, Nick. "Future Forecasts." *Extropy* 15, no. 7:2 (2nd/3rd Quarter 1995): 10–13.

———. "Secure Property Titles with Owner Authority." Nick Szabo's E-Commerce and Security White Papers (website), 1998. http://szabo.best.vwh.net/securetitle .html.

———. "Intrapolynomial Cryptography." Nick Szabo's E-Commerce and Security White Papers (website), 1999. https://web.archive.org/web/20010802174702 /http://www.best.com:80/~szabo/intrapoly.html.

———. "Trusted Third Parties Are Security Holes." Nick Szabo's Essays, Papers, and Concise Tutorials (website), 2001. https://web.archive.org/web/20160705000502 /http://szabo.best.vwh.net/ttps.html.

———. "Bit Gold." *Unenumerated* (blog), December 29, 2005. http://unenumerated .blogspot.com/2005/12/bit-gold.html.

Szilard, Leo. "The Mark Gable Foundation." Leo Szilard Papers. MSS 32, Box 27, Folder 11. Special Collections & Archives, UC San Diego Library, July 28, 1948.

———. "Memoirs." Leo Szilard Papers. MSS 32, Box 40, Folder 10. Special Collections & Archives, UC San Diego Library, 1960.

Taaki, Amir. "Why Do We Want to Make unSYSTEM, DarkWallet and All These Things?" Darkwallet (website), 2013. https://www.darkwallet.is/whydw.html.

Taylor, Frederick. *The Downfall of Money: Germany's Hyperinflation and the Destruction of the Middle Class.* New York: Bloomsbury, 2013.

Technocracy, Inc. "Total Conscription! Your Questions Answered." New York: Technocracy Inc. Continental Headquarters, 1942. https://archive.org/details/Total ConscriptionYourQuestionsAnswered.

Thaler, Richard. "Mental Accounting and Consumer Choice." *Marketing Science* 4, no. 3 (1985): 199–214.

Thiel, Peter. "The Education of a Libertarian." *Cato Unbound,* April 13, 2009. https:// www.cato-unbound.org/2009/04/13/peter-thiel/education-libertarian.

Tresch, John. "Cosmogram." In *Cosmograms,* edited by Melik Ohanian and Jean-Christophe Royoux. New York: Lukas & Sternberg, 2005.

———. *The Romantic Machine: Utopian Science and Technology after Napoleon.* Chicago: University of Chicago Press, 2012.

Trettien, Whitney Anne. "Leaves." In *Paid: Tales of Dongles, Checks, and Other Money Stuff,* edited by Bill Maurer and Lana Swartz. Cambridge, MA: MIT Press, 2017.

Turner, Fred. *From Counterculture to Cyberculture: Stewart Brand, the Whole Earth Network, and the Rise of Digital Utopianism.* Chicago: University of Chicago Press, 2006.

———. "Prototype." In *Digital Keywords: A Vocabulary of Information Society and Culture*, edited by Benjamin Peters. Princeton, NJ: Princeton University Press, 2016.

———. "Can We Write a Cultural History of the Internet? If So, How?" *Internet Histories* 1 (2017): 39–46.

US Congress, Office of Technology Assessment. "Federal Government Information Technology: Electronic Record Systems and Individual Privacy." OTA-CIT-296. Washington, DC: US Government Printing Office, 1995.

van Fossen, Anthony. *Tax Havens and Sovereignty in the Pacific Islands.* St. Lucia: University of Queensland Press, 2012.

Vinge, Vernor. "The Coming Technological Singularity: How to Survive in the Posthuman Era." *Vision-21: Interdisciplinary Science and Engineering in the Era of Cyberspace* (NASA Conference publication 10129). NASA Office of Management, 1993.

———. *True Names and the Opening of the Cyberspace Frontier.* New York: Tor, 2001.

von Glahn, Richard. *Fountain of Fortune: Money and Monetary Policy in China, 1000–1700.* Berkeley: University of California Press, 1996.

von NotHaus, Bernard. "To Know Value—An Economic Research Paper." 1974. http://bernardvonnothaus.org/wp-content/uploads/To-Know-Value.pdf.

———. "The Nazi-ization of America." In *The Liberty Dollar Solution to the Federal Reserve.* Evansville, IN: American Financial Press, 2003.

Waldrop, M. Mitchell. *The Dream Machine: J. C. R. Licklider and the Revolution That Made Computing Personal.* New York: Penguin, 2001.

Walker, John. *The Autodesk File: Bits of History, Words of Experience.* 4th ed. 1994. https://www.fourmilab.ch/autofile/.

Wallace, Robert, and Harold Keith Melton. *Spycraft: The Secret History of the CIA's Spytechs from Communism to Al-Qaeda.* New York: Plume, 2006.

Waring, Marilyn. *If Women Counted: A New Feminist Economics.* New York: Harper & Row, 1988.

Weatherford, John. *The History of Money: From Sandstone to Cyberspace.* New York: Three Rivers, 1997.

Wells, H. G. *The Shape of Things to Come.* New York: Penguin, 2005.

Widdig, Bernd. *Culture and Inflation in Weimar, Germany.* Berkeley: University of California Press, 2001.

Williams, Kathleen. "Improbable Warriors: Mathematicians Grace Hopper and Mina Rees in World War II." In *Mathematics and War,* edited by Bernhelm Booß-Bavnbek and Jens Hoyrup. Basel: Springer Basel AG, 2003.

Wilson, Cody. *Come and Take It: The Gun Printer's Guide to Thinking Free.* New York: Gallery Books, 2016.

Wolf, Gary. "The Curse of Xanadu." *Wired* 3, no. 6 (June 1995). https://www.wired.com/1995/06/xanadu/.

Wolfson, Shael N. "Bitcoin: The Early Market." *Journal of Business & Economics Re-search* 13, no. 4 (Fourth Quarter 2015): 201–14.

Yow. "Mindsurfing: The Tia Transformation." *Extropy* 15, no. 7:2 (2nd/3rd Quarter 1995): 47.

Zaloom, Caitlin. *Out of the Pits: Trading and Technology from Chicago to London.* Chicago: University of Chicago Press, 2006.

———. "How to Read the Future: The Yield Curve, Affect, and Financial Prediction." *Public Culture* 21, no. 2 (2009): 245–268.

Zelizer, Viviana. "The Social Meaning of Money: 'Special Monies.'" *American Journal of Sociology* 95, no. 2 (September 1989): 342–77.

———. *Economic Lives: How Culture Shapes the Economy.* Princeton, NJ: Princeton University Press, 2011.

Zielinski, Siegfried. *Deep Time of the Media: Toward an Archaeology of Hearing and Seeing by Technical Means.* Cambridge, MA: MIT Press, 2008.

Zimmerman, Philip R. *PGP Source Code and Internals.* Cambridge, MA: MIT Press, 1995.

INDEX